T0320173

Machine Learning in Healthcare and Security

This book brings together a blend of different areas of machine learning and recent advances in the area. From the use of ML in healthcare to security, this book encompasses several areas related to ML while keeping a check on traditional ML algorithms.

Machine Learning in Healthcare and Security: Advances, Obstacles, and Solutions describes the predictive analysis and forecasting techniques in different emerging and classical areas using the approaches of ML and AI. It discusses the application of ML and AI in medical diagnostic systems and deals with the security prevention aspects of ML and how it can be used to tackle various emerging security issues. This book also focuses on NLP and understanding the techniques, obstacles, and possible solutions.

This is a valuable reference resource for researchers and postgraduate students in healthcare systems engineering, computer science, cyber-security, information technology, and applied mathematics.

Artificial Intelligence in Smart Healthcare Systems

Series Editors: Vishal Jain and Jyotir Moy Chatterjee

The progress of the healthcare sector is incremental as it learns from associations between data over time through the application of suitable big data and IoT frameworks and patterns. Many healthcare service providers are employing IoT-enabled devices for monitoring patient health care, but their diagnosis and prescriptions are instance-specific only. However, these IoT-enabled healthcare devices are generating volumes of data (Big-IoT Data), that can be analyzed for more accurate diagnosis and prescriptions. A major challenge in the above realm is the effective and accurate learning of unstructured clinical data through the application of precise algorithms. Incorrect input data leading to erroneous outputs with false positives shall be intolerable in healthcare as patient's lives are at stake. This new book series addresses various aspects of how smart healthcare can be used to detect and analyze diseases, the underlying methodologies, and related security concerns. Healthcare is a multidisciplinary field that involves a range of factors like the financial system, social factors, health technologies, and organizational structures that affect the healthcare provided to individuals, families, institutions, organizations, and populations. The goals of healthcare services include patient safety, timeliness, effectiveness, efficiency, and equity. Smart healthcare consists of m-health, e-health, electronic resource management, smart and intelligent home services, and medical devices. The Internet of Things (IoT) is a system comprising real-world things that interact and communicate with each other via networking technologies. The wide range of potential applications of IoT includes healthcare services. IoT-enabled healthcare technologies are suitable for remote health monitoring, including rehabilitation, assisted ambient living, etc. In turn, healthcare analytics can be applied to the data gathered from different areas to improve healthcare at a minimum expense.

This new book series is designed to be a first choice reference at university libraries, academic institutions, research and development centres, information technology centres, and any institutions interested in using, design, modelling, and analysing intelligent healthcare services. Successful application of deep learning frameworks to enable meaningful, cost-effective personalized healthcare services is the primary aim of the healthcare industry in the present scenario. However, realizing this goal requires effective understanding, application, and amalgamation of IoT, Big Data and several other computing technologies to deploy such systems in an effective manner. This series shall help clarify the understanding of certain key mechanisms and technologies helpful in realizing such systems.

Immersive Virtual and Augmented Reality in Healthcare: An IoT and Blockchain Perspective
Rajendra Kumar, Vishal Jain, Garry Han, and Abderezak Touzene

Handbook on Augmenting Telehealth Services: Using Artificial Intelligence
Edited by Sonali Vyas, Sunil Gupta, Monit Kapoor, and Samiya Khan

Machine Learning in Healthcare and Security: Advances, Obstacles, and Solutions
Edited by Prashant Pranav, Archana Patel, and Sarika Jain

Machine Learning in Healthcare and Security

Advances, Obstacles, and Solutions

Edited by
Prashant Pranav, Archana Patel, and Sarika Jain

CRC Press
Taylor & Francis Group
Boca Raton London New York

CRC Press is an imprint of the
Taylor & Francis Group, an **informa** business

Designed cover image: Shutterstock

First edition published 2024
by CRC Press
2385 NW Executive Center Drive, Suite 320, Boca Raton FL 33431

and by CRC Press
4 Park Square, Milton Park, Abingdon, Oxon, OX14 4RN

CRC Press is an imprint of Taylor & Francis Group, LLC

Library of Congress Cataloging-in-Publication Data

Names: Pranav, Prashant, editor. | Patel, Archana (Lecturer in software engineering), editor. | Jain, Sarika, editor.
Title: Machine learning in healthcare and security : advances, obstacles, and solutions / edited by Prashant Pranav, Archana Patel, and Sarika Jain.
Description: First edition. | Boca Raton : CRC Press, 2024. | Series: Artificial Intelligence in smart healthcare systems | Includes bibliographical references and index.
Identifiers: LCCN 2023033734 (print) | LCCN 2023033735 (ebook) | ISBN 9781032478418 (hbk) | ISBN 9781032483993 (pbk) | ISBN 9781003388845 (ebk)
Subjects: LCSH: Artificial intelligence--Medical applications. | Medicine--Data processing. | Machine learning. | Data protection.
Classification: LCC R859.7.A78 M334 2024 (print) | LCC R859.7.A78 (ebook) | DDC 610.285--dc23/eng/20231031
LC record available at https://lccn.loc.gov/2023033734
LC ebook record available at https://lccn.loc.gov/2023033735

ISBN: 978-1-032-47841-8 (hbk)
ISBN: 978-1-032-48399-3 (pbk)
ISBN: 978-1-003-38884-5 (ebk)

DOI: 10.1201/9781003388845

Typeset in Times
by KnowledgeWorks Global Ltd.

Contents

PART I Natural Language Processing Using ML

PART II AI and ML in Healthcare

PART III   Security Aspects of ML

Preface

In recent years, machine learning has become a developing topic with applications in many fields. Machine learning has made tremendous strides in the fields of security and healthcare in recent years. Machine learning has evolved into a crucial tool for security and healthcare. Experts thanks to improvements in computer hardware, the accessibility of large amounts of data, and the creation of complex algorithms.

By facilitating effective decision-making, precise predictions, and real-time monitoring, machine learning has the potential to revolutionize the healthcare and security industries. Machine learning algorithms can analyze medical data in the healthcare industry and offer insights that were previously unattainable. It can support disease diagnosis, patient outcome prediction, and individualized care. The ability of machine learning to sift through massive volumes of data and find prospective medication candidates could also revolutionize drug discovery and clinical trials.

Machine learning algorithms can be used to find threats, identify threats, and stop assaults in the security area. Cyber risks can be recognized with the aid of machine learning, which also offers real-time monitoring to find and stop attacks. It can also aid in the detection of fraud and the avoidance of financial crimes.

However, there are difficulties in using machine learning in security and healthcare. In all fields, data security and privacy are major problems. Healthcare data must be safeguarded against unauthorized access and breaches due to its sensitivity. Similar to that, important security data frequently needs to be protected from bad actors.

The development of machine learning models for healthcare and security is also significantly hampered by the lack of standardized data formats and the variation in data quality. Inaccurate predictions and unreliable models can come from a lack of high-quality training data since machine learning models are only as good as the data on which they are trained.

The goal of this book is to give a thorough review of the developments, challenges, and solutions in machine learning for security and healthcare. Predictive modeling in healthcare, image analysis, natural language processing, cybersecurity, and fraud detection are just a few of the topics covered in this book. The problems and ethical issues surrounding the application of machine learning in these sectors are also covered in this book.

The authors of this book are experts in their fields, with a plethora of expertise in security, healthcare, and machine learning, thanks to their viewpoints and insights. Readers will gain a thorough knowledge of the state of machine learning in healthcare and security today and the possibilities for future advancements.

We hope this book will be a valuable resource for academics, practitioners, and students interested in the nexus of machine learning, healthcare, and security. We sincerely hope that this book will promote these subjects and help society find creative answers to some of the most critical problems it is currently experiencing.

About the Editors

Dr. Prashant Pranav is Assistant Professor in the Department of Computer Science and Engineering, Birla Institute of Technology, Mesra. He completed his Bachelor of Technology in Computer Science and Engineering from College of Engineering Bhubaneswar. He then pursued Master of Engineering in Software Engineering from Birla Institute of Technology, Mesra. His research interests include Cryptography, Cyber Security, Biometric Security, Digital Forensics, Algorithm Analysis, Network Security, Statistical Analysis, and Musical Cryptography. He has published many research articles and conference proceedings in journals of repute. He has also authored four reference books with well-known publishers.

Dr. Archana Patel is Assistant Professor, National Forensic Sciences University, Gandhinagar, Gujarat, India. She has worked as a full-time faculty at the School of Computing and Information Technology, Eastern International University, Binh Duong Province, Vietnam. She has completed her Postdoc from the Freie Universität Berlin, Berlin, Germany. She has filed a patent entitled "Method and System for Creating Ontology of Knowledge Units In A Computing Environment" in November 2019. She has received Doctor of Philosophy (PhD) in Computer Applications and PG degree, both from the National Institute of Technology (NIT) Kurukshetra, India in 2020 and 2016, respectively. She has qualified GATE and UGC-NET/JRF exams in 2017. Dr. Patel has also contributed in research project funded by Defence Research and Development Organization (DRDO), for the period of two year. Dr. Patel is the author or co-author of more than 40 publications in numerous referred journals and conference proceedings. She has been awarded best paper award (four times) in international conferences. She has served as a reviewer for various reputed journal and conferences. Dr. Patel has received various awards for presentation of research work at various international conferences, teaching and research institutions. She has edited six books and served as a guest editor in many well-reputed journals. Dr. Patel served as the keynote speaker at ICOECA-2022 and ICSADL 2022. Her research interests are Ontological Engineering, Semantic Web, Big Data, Expert System, and Knowledge Warehouse.

Dr. Sarika Jain graduated from Jawaharlal Nehru University (India) in 2001. Her doctorate, awarded in 2011, is in the field of knowledge representation in Artificial Intelligence. She has served in the field of education for more than 19 years and is currently in service at the National Institute of Technology Kurukshetra, India. Dr. Jain has authored or co-authored more than 150 publications, including books.

Dr. Jain has supervised four doctoral scholars who are well-placed now. She has received grants from DRDO, DST, CSIR, and NIT Kurukshetra for research projects; from AICTE (thrice) for FDPs; from DAAD RISE worldwide (thrice) for hosting research interns from Germany; and MHRD (twice) for hosting a reputed international faculty and for FDP. She works in collaboration with various researchers across the globe, including in Germany, Austria, Australia, Malaysia, Spain, the USA, and Romania. She is a senior member of the IEEE, a member of the ACM, and a Life Member of the CSI. Among the awards and honors she has received are the Best Paper Awards, February 2021 (two), August 2020, August 2017; and the Best Faculty Award, September 2019 from NIT Kurukshetra.

Contributors

Shamama Anwar
Birla Institute of Technology, Mesra
Ranchi, Jharkhand, India

Hemantha Kumar Bhuyan
Vignan's Foundation for Science,
    Technology & Research
Guntur, Andhra Pradesh, India

Anup W. Burange
Prof. Ram Meghe Institute of
    Technology & Research
Amravati, Maharashtra, India

Deepika Chaudhary
Chitkara University Institute of
    Engineering & Technology
Chitkara University
Rajpura, Punjab, India

Dilip Kumar Choubey
Indian Institute of Information
    Technology, Bhagalpur
Bhagalpur, Bihar, India

Ritwik Dalmia
Sri Sri University
Cuttack, Odisha, India

Vaishali M. Deshmukh
Prof. Ram Meghe Institute of
    Technology & Research
Amravati, Maharashtra, India

Sandip Dutta
Birla Institute of Technology, Mesra
Ranchi, Jharkhand, India

Kirti Jain
University of Delhi
Delhi, India

Sarika Jain
NIT Kurukshetra
Kurukshetra, Haryana,
    India

Mousumi Karmakar
University of Petroleum and Energy
    Studies
Dehradun, Uttarakhand, India

Puneet Kaur
Chitkara University Institute of
    Engineering & Technology
Chitkara University
Rajpura, Punjab, India

Sharanjit Kaur
Acharya Narendra Dev
    College
University of Delhi
Delhi, India

Naghma Khatoon
Usha Martin University
Ranchi, Jharkhand, India

Ankita Kumari
Birla Institute of Technology,
    Mesra
Ranchi, Jharkhand, India

Shalini Mahato
Indian Institute of Information
    Technology, Ranchi
Ranchi, Jharkhand, India

Ramakrishna Murthy M.
Anil Neerukonda Institute of
    Technology and Sciences
Visakhapatnam, Andhra Pradesh,
    India

Pallavi Nagpal
Chitkara University Institute of
    Engineering & Technology
Chitkara University
Rajpura, Punjab, India

Ritushree Narayan
Usha Martin University
Ranchi, Jharkhand, India

Laxmi Kumari Pathak
CHRIST (Deemed to be University)
Bangalore, India

R.S.M. Lakshmi Patibandla
Koneru Lakshmaiah Education
    Foundation
Vaddeswaram, Andhra Pradesh, India

Prashant Pranav
Birla Institute of Technology, Mesra
Ranchi, Jharkhand, India

B. Tarakeswara Rao
Kallam Haranadhareddy Institute of
    Technology
Guntur, Andhra Pradesh, India

Sharmistha Roy
Usha Martin University
Ranchi, Jharkhand, India

Gunjan Rani
Acharya Narendra Dev College
University of Delhi
Delhi, India

Atef Shalan
Georgia Southern University
Statesboro, GA, USA

Jaiteg Singh
Chitkara University Institute of
    Engineering & Technology
Chitkara University
Rajpura, Punjab, India

Nikita Singh
IIT (ISM) Dhanbad
Dhanbad, Jharkhand, India

Pratiksha Singh
Dr B R Ambedkar National Institute of
    Technology Jalandhar
Jalandhar, Punjab, India

Purushottam Singh
Birla Institute of Technology,
    Mesra
Ranchi, Jharkhand, India

Keshav Sinha
University of Petroleum and Energy
    Studies
Dehradun, Uttarakhand, India

Soni Sweta
MPSTME, NMIMS (Narsee
    Monjee Institute of Management
    Studies, Mukesh Patel School
    of Technology Management and
    Engineering)
Mumbai, Maharashtra, India

Urvashi
Dr B R Ambedkar National Institute of
    Technology Jalandhar
Jalandhar, Punjab, India

Part I

Natural Language Processing Using ML

1 Application of Classification and Regression Techniques in Bank Fraud Detection

Nikita Singh

1.1 INTRODUCTION

Machine learning (ML) is becoming a powerful field for solving real-life problems [1]. It is extensively applied in almost every field, such as healthcare, banking, insurance, agriculture, and e-commerce. Earlier, all of the reviewing tasks were completed manually. However, as computing power has improved and statistical modeling has advanced, ML has become more widely accepted across all industries [2]. ML is the ability of systems to "learn" directly from "examples," "data," or "past experience." It is a method by which a system learns from its experience and improves performance. A study by Sharma et al. [3] focused on loan amount prediction and distribution using ML.

According to Tom Mitchel, "Machine learning is the study of algorithms that improve their performance (P) at some task (T) with experience (E)."

This chapter focuses on discussing how ML helps in the classification, prevention, and detection of financial frauds, especially bank frauds. The main focus will be on various classification and regression models of ML and how they can be applied to scenarios. Concepts and differences between classification and regression will also be covered in the following sections.

Financial fraud is a significant issue that has an impact on both the financial world and daily life [4]. It has a significant negative impact on the integrity and confidence of the financial world as well as the cost of living for people. According to the Oxford English Dictionary, "Fraud is a wrongful or criminal deception intended to result in financial or personal gain." Financial frauds come in many forms, including those involving insurance, banking, agriculture, securities, and commodities, among others. Financial fraud, especially banking fraud, is a problem that is getting worse economically. A compelling example of this is the Punjab National Bank scam by Neerav Modi of Rs. 11,400 crore, the Vijay Mallya Bank Scam of Rs. 9,432 crore, the Scam by Allahabad Bank of Rs. 2,363 crores, the Rotomac Pen Scam of Rs. 3,695 crore, and many other cases. Financial fraud results in enormous losses that are impossible to calculate.

Financial fraud detection (FFD) is essential to preventing the often disastrous consequences of financial fraud. In order to expose fraudulent behavior or acts and

DOI: 10.1201/9781003388845-2

provide decision-makers with the knowledge they need to develop efficient fraud defenses, FFD requires differentiating fraudulent financial data from valid data.

One of the most well-established uses of ML in business and government today is fraud detection. ML is frequently employed in fraud detection to evaluate vast amounts of data, spot trends and abnormalities, and forecast probable fraudulent behaviors [5]. It can be trained on historical data to learn what constitutes normal behavior and detect deviations from it that might indicate fraud. The algorithms can be continuously improved as new data are collected, leading to better accuracy over time. ML models can be used for various types of fraud, including credit card fraud, bank fraud, agricultural fraud, insurance fraud, and financial fraud. Additionally, ML can also help prioritize fraud cases for investigation by automatically flagging high-risk transactions. Various ML techniques applied in bank fraud detection include the neural network, logistics regression models, Naïve Bayes method, decision trees, and many others.

1.1.1 Bank Fraud

Financial institutions play a crucial role in shaping the economy of any country [6], but as the advancement in financial institutions is increasing, the cases of fraud are also increasing. The misuse of a financial institution or its services for one's own gain or to engage in other illegal activity is known as bank fraud. It may involve several strategies, including fabricating accounts, assuming fraudulent identities, or altering account records. Additionally, it could entail utilizing ATM cards, credit cards, or other unauthorized methods to access money from a financial institution. Connell University Law School defines bank fraud as "whoever knowingly executes, or attempts to execute, a scheme or artifice (1) to defraud a financial institution; or (2) to obtain any of the money, funds, credits, assets, securities, or other property owned by, or under the custody or control of, a financial institution, using false or fraudulent pretenses, representations, or promises." There are several types of bank fraud, such as accounting, bill discounting, check kiting, fraudulent documents, forgery, altered checks, money laundering, credit card fraud, and mortgage fraud. Classification and regression techniques of ML can be applied to the scenarios of credit card fraud, money laundering, and mortgage fraud [7]. Different types of ML models can be used for different types of financial and banking fraud.

1.1.1.1 Credit Card Fraud

This is a kind of financial fraud in which someone obtains cash advances or makes illicit transactions using the credit card details of another individual [8]. This can be done in a variety of ways, including skimming, where a device is attached to a card reader to capture card information; phishing, where a criminal tricks the cardholder into revealing their information; and exploiting vulnerabilities in a merchant's payment system. Credit card fraud can cause significant financial loss for both the cardholder and the issuer, as well as damage to the cardholder's credit score. To combat fraud, financial institutions and credit card companies use a combination of fraud detection systems, security measures such as chip cards and security codes, and consumer education to help prevent fraud and detect it quickly if it does occur. Credit card fraud can occur both online and offline.

1.1.1.2   Online Fraud

This type of bank fraud involves the unauthorized or illegal use of a credit card to make purchases or access sensitive information over the internet. Examples include phishing, card-not-present fraud, and account takeover.

1.1.1.3   Offline Fraud

This type of fraud involves the unauthorized use of a credit card in a physical setting, such as at a store or an ATM. Examples include skimming, counterfeit card fraud, and lost or stolen card fraud.

Regardless of the type of fraud, it is important to monitor your credit card statements regularly, report any suspicious activity promptly, and follow best practices for protecting your credit card information.

1.1.1.4   Money Laundering

It is the process of making money obtained unlawfully (sometimes known as "dirty or black money") appear legitimate (i.e. "clean"). Fraudulent activities such as embezzlement, tax evasion, and racketeering often result in the generation of large amount of cash, which must be laundered in order to avoid detection by law enforcement. The process of money laundering normally involves three steps: placement, layering, and integration [9–11]. The launderer introduces "illegal money" into the financial system during the placement stage. To separate the "illegal money" from its source, the launderer engages in intricate financial activities throughout the layering stage. In the integration stage, the launderer reintegrates the "clean money" back into the economy so it can be used without detection.

1.1.1.5   Mortgage Fraud

Mortgage fraud refers to the deliberate misstatement, misrepresentation, or omission of information on a mortgage loan application for the purpose of obtaining a loan or a larger amount of loan than would have been possible based on truthful information. This can be done by borrowers, lenders, or others involved in the mortgage process. Examples of mortgage fraud include inflating income or assets, providing false information about employment, and failing to disclose debts or liens. Mortgage fraud can have serious consequences, including financial loss, criminal charges, and damage to credit scores.

1.1.2   Meaning of Classification and Regression

Classification is a supervised ML algorithm that involves assigning a class label to an input dataset based on its features [12]. The objective of a classification model is to learn a mapping function from input features to class labels based on a training dataset that contains data with known class labels. The resulting model can then be used to predict the class label of unseen new data. Many algorithms and methods are available for classifying data, including decision trees, random forests, logistic regression, support vector machines (SVMs), and neural networks. The specific problem and the data's properties, such as the number of classes, the number of features, and the distribution of the data, determine the classification model to be used. Classification is a widely used technique in many applications, including image classification, text classification, and fraud detection, among others.

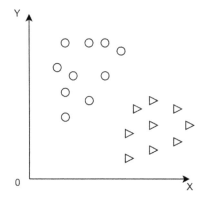

FIGURE 1.1   Classification.

In the context of bank fraud, classification is the process of analyzing transaction data using statistical and ML techniques to determine if a transaction is fraudulent or not. Since the model was trained on a labeled dataset that includes both fraudulent and non-fraudulent transactions, it can find trends and relationships in the data that are indicative of fraud [13]. The resulting model is then applied to fresh, previously unexplored transaction data, and it generates a class label for each transaction that denotes whether or not it is fraudulent. This approach can greatly improve a bank's ability to detect fraud, as it can identify suspicious transactions in real-time and allow bank staff to take appropriate action to prevent losses.

Using the statistical method of regression, an output (the dependent variable) and one or more independent variables are investigated. The regression model fits a line or curve through the data to show this relationship [14]. The dependent variable is then predicted using the model, given the new values for the independent variables. There are many different types of regression models, including logistic regression, support vector regression (SVR), polynomial regression, and linear regression. The model chosen depends on the nature of the relationship between the dependent and independent variables as well as the quantity and type of data available. Figures 1.1 and 1.2 depict a classification and regression model.

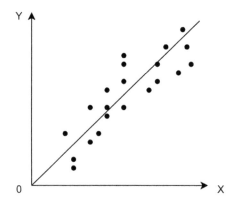

FIGURE 1.2   Regression.

TABLE 1.1

Difference between Classification and Regression

Classification	Regression
The output variable for classification must have a discrete value.	The output variable in regression must have a continuous or real value.
When classifying data, we seek out the decision boundary that can categorize the dataset.	We look for the best-fit line in regression in order to forecast the result.
Binary classifiers and multi-class classifiers are two different classification algorithms.	Linear regression and nonlinear regression are two different regression algorithms.
The predicted data in classification are typically unordered.	The predicted data in regression are typically ordered.
Examples of classification models are support vector machines, Naïve Bayes, and decision trees.	Examples of regression models are simple linear regression, polynomial regression, and multiple linear regression.

1.1.3 DIFFERENCE BETWEEN CLASSIFICATION AND REGRESSION

Table 1.1 highlights the key difference between classification and regression.

The main distinction between classification and regression is that classification offers a prediction model that, given historical data, predicts future data with discrete labels, while regression predicts data with continuous values.

1.2 CLASSIFICATION OF BANK FRAUD

Classification models are widely used in the field of bank fraud detection to identify fraudulent transactions and protect financial institutions and customers from financial losses. These models can be based on traditional ML algorithms, such as decision trees and logistic regression, or more advanced algorithms, such as neural networks and ensemble methods.

1.2.1 LOGISTIC REGRESSION

The statistical method known as logistic regression is commonly employed in ML when attempting to predict a binary outcome based on a set of input data [15]. It is a kind of generalized linear model that uses a logistic function to represent the relationship between the dependent variable and independent variables. In logistic regression, the dependent variable is modified using the logistic function, which changes the predicted values to a probability range of 0–1 [16]. As a result, the model can forecast the probability that a particular instance will belong to a positive class (like class 1) rather than a negative class (like class 0). A labeled dataset is used to train the model, and maximum likelihood estimation is used to determine the relationship between the input features and the target variable. Then, predictions for fresh cases are made using the model's coefficients.

Logistic classification is a simple yet efficient approach that is extensively used for binary classification problems and has several desirable properties, such as being easy to implement, providing probabilistic predictions, and being robust to outliers [17]. However, it may not be appropriate for more complex classification problems, such as multi-class classification, where other algorithms such as Support Vector Machines or Random Forest may be more suitable.

Logistic regression is a statistical method that is commonly utilized for binary classification, including the classification of bank fraud. In this context, the goal is to develop an algorithm that can predict whether a transaction is fraudulent or not. Logistic regression's main goal is to establish a connection between transaction data characteristics (such as value, location and so on) and the likelihood that a transaction is fraudulent. The model is then trained using a dataset that has been labeled with the terms "fraud" or "not fraud" for each transaction in the dataset. In logistic regression, the independent variables are characteristics of the transaction data, while the dependent variable is a binary outcome (fraud or not fraud) [18]. The model calculates the likelihood that a transaction is fraudulent based on the values of the independent variables. The predictions made by the model can then be thresholded to make binary classifications. The logistic regression model can be used to make predictions on fresh, unused data after being trained. This makes it a useful method for detecting bank fraud in real-time, as new transactions can be processed and their fraud risk assessed quickly. In conclusion, logistic regression is a useful method for classifying bank fraud, as it can model the relationship between the transaction data and the probability of it being a fraud. With the right data and proper training, it can produce accurate predictions and help prevent financial losses from fraudulent transactions.

Here's an example of how logistic regression could be applied to detect bank fraud in the context of a bank, as shown in Figure 1.3.

Assume the bank has a dataset of previous transactions, where each transaction is represented by a number of variables, including the money, the location, the time of day, and the customer's account history. These transactions have been marked in the dataset as "fraud" because some of them were found to be fake. The bank wants to

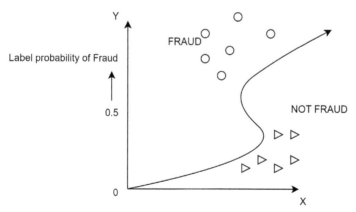

FIGURE 1.3 Logistic regression model.

utilize this information to develop a model that can assess the likelihood of fraud in a new transaction. To do this, they use logistic regression.

First, the bank trains a logistic regression model on the labeled dataset. The transaction characteristics (amount, location, time of day, etc.) are utilized as independent factors in the model, while the binary outcome of "fraud" or "not fraud" is used as the dependent variable. The model then learns the relationship between these variables and the probability of a transaction being a fraud. For each new transaction, the model calculates the probability that the transaction is a fraud based on its features. The bank can set a threshold value, such as 0.5, to determine whether the predicted probability is high enough to indicate fraud. Transactions with a predicted probability above the threshold are flagged as potential frauds and are subject to further investigation.

In this way, logistic regression can help the bank identify fraudulent transactions in real-time and prevent financial losses. With the right data and proper training, logistic regression can be an effective tool for detecting bank fraud.

1.2.2 DECISION TREE

An efficient supervised ML approach called a decision tree is utilized to resolve classification and regression issues [19]. By creating a tree-like structure of decisions and possible outcomes, the algorithm learns and generates predictions based on input features. The method divides the dataset into smaller subsets starting at the root node depending on the criteria that help classify the data into different groups or forecast the desired variable [20]. Each leaf node in the tree represents the ultimate prediction or conclusion, whereas each internal node in the tree represents a feature or trait. Before splitting can halt, conditions like a minimum number of samples in a leaf node, a maximum tree depth, or a minimum information gain must be satisfied.

The ultimate output of the decision tree is a set of if–then rules that can be used to forecast the target variable for new transactions [21]. Decision trees can be used to solve a range of issues, including credit risk assessment, consumer segmentation, and medical diagnosis. They can handle both numerical and categorical features.

The interpretability of decision trees is one of their benefits since the tree structure clearly illustrates the connections between the features and the goal variable. The disadvantage of overfitting is that decision trees may not generalize effectively to new data because they may fit the training data too closely. Techniques like pruning, ensemble approaches, and cross-validation can be used to overcome this.

A decision tree can be used to determine if a transaction is fraudulent or not depending on a number of transactional variables, such as the transaction's value, location, past transactional history, and so on. [22]. The tree begins with a root node that demonstrates the entire dataset and splits it into branches based on the feature that provides the most information about the target class. The process is repeated for each branch, which represents a distinct feature outcome, until a stopping condition is satisfied, such as the fulfilment of a minimum number of leaf node samples or a maximum tree depth. For example, a rule may state that if a transaction has an amount greater than $1000 and is located in a foreign country, it is considered fraudulent.

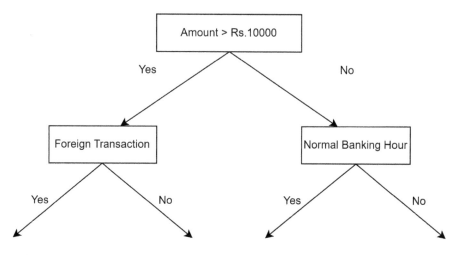

FIGURE 1.4 Decision tree model.

The process would involve gathering data on past fraudulent transactions and using it to train the algorithm, as shown in Figure 1.4.

Here's a simple example:

Root node: Is the transaction amount greater than Rs. 10,000?
Yes branch: Is the transaction made from a foreign country?
No branch: Is the transaction made outside of normal banking hours?
Yes branch (of 3): Flag the transaction as potentially fraudulent.
No branch (of 3): Continue to monitor the transaction.

Other pertinent considerations, such as the customer's previous behavior, the kind of goods or services being purchased, and the source of the funds being used, might cause the decision tree to branch out in further directions. The algorithm would use these factors to make a prediction about whether a transaction is likely to be fraudulent or not. The result of the prediction would be used to flag transactions for review by fraud analysts.

This example is a very basic illustration of how decision trees can be used for bank fraud classification, and in practice, much more complex trees with many more branches would be used, taking into account many more features and data points. The objective is to reduce false positives (legitimate transactions being labeled as fraudulent) and false negatives by developing a model that can accurately identify between fraudulent and nonfraudulent transactions (fraudulent transactions going undetected).

1.2.3 RANDOM FOREST

A supervised ML approach called "Random Forest Classification" use a number of decision trees to produce a more accurate and reliable prediction. It operates by building several decision trees, each one made from a randomly chosen portion of the training data and characteristics [23]. The outcome is then determined by combining all of the trees' predictions, usually through a voting process or by taking the average.

Using random forest classification over single decision tree models reduces overfitting, an issue with decision trees that happens when the model becomes too complicated and memorizes the training data instead of generalizing it to new, unexpected data. By combining many trees, the random forest model is less likely to overfit and is more robust to noisy or irrelevant features.

Text classification, picture classification, and fraud detection are just a few of the numerous applications that make use of random forest classification. It is an extremely practical and adaptable technique that handles massive datasets with a ton of characteristics and is comparatively simple to understand and utilize. It works by building a decision tree model that uses random sampling of features to split the data into smaller groups and make predictions based on patterns in the data. This technique can handle nonlinear correlations between the characteristics and the target variables as well as huge and complicated datasets. The algorithm is trained on historical data to identify trends that may indicate fraud and is then applied to new data to predict whether a transaction is likely to be fraudulent or not.

Example – Let's take a hypothetical situation in which a bank wants to utilize ML to foretell fraud in credit card transactions. Here's how they might use a random forest algorithm in this context:

Step 1 Data preparation: The bank first collects and preprocesses data on past credit card transactions, including features such as transaction amount, location, time of day, and previous transaction history. They also label transactions as either fraudulent or non-fraudulent.

Step 2 Model training: The bank uses preprocessed data to train a random forest algorithm. The algorithm builds multiple decision trees by randomly selecting a subset of features and using those features to split the data into smaller groups. The algorithm continues this process until it can accurately predict the target variable (fraud vs. nonfraud).

Step 3 Model evaluation: The bank evaluates the performance of the random forest algorithm on a test dataset, assessing its accuracy, precision, and recall in detecting fraud. Based on the results, the bank may tweak the algorithm or try alternative algorithms to improve performance.

Step 4 Deployment: Once the random forest algorithm is deemed effective in detecting fraud, the bank deploys it in production, using it to screen each new credit card transaction. If the algorithm predicts a transaction as fraudulent, the bank may flag it for further review or decline the transaction altogether.

By using a random forest algorithm, as shown in Figure 1.5, the bank can benefit from the ability of the algorithm to handle large and complex datasets and make accurate predictions based on multiple features. This can help the bank catch fraud more effectively while also reducing false-positive rates and minimizing the impact on legitimate transactions.

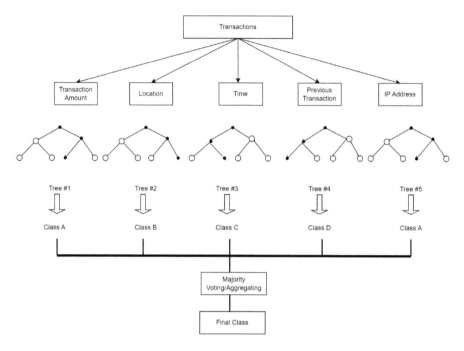

FIGURE 1.5   Random forest model.

1.2.4   NEURAL NETWORK

Neural network classification is a ML algorithm used to categorize data into different classes. It is a specific kind of artificial neural network created with categorization in mind. Artificial neurons, or layers and layers of interconnected nodes in neural network classification models, are trained to recognize patterns in incoming data [24]. The way the human brain functions served as inspiration for the idea of neural networks. Different layers are used by neural networks in ML to compute. Data mining, pattern recognition, and natural language processing are used to create machines that can apply self-learning algorithms. Cognitive computing is used in this process. It is trained on a dataset by repeatedly running it through various layers.

In the context of bank fraud detection, a neural network classification model could be trained on historical transaction data, with features such as transaction amount, location, and time of day, and a target variable indicating whether a transaction is fraudulent or not, as shown in Figure 1.6 [25]. The model would then use this information to make predictions on new transactions, assigning them to one of the two categories. The outputs of the network would be the predictions of fraud or non-fraud for each transaction. The neural network would be trained using a supervised learning approach, where the goal is to minimize the prediction error between the actual and predicted classes.

Because they can handle huge and complicated datasets and can discover nonlinear correlations between features and the target variable, neural network classification methods are frequently preferred. However, they can also be more computationally intensive and require more data to train effectively compared to other ML techniques.

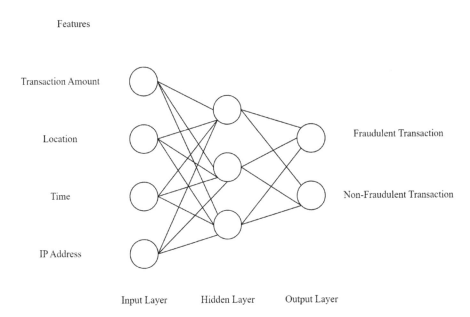

Features

Transaction Amount

Location

Time

IP Address

Fraudulent Transaction

Non-Fraudulent Transaction

Input Layer   Hidden Layer   Output Layer

FIGURE 1.6   Neural network model

1.3   REGRESSION MODELS IN MACHINE LEARNING

In ML, regression is a statistical method used to analyze the connection between a dependent variable and one or more independent variables. Making predictions about the value of the dependent variable based on the values of the independent variables is the goal of a regression model. Regression makes use of the continuous dependent variable to forecast what the independent variable's value will be. The independent variables could be continuous or categorical. Based on the values of the independent variables, predictions can be made using the mathematical model produced by the regression process.

Regression models come in various types, including logistic, polynomial, and linear models. Each form of the regression model is used for a unique set of applications, depending on the type of data being analyzed and the desired outcome of the study. For instance, logistic regression is useful for binary classification issues where the dependent variable has only two possible values, whereas linear regression is used to describe linear connections between two variables.

Regression is a very helpful tool in ML that enables the prediction of future outcomes based on past data and trends.

Related key terms of the regression algorithm:

1. **Dependent Variable:** The dependent variable in a regression is the key element that we wish to predict or forecast. It is also referred to as the target variable.
2. **Independent Variable:** The term "independent variable," also known as a "predictor," refers to the variable that has an impact on the dependent variables or that is employed to predict their values.

3. **Multicollinearity:** Multicollinearity is a circumstance where the independent variables have a higher correlation with one another than with other variables. It should not be included in the dataset because it causes issues when determining which variable has the greatest impact.
4. **Outliers:** An outlier is an observation that has a very low or very high value compared to other values that have been seen. An outlier should be avoided, as it might hurt the outcome.
5. **Overfitting or Underfitting:** Overfitting is a problem that occurs when our system performs well with the training dataset but poorly with the test dataset. Underfitting is the term used when an algorithm does not perform well even with training data.

Regression models give us the ability to anticipate or predict the value of the dependent variable based on the values of the independent variables as well as to evaluate the strengths and weaknesses of the connection between the variables. Making data-driven judgments and comprehending underlying patterns and linkages in the data are important in a range of industries, including economics, finance, marketing, and engineering.

Regression models have proven to be an effective tool for identifying fraudulent transactions in the banking industry [26]. With the ever-increasing amount of data generated by banks, ML techniques have become increasingly important in detecting and preventing fraud. Regression models are a sort of ML technique used to find patterns and connections between data, making it possible to accurately detect fraudulent transactions. The use of regression models in bank fraud detection has proven to be highly effective. By analyzing large datasets and identifying patterns and trends, banks can take proactive steps to prevent fraud and protect their customers' financial assets. In addition to being used to evaluate transaction data to find patterns and trends that point to fraudulent conduct, regression models can be used to create predictive models that spot potentially fraudulent transactions before they happen. These techniques can help banks detect and prevent fraudulent activity, reducing financial losses and protecting their reputation.

Some of the important regression models that are widely used are explained below.

1.3.1 LINEAR REGRESSION

To determine the relationship between a dependent variable (also known as the target or response variable) and one or more independent variables, regression models such as linear regression are utilized (also known as predictors, inputs, or features). It assumes that there is a linear relationship between the variables, meaning that changing one always results in a change in the other [27].

Finding the best-fit line, or the line that most accurately illustrates the relationship between the variables, is the goal of linear regression. For prediction, inference, and causal inference, the straightforward yet effective method of linear regression is widely utilized in a variety of disciplines, including engineering, finance, economics, and marketing.

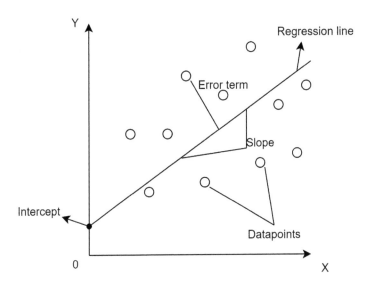

FIGURE 1.7   Linear regression model

A scatterplot of the data points and the regression line of a linear regression model are commonly shown in Figure 1.7. With each data point reflecting a mix of values for the variables, the scatterplot shows the relationship between the independent variable(s) and the dependent variable. The total of the squared distances between the regression line and the data points is minimized when the line is drawn through the scatterplot. The best linear approximation of the relationship between the variables is represented by this line. The regression line's slope and intercept are among the additional details shown in the figure.

A model that forecasts the likelihood of fraudulent behavior in the context of bank fraud can be created using a collection of independent variables and linear regression [28]. The amount of money transferred, the time of day the transaction was performed, and the location of the transaction are a few examples of the types of information a bank might gather about various customer transactions. The bank can next apply linear regression to determine which of these factors has the strongest correlation with fraud.

The bank can create a linear regression model that forecasts the chance of fraud for each transaction using the pertinent independent factors it has found. The bank's fraud prevention staff can then use the model to flag transactions that are thought to be high risk for further examination.

In essence, linear regression can help banks identify patterns and trends in customer behavior that may be indicative of fraudulent activity. By using this method, banks can more effectively detect and prevent fraud, protecting both their own financial interests and those of their customers.

Simple linear regression and multiple linear regression are the two subcategories of linear regression.

1.3.1.1 Simple Linear Regression

A single independent variable and a dependent variable are connected using a statistical model called simple linear regression. It is based on the assumption that the variables are related linearly, which is symbolized by a straight line.

Simple linear regression aims to find the best-fit line that depicts the relationship between the single dependent variable and the single independent variable. The line of simple linear regression is represented by the following equation:

$$y = \beta 0 + \beta 1 x$$

where:
 y = dependent variable
 x = independent variable
 $\beta 0$ = y-intercept, the point where the line crosses the y-axis
 $\beta 1$ = slope, the rate at which the dependent variable changes concerning the independent variable

Several techniques, including ordinary least squares (OLS), maximum likelihood, and gradient descent, are used to estimate the values of 0 and 1. On the basis of the estimated values of the independent variable, the values of 0 and 1 can be used to forecast the values of the dependent variable.

Simple linear regression is useful when we want to understand the connection between two variables and make predictions based on that relationship. It is a simple approach that can be easily extended to more complex models like multiple linear regression.

1.3.1.2 Multiple Linear Regression

It is possible to represent the relationship between a dependent variable and multiple independent variables using multiple linear regression, a form of linear regression (also known as predictors, inputs, or features). It is a development of simple linear regression, in which the dependent variable is predicted using only one independent variable.

Finding the equation that best captures the relationship between the dependent variable and various independent factors is the goal of multiple linear regression [29]. The following is a representation of the multiple regression equation:

$$y = \beta 0 + \beta 1 x 1 + \beta 2 x 2 + \ldots + \beta n x n$$

where:
 y = dependent variable
 $x1, x2, \ldots, xn$ = independent variables
 $\beta 0$ = y-intercept, the point where the plane crosses the y-axis
 $\beta 1, \beta 2, \ldots, \beta n$ = coefficients that describe the relationship between each independent variable and the dependent variable

A number of techniques, including gradient descent, maximum likelihood, and OLS, are used to estimate the values of 0 through n. Predictions about the dependent variable based on the values of the independent variables can be made after the values have been estimated.

Multiple linear regression is helpful when we wish to comprehend the link between several independent variables and a dependent variable and make predictions based on that relationship. We can use it to determine the most significant factors influencing the dependent variable and calculate their influence. However, it makes the assumption that the variables have a linear connection, which may not always be the case. In such situations, other regression techniques like polynomial regression or nonlinear regression may be more appropriate.

1.3.2 POLYNOMIAL REGRESSION

Polynomial regression is a type of regression analysis that ties the relationship between independent variable x and dependent variable y, and it is modeled as an nth-degree polynomial. Polynomial regression is a technique for modeling nonlinear connections between variables [30]. The data in this model are fitted to a polynomial equation, and a least squares optimization technique is used to determine the coefficients of the equation. Based on fresh values for the independent variable, predictions regarding the dependent variable can be made using the resulting equation.

Polynomial regression has various applications in fields such as finance, physics, biology, and engineering. For example, it can be used to model the relationship between atmospheric pressure and temperature or to predict stock prices by modeling the relationship between time and stock prices.

Polynomial regression can be used to create a more intricate model for bank fraud that can account for the nonlinear relationship between the independent and dependent variables [31]. For instance, polynomial regression can be used to simulate the connection between the amount of money transferred during a transaction and the possibility of fraudulent behavior in the case of bank fraud. The relationship between these two variables may not be linear, as larger transactions may be more likely to be fraudulent, but only up to a certain point beyond which the relationship may flatten out.

Polynomial regression can be employed in this case, as shown in Figure 1.8, to fit a curve rather than a straight line to the data, enabling the capture of more complex

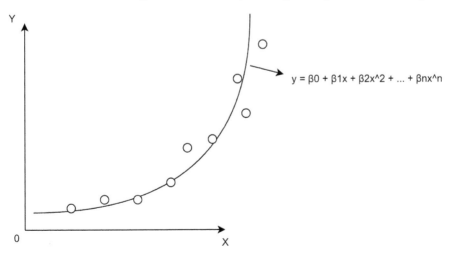

$$y = \beta 0 + \beta 1x + \beta 2x^2 + \ldots + \beta nx^n$$

FIGURE 1.8   Polynomial regression model

relationships between the variables. The degree of the polynomial equation can be adjusted to fit the data appropriately, and higher degree polynomials can capture even more complex relationships. The likelihood of fraudulent activity for new transactions can be predicted using the polynomial regression model after it has been constructed using the model's independent variables. This can help banks detect and prevent fraudulent activity more effectively by providing a more accurate and nuanced understanding of the factors that contribute to fraud.

For a certain set of data, polynomial regression can offer a reasonable fit, but it can also be prone to overfitting. It's important to validate the model using cross-validation techniques to ensure it generalizes well to new data.

The polynomial regression model's mathematical equation is as follows:

$$y = \beta0 + \beta1x + \beta2x^2 + \beta nx^n$$

where:

y = dependent variable or output
x = independent variable or input
$\beta0, \beta1, \beta2, ..., \beta n$ = coefficients to be estimated
n = degree of the polynomial regression.

The weights assigned to each term in the polynomial are represented by the coefficients, which are commonly calculated using methods like least squares regression or maximum likelihood estimation. The complexity of the relationship between the independent and dependent variables is determined by the degree of the polynomial (n).

1.3.3 SUPPORT VECTOR REGRESSION

A supervised ML technique called SVR is used to solve regression problems. It is an improvement on SVMs, a method commonly used to address classification problems [32].

The purpose of SVR is to locate the line or hyperplane that best matches the data as well as to optimize the margin—the distance between the line and the nearest data points. Figure 1.9 shows the SVM model. Support vectors are used to describe these nearby data points.

SVR can be used to create a model that forecasts the likelihood of fraudulent behavior in client transactions in the context of bank fraud based on a number of independent variables. In order to divide the data into two groups based on the independent variables and maximize the margin between the classes, SVR seeks out a hyperplane. In the context of bank fraud, the two classes might be fraudulent and non-fraudulent transactions. SVR can be used to forecast the likelihood of fraudulent conduct for future transactions depending on the values of their independent variables once the hyperplane has been located. Transactions that fall above the hyperplane are more likely to be fraudulent, while transactions that fall below the hyperplane are more likely to be non-fraudulent.

In practice, building an SVR model for bank fraud might involve collecting data on various independent variables such as the transaction amount, the location of the

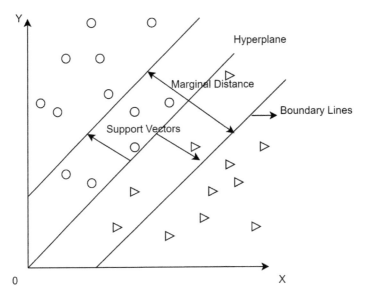

FIGURE 1.9 Support vector regression model

transaction, and the time of day the transaction was made. The SVR model can then be trained on this data to identify the hyperplane that best separates fraudulent and nonfraudulent transactions and used to predict the likelihood of fraudulent activity for new transactions.

By using SVR to predict the likelihood of fraudulent activity, banks can more effectively detect and prevent fraud, minimizing the financial losses and reputational damage that can result from fraudulent activity.

The mathematical equation for SVR is

$$y = wx + b$$

where:

   y is the predicted output value
   x is the input data
   w is the weight vector
   b is the bias term

The goal of SVR is to find the weight vector w and bias term b that minimize the following cost function:

$$minimize \left(\frac{1}{2}\right) * \|w\|^2 + C * \sum \left[\left(y - f(x)\right)^2 - \varepsilon^2\right] +$$

where:

   $\|w\|^2$ is the square of the magnitude of the weight vector w

The regularization parameter C regulates the trade-off between the margin's breadth and the prediction errors.

$\Sigma[(y - f(x))^2 - \varepsilon^2]$ Y is the actual output and a tolerance parameter that allows for some variation from the real output value. _+ is the sum of the loss function over all data points.

The "+" sign denotes that only points outside the margin—i.e., ones for which the discrepancy between the actual output and the anticipated output is greater than— are computed to determine the loss.

The solution to this optimization problem is found using a technique called Lagrange duality, which involves transforming the original problem into a dual problem that can be solved more efficiently. The weight vector w and bias term b's optimal values are produced by the dual problem solution, which may then be applied to forecast the values of brand-new data points.

1.3.4 RIDGE REGRESSION AND LASSO REGRESSION

With a high degree of correlation between the independent variables in a regression model, multicollinearity is a problem that ridge regression seeks to solve [33]. This may lead to overfitting of the model and unstable and unreliable coefficients.

In order for ridge regression to function, a penalty term must be added to the linear regression's least squares objective function. The purpose of this penalty term, sometimes referred to as L2 regularization, is to reduce the size of the coefficients towards zero by summing the squares of the coefficients. The magnitude of the penalty term is controlled by a hyperparameter referred to as lambda, which determines the strength of the regularization.

The goal of the ridge regression approach is to identify the coefficients and their values that minimize the sum of the squared residuals. Compared with a typical linear regression model, the resulting model will have smaller coefficients and be less prone to overfitting.

Here is an example:

Let's say you wish to fit a linear regression model to a dataset that has two predictor variables ($x1$, $x2$) and one response variable (y). The model's equation will resemble this:

$$y = \beta 0 + \beta 1 x1 + \beta 2 x2$$

The cost function will be changed in ridge regression to include a penalty term lambda times the sum of squares of the coefficients:

$$J(\beta 0, \beta 1, \beta 2) = (1/2n) * \Sigma(y - y)^2 + \lambda(\beta 1^2 + \beta 2^2)$$

where n is the number of observations and λ is the tuning parameter that determines the strength of the penalty term.

The goal is to determine the ideal values of $\beta 0$, $\beta 1$, and $\beta 2$ by minimizing this cost function. The coefficients will be less after the penalty term is added, leading to a less complex model with less overfitting.

Lasso regression is a regression method that addresses multicollinearity and overfitting issues by using L1 regularization. The least squares objective function is subjected to L1 regularization by introducing a penalty term whose absolute value is proportionate to the coefficients' values [34].

A hyperparameter called lambda, which controls the regularization's strength, controls the size of the regularization term. When lambda is set to a small value, the lasso regression is similar to a standard linear regression. When lambda is set to a high value, the lasso regression is similar to a feature selection method that selects only a subset of the predictor variables.

When there are many predictor variables and some of them are highly connected, lasso regression is especially helpful. The lasso regression may automatically determine and choose the model's most crucial variables while reducing the coefficients of the less crucial ones until they are zero. Figure 1.10 depicts the ridge and lasso regression model.

Here is an example:

Let's say you wish to fit a linear regression model to a dataset that contains one response variable (y) and two predictor variables ($x1$, $x2$). The model's equation will resemble this:

$$y = \beta 0 + \beta 1 x1 + \beta 2 x2$$

Lasso regression will add a penalty term lambda times the sum of the absolute values of the coefficients to the cost function:

$$J(\beta 0, \beta 1, \beta 2) = (1/2n) * \sum (y - y)^2 + \lambda (|\beta 1| + |\beta 2|)$$

where n is the number of observations and λ is the tuning parameter that determines the strength of the penalty term.

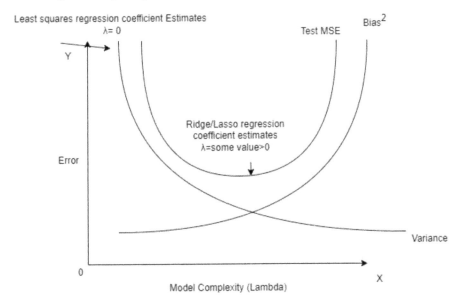

FIGURE 1.10   Ridge and lasso regression model

The goal is to determine the ideal values of $\beta 0$, $\beta 1$, and $\beta 2$ by minimizing this cost function. The penalty term will force the coefficients to be near zero, effectively lowering the number of variables in the model. This results in a more parsimonious model with improved interpretability compared to a standard linear regression model.

In conclusion, ML and data analysis frequently employ the techniques of regression and classification. Both methods can be used in bank fraud detection to spot patterns and fraudulent transactions [35]. In order to predict a continuous outcome variable, regression analysis is utilized to identify a link between two or more variables. Based on previous transactions and account history, a regression can be used to estimate the risk of fraudulent behaviors in bank fraud detection. By using historical data from previous fraudulent transactions, regression analysis, for instance, can be used to forecast the expected value of a fraudulent transaction. Contrarily, classification is a method for grouping data into predetermined classes or categories. Transactions can be categorized as fraudulent or non-fraudulent in the context of bank fraud detection. This can be achieved by leveraging past data on fraudulent and non-fraudulent transactions to train a ML model and then using the model to categorize fresh transactions in real time.

In summary, regression and classification techniques can be applied in bank fraud detection to predict the likelihood and identify patterns of fraudulent transactions, respectively. By leveraging these techniques, banks can reduce their exposure to financial losses due to fraudulent activities.

REFERENCES

1. Olivas, E. S., Guerrero, J. D. M., Martinez-Sober, M., Magdalena-Benedito, J. R., & Serrano, L. (Eds.). (2009). *Handbook of Research on Machine Learning Applications and Trends: Algorithms, Methods, and Techniques: Algorithms, Methods, and Techniques*. IGI global.
2. Shen, C. (2018). A transdisciplinary review of deep learning research and its relevance for water resources scientists. *Water Resources Research*, *54*(11), 8558–8593.
3. Sharma, H. K., Choudhury, T., Ahlawat, P., Mohanty, S. N., & Jain, S. (2021). Machine Learning based model for Loan Amount Prediction and Distribution. *CEUR Workshop Proceedings*, *3283*.
4. Zhang, Y. F., Lu, H. L., Lin, H. F., Qiao, X. C., & Zheng, H. (2022). The optimized anomaly detection models based on an approach of dealing with imbalanced dataset for credit card fraud detection. *Mobile Information Systems*, *2022*. https://doi.org/10.1155/2022/8027903.
5. Kapoor, A. (2022). Deception Detection and Vulnerability Analysis Using a Multi-Level Clustering Machine Learning Algorithm in Business Transactions. http://dx.doi.org/10.2139/ssrn.4267942.
6. Mishra, A. K., Patel, A., & Jain, S. (2021, January). Impact of Covid-19 Outbreak on Performance of Indian Banking Sector. In *ISIC* (pp. 368–375).
7. Leo, M., Sharma, S., & Maddulety, K. (2019). Machine learning in banking risk management: A literature review. *Risks*, *7*(1), 29.
8. Singh, A., Singh, A., Aggarwal, A., & Chauhan, A. (2022, November). Design and Implementation of Different Machine Learning Algorithms for Credit Card Fraud Detection. In *2022 International Conference on Electrical, Computer, Communications and Mechatronics Engineering (ICECCME)* (pp. 1–6). IEEE.

9. Gilmour, P. M. (2022). Reexamining the anti-money-laundering framework: A legal critique and new approach to combating money laundering. *Journal of Financial Crime*, 30(1), 35–47.

10. Matanky-Becker, R., & Cockbain, E. (2022). Behind the criminal economy: Using UK tax fraud investigations to understand money laundering myths and models. *Crime, Law and Social Change*, 77(4), 405–429.

11. Arman, M. (2023). Money laundering: A three step secret game. *Partners Universal International Innovation Journal*, 1(1), 34–45.

12. Bhavsar, H., & Ganatra, A. (2012). A comparative study of training algorithms for supervised machine learning. *International Journal of Soft Computing and Engineering (IJSCE)*, 2(4), 2231–2307.

13. Lokanan, M. E., & Sharma, K. (2022). Fraud prediction using machine learning: The case of investment advisors in Canada. *Machine Learning With Applications*, 8, 100269.

14. Salem, H., Kabeel, A. E., El-Said, E. M., & Elzeki, O. M. (2022). Predictive modelling for solar power-driven hybrid desalination system using artificial neural network regression with Adam optimization. *Desalination*, 522, 115411.

15. Nabipour, M., Nayyeri, P., Jabani, H., Shahab, S., & Mosavi, A. (2020). Predicting stock market trends using machine learning and deep learning algorithms via continuous and binary data; A comparative analysis. *IEEE Access*, 8, 150199–150212.

16. Tu, J. V. (1996). Advantages and disadvantages of using artificial neural networks versus logistic regression for predicting medical outcomes. *Journal of Clinical Epidemiology*, 49(11), 1225–1231.

17. Feng, J., Xu, H., Mannor, S., & Yan, S. (2014). Robust logistic regression and classification. *Advances in Neural Information Processing Systems*, 27.

18. Dighe, D., Patil, S., & Kokate, S. (2018, August). Detection of credit card fraud transactions using machine learning algorithms and neural networks: A comparative study. In *2018 Fourth International Conference on Computing Communication Control and Automation (ICCUBEA)* (pp. 1–6). IEEE.

19. Jijo, B. T., & Abdulazeez, A. M. (2021). Classification based on decision tree algorithm for machine learning. *Evaluation*, 6, 7.

20. Podgorelec, V., Kokol, P., Stiglic, B., & Rozman, I. (2002). Decision trees: An overview And their use in medicine. *Journal of Medical Systems*, 26, 445–463.

21. Chitra, K., & Subashini, B. (2013). Data mining techniques and its applications in banking sector. *International Journal of Emerging Technology and Advanced Engineering*, 3(8), 219–226.

22. Patil, D. D., Wadhai, V. M., & Gokhale, J. A. (2010). Evaluation of decision tree pruning algorithms for complexity and classification accuracy. *International Journal of Computer Applications*, 11(2), 23–30.

23. Zhang, Q. (2022). Financial data anomaly detection method based on decision tree and random forest algorithm. *Journal of Mathematics*, 2022, Article ID 9135117, 10 pages, 2022. https://doi.org/10.1155/2022/9135117

24. Mohamed, N. (2022, December). Importance of Artificial Intelligence in Neural Network through using MediaPipe. In *2022 6th International Conference on Electronics, Communication and Aerospace Technology* (pp. 1207–1215). IEEE.

25. Lokanan, M. E. (2022). Predicting money laundering using machine learning and artificial neural networks algorithms in banks. *Journal of Applied Security Research*, 1–25.

26. Asuni, J., & Koshiya, K. (2022). Application of Data Mining Techniques in the Banking Sector. http://dx.doi.org/10.13140/RG.2.2.21091.43042.

27. Lee, S. W. (2022). Regression analysis for continuous independent variables in medical research: Statistical standard and guideline of life cycle committee. *Life Cycle*, 2.

28. Mehbodniya, A., Alam, I., Pande, S., Neware, R., Rane, K. P., Shabaz, M., & Madhavan, M. V. (2021). Financial fraud detection in healthcare using machine learning and deep learning techniques. *Security and Communication Networks, 2021*, 1–8.

29. Maulud, D., & Abdulazeez, A. M. (2020). A review on linear regression comprehensive in machine learning. *Journal of Applied Science and Technology Trends, 1*(4), 140–147.

30. Shah, V., Jagupilla, S. C. K., Vaccari, D. A., & Gebler, D. (2021). Non-linear visualization and importance ratio analysis of multivariate polynomial regression ecological models based on river hydromorphology and water quality. *Water, 13*(19), 2708.

31. Amjad, R. M., Rafay, A., Arshed, N., Munir, M., & Amjad, M. M. (2022). Non-linear impact of globalization on financial crimes: A case of developing economies. *Journal of Money Laundering Control, 25*(2), 358–375.

32. Maity, R., Bhagwat, P. P., & Bhatnagar, A. (2010). Potential of support vector regression for prediction of monthly streamflow using endogenous property. *Hydrological Processes: An International Journal, 24*(7), 917–923.

33. McDonald, G. C. (2009). Ridge Regression. *Wiley Interdisciplinary Reviews: Computational Statistics, 1*(1), 93–100.

34. Vidaurre, D., Bielza, C., & Larranaga, P. (2013). A survey of L1 regression. *International Statistical Review, 81*(3), 361–387.

35. Karthik, V. S. S., Mishra, A., & Reddy, U. S. (2022). Credit card fraud detection by modelling behaviour pattern using hybrid ensemble model. *Arabian Journal for Science and Engineering*, 1–11.

2 A Survey on Water Quality Monitoring and Controlling Using Different Modality of Machine Learning Model

Pratiksha Singh and Urvashi

2.1 INTRODUCTION

Water is now and always will be a necessity for modern life. The environment and human health both benefit from clean water. Various types of chemicals mixed in industrial wastewater are harmful to the environment and indirectly harm the human body. Different governments have attempted to purify industrial water and polluted water through purification programs, but they have not succeeded in purifying polluted water into pure natural water. Water-borne illnesses, an increase in the water's toxicity, eutrophication of the body of water, and changes in the water's flavor, color, and odor could arise from these [1].

Sensors can be used to measure biological, chemical, and physical sensor parameters, depending on the application and requirements. Sensors can help improve decision-making and provide valuable insights by precisely measuring and monitoring these physical, chemical, and biological parameters in a variety of industries and fields, including manufacturing, environmental monitoring, and healthcare.

Water quality assessment (WQA) is a crucial component of environmental monitoring since it has a significant impact on both aquatic life and human health. Elimination of some or all contaminants from waste water to enhance and purify its quality so that it can be released back into the environment is a major technique of WQA. Waste water that has not been properly treated or that has not been treated at all pollutes water sources and lowers the quality of water [2–4].

Water quality (WQ) prediction is an important task in various fields, including aquaculture. The most commonly used methods for predicting WQ are traditional methods [5], such as autoregressive moving average model [6], autoregressive integrated moving average model (ARIMA) [7], seasonal autoregressive integrated moving average model [8], seasonal autoregressive integrated moving average model [9] with exogenous factors [10], gray model, Markov model [11], and support vector

DOI: 10.1201/9781003388845-3

regression [12]. These methods are used to analyze past WQ data and make predictions about future values [13].

However, these conventional techniques depend on a linear connection between the data and WQ. This means that they are limited in their ability to capture nonlinear relationships between variables that may affect WQ in aquaculture systems. As a result, these methods may be less suitable for predicting WQ in aquaculture systems, where nonlinear relationships between variables are more common. Other methods, such as machine learning (ML), deep learning (DL), and artificial neural networks (ANNs), may be more appropriate for these situations, as they are better suited to handle nonlinear relationships.

The purpose of this literature review is to examine approaches and developments in WQ and treatments that support environmentally responsible wastewater management. In addition to demonstrating a variety of applications in aquaculture and surface regions, this chapter focuses on machine learning methods for estimating and forecasting WQ. In this regard, this study's primary contributions are as follows:

- The importance of WQ cannot be overstated by pointing out the difficult conditions facing wastewater habitats mostly because of the human activity and so there is a need to move towards maintenance-free use of purification systems through intelligent control.
- It examines unsolved research questions in this area and outlines potential future research directions to address the concerns identified.

This chapter presents an integrated test of WQ based on an AI model to observe the inflow of garbage to the water reclamation plant. This chapter is structured as follows: Section 2.2 discusses related work, Section 2.3 presents the water application parameters, Section 2.4 describes the water quality testing organization, Section 2.5 presents the data sets, Section 2.6 describes the methods and model, Section 2.7 provides a work description. Section 2.8 concludes with future work.

2.2   RELATED WORK

There are various proposals and techniques available for assessing WQ, and some of these models are explained below. This study aims to safeguard the natural balance of the aquatic ecosystem. Based on a comparative analysis, the proposed system performs better than past technologies and is more environmentally friendly.

Bansal and Ganesan [14] offer a technique for computing the Water Quality Index (WQI) based on artificial neural networks (ANNs) [14]. The WQI serves as a single indicator that provides an overall view of multiple water test findings. However, determining the weight values for the WQ criteria to be used in the WQI calculation can be a tedious process. The study finds that the ANN approach is useful for quickly calculating the connection weights and WQI. The results of the proposed model show improved accuracy compared with conventional techniques, with the computed WQI accuracy reaching 98.3%.

Meng and Yang [15] have used direct heuristics dynamic programming (DHDP)-based reinforcement model control [16] to solve a multivariate monitoring control problem. The proposed DHDP methodology, as an online learning control technique, develops an optimal control strategy driven by domestic sewage process data. To evaluate and compare its performance with other approaches, extensive and meticulous studies have also been conducted on the tested Benchmark Simulation Model platform of a water reclamation plant run by DHDP.

Malisa, Schwella, and Batinge [17] have an evaluation of the effects of urban wastewater recycling on water accessibility in the Stellenbosch urban water system as the primary objective of this chapter. Using the system dynamic modeling tools in Vensim PLE 7.2, they created quality and quantity system dynamics models. The results of the simulation showed that urban wastewater recycling in Stellenbosch has a good chance of increasing the water supply over the next ten years. Furthermore, data extrapolated from supply index graphs indicated that water availability indices were higher for each of the urban wastewater recycling scenarios examined, i.e., 10%, 30%, and 50%, respectively.

Liu, Zhang, and Zhang [18] have enhanced the modeling capability of wastewater treatment plants (WWTPs) in this chapter by suggesting a fuzzy partial least-square dynamic Bayesian network (FPLS-DBN). They presented fuzzy partial least squares, which use a fuzzy rule base to extract nonlinear characteristics from process data, to customize the nonlinear process data. In order to handle uncertainty and moment characteristics, augmented matrices were included as a dynamic expansion of Bayesian networks. With respect to the quality indicators for effluent-suspended solids (ESS) in a water reclamation plant, the FPLS-DBN model's mean square error decreased by 28.63% and 69.47%, respectively [19].

Sandeep Bansal and Geeta [20] have assessed WQ for usage and provided a machine learning (ML) technique for computing the WQI and classifying water attributes. They estimated WQ information using the decision tree approach and based on the standard values of parameters as per the World Health Organization's (WHO) recommendations. The results estimated with ML approaches were significantly more accurate than those from conventional methods, with an accuracy of 98% being particularly noteworthy.

Noman Haider, Muhammad Imran, and Hakak [21] have recognized in this chapter that industrial wastewater poses a major threat to aquatic life and the surrounding ecosystem, and it is necessary to address this issue. To ensure thorough treatment of sewage before it is discharged into water bodies, the authors propose using blockchain-based regulation of industrial effluent. They have suggested a conceptual architecture built on blockchain and provided case examples to illustrate the need for integrating blockchain into wastewater management. They have also covered the approach for future work in this field.

Solano, Krause, and Wollegns [22] have written an article titled "Industrial Wastewater Management using Blockchain Technology: Architecture, Essentials, and Future Directions for an IoT-Enabled Smart System for Wastewater Monitoring."

Mandal and Mitra [23] have successfully validated the sensors using actual samples. Before the validation, the sensors were defined and calibrated using known concentrations of countermeasures. The sensors were then illuminated from one side by a light-emitting diode, and on the other side, a light-dependent resistor was used to collect the transmitted light passing through the sensor. The results of this process were achieved via a precise, reliable, and user-friendly point-of-care testing (POCT) device that enables low-cost spot pollution detection in drinking water.

Mitra and Bandyopadhyay [24] have proposed a novel cloud-based industrial IoT approach for real-time monitoring and regulation of wastewater. The proposed system monitors the temperature and pH parameters of the processed wastewater inflow at the treatment facility. The flow of the waste is redirected to a facility equipped to handle industrial waste. An experimental study is conducted to compare the efficiency of the proposed system with previous ones, and the results demonstrate its effectiveness.

Maha, Omar, and Tawfik [25] have identified that the groundwater system is in danger due to the sharp rise in various human activities near and on the Wadi Canal. The sustainability of groundwater as a primary and secondary source for drinking water requires examining its suitability for that purpose. The authors have proposed using the WQI as a method for determining and rating the acceptability of drinking-quality groundwater.

Ling Cheng and Adnan M. Abu-Mahfouz [26] have reduced the differences in model prediction performance that occur when a method is applied to various data sets. This work focuses on enhancing the tolerance of the long short-term memory (LSTM) model. With regard to the volume of dissolved oxygen (DO) present in river water, the model has been effective in making predictions [19]. The root mean squared error (RMSE) values of the Baffle model decreased by 42.42 and 10.71, respectively, after genetic algorithm (GA) optimization. The RMSE values of the GA-Baffle model decreased by 5.05 for the average ensemble, 6.06 for the weighted ensemble, and 7.84, 8.82, and 8.82, respectively, for other ensembles.

Chai, Chen, and Xing [27] retrieved the WQI using specific wavelengths that were also detected by the random forest (RF) algorithm [28]. Our findings show that both the RF algorithm and the 1D-convolutional neural network (1D-CNN) model were effective in calculating the WQI. Particularly, the 1D-CNN model outperformed the RF model when it came to samples with a high WQI. The best performance of the 1D-CNN model was achieved when using the top 10% of the crucial spectrum data, resulting in an R-square of 0.87, an RMSE of 0.574, and relative performance index (RPIQ) of 3.082 [19]. The hyperspectral data smoothing did not impact either model [29].

Aktar, Md. Al Mamun, and Md. S. R. Shuvo [30] have assessed WQ using histogram comparisons and satellite pictures. The original image, a satellite image, was chosen because its water body met the criteria for a typical clean water body. The histograms of the standard and tested images were separated by a Euclidean distance. The WQ was rated as excellent, better, good, low, or poor using a tolerance threshold.

Rasheed and Hari [31] investigated aquaculture water quality prediction (WQP) and proposed hybrid deep learning (HDL) models that combine a convolutional neural network (CNN) with an LSTM network and a gated recurrent unit (GRU) [32]. The scientists discovered that for determining the characteristics of aquaculture WQ, LSTM and GRU outperform CNN at spotting long-term relationships in time series data. The performance of the combined CNN-LSTM and CNN-GRU models was evaluated using attention-based LSTM and attention-based GRU-DL models, in addition to the baseline LSTM, GRU, and CNN-DL models. The hybrid CNN-LSTM model performed better than all other models in terms of prediction accuracy and processing speed, according to the results.

Angel, Eduard, Jesus, Marco, and Paolo Dini [33] have examined WQA approaches and technologies that support the ecological sustainability of marine habitats. They have particularly concentrated on deep learning (DL) methodologies for estimating and forecasting WQ. The literature reviewed has been categorized depending on the type of work, situation, and architecture. Finally, the authors have examined unresolved challenges and future directions, where edge computing, decision-making policies, reinforcement learning, transfer learning, and knowledge fusion are anticipated to be the primary agents engaged [34].

Qi, Huang, and Wang [35] have emphasized the importance of long-term dynamic monitoring (LTDM) [36] of the quality of aquatic resources for the smooth and orderly operation of human society. In monitoring WQ, shallow neural networks often perform less than optimally. To address these issues, the researchers have presented an LSTM [36] model to invert four important water parameters, including CODM, pH, DO, and NH_3-H. Additionally, the algorithm has been used to create an inverted representation of each WQ metric using satellite photographs taken at different times. With relative mean squared error (RMSE), mean relative error (MRE), and R-squared (R^2) values of 0.83, 0.16, and 0.18, respectively, the suggested model performed exceptionally well in the project's WQ evaluation [19].

Olasupo, Ajayi, and Bagula [37] have assessed if water samples are suitable for drinking and irrigation. The study suggests a node architecture for real-time data collection on water characteristics, and the results of simulations performed in radio mobile found that a partial mesh network design was the most suitable. The categorization of water was done using three machine learning models: RF [13], logistic regression (LR) [38], and support vector machine (SVM) [39]. The results showed that SVM was more effective for agricultural production, while LR performed best for drinking purposes. Table 2.1 shows some related literatures on water quality parameter.

2.3 WATER APPLICATION AND PARAMETER-SENSING DEVICES

Water application and parameters-sensing devices are tools or instruments made to measure and monitor water parameters (such as pH, temperature, turbidity, dissolved oxygen, and many more) and the use of water (for drinking, irrigation,

TABLE 2.1
Old Work of Water Quality Parameter

R. No	Author	Title	Publication	Year	Proposal
[14]	S. Bansal and G. Ganesan	Advanced evaluation methodology for water quality assessment using artificial neural network approach	–	2019	The study proposes a method for calculating the WQI using ANN. The WQI is a comprehensive indicator of WQ based on various water test results. The study suggests that the ANN method can be used to quickly calculate the connection weights and WQI, with an estimated accuracy of 98.3%
[16]	Q. Yang, W. Cao, W. Meng, and J. Si	Reinforcement learning based tracking control of waste water treatment process under realistic system conditions and control performance requirements	IEEE	2021	This chapter presents a solution for a multivariate monitoring control problem using Direct Heuristics Dynamic Programming (DHDP)-based Reinforcement Model Control. The DHDP methodology generates an optimal control plan based on online learning and information about home sewage processing. The study evaluates the performance of the DHDP approach using the Benchmark Simulation Model platform of a water reclamation plant and compares it with other methodologies, indicating that DHDP is a promising approach for addressing the multivariate monitoring and control problem
[20]	S. Bansal and G. Geetha	"A machine learning approach towards automatic water quality monitoring," Journal of Water Chemistry and Technology	–	2020	This study evaluated the quality of water and developed a machine learning (ML) method for calculating the WQI and categorizing water properties. The researchers used the World Health Organization's guidelines for the standard values of the parameters to estimate the WQ information using the decision tree technique. The findings obtained using the ML techniques were highly accurate, with a 98% accuracy rate, which is much higher than that of traditional methods
[17]	R. Malisa, E. Schwella, and B. Batinge	Augmenting water supplies through urban wastewater recycling (March 2019)	IEEE	2019	This study assesses the impact of urban wastewater recycling on water availability in the Stellenbosch urban water system. The researchers developed quantity and quality system dynamics models using Vensim PLE 7.2's system dynamic modeling capabilities. The simulation results suggest that Stellenbosch's urban wastewater recycling program has a strong potential to expand the

(Continued)

TABLE 2.1 (*Continued*)
Old Work of Water Quality Parameter

R. No	Author	Title	Publi-cation	Year	Proposal
					city's water supply over the next 10 years. The study also found that water availability indices were greater for each of the three analyzed scenarios for urban wastewater recycling, which were 10%, 30%, and 50%, respectively, based on extrapolated data from supply index graphs
[18]	H. Liu, H. Zhang, Y. Zhang, F. Zhang, and M. Huang	Modeling of wastewater treatment processes using dynamic Bayesian networks based on fuzzy PLS	IEEE	2020	This study proposes a FPLS-DBN as an improved modeling approach for WWTPs. The FPLS-DBN approach utilizes fuzzy partial least squares to capture nonlinear characteristics of process data and augmented matrices to manage uncertainty and moment features. The study demonstrates the effectiveness of the FPLS-DBN approach by showing a 28.63% and 69.47% decrease in mean square error for the ESS quality indicators at a water reclamation facility
[24]	R. M. Salem, M. S. Saraya, and A. M. Ali-Eldin	An industrial cloud-based IoT system for real-time monitoring and controlling of wastewater	IEEE	2022	This study proposes a unique cloud-based industrial IoT strategy for real-time monitoring and control of wastewater. The system tracks the temperature and pH levels of the treated wastewater entering the treatment plant and diverts the flow of garbage to an appropriate location for industrial waste management. The effectiveness of the proposed approach is demonstrated through an experimental study that compares it to earlier studies
[19]	R. Chai and R. Draxler	Using Machine Learning Algorithm with in situ Hyper spectral Reflectance data to Assess Comprehensive water quality of urban Rivers	–	2014	The study aimed to determine the WQI using certain wavelengths that the RF algorithm had identified. The researchers found that both the 1D-CNN model and the RF model performed well in determining the WQI, but the 1D-CNN model outperformed the RF model for data with a high WQI. The top 10% of the important spectrum data produced the best results for the 1D-CNN model, with an R-square of 0.87, an RMSE of 0.574, and a relative performance index (RPIQ) of 3.082. The hyper-spectral data smoothing did not affect the performance of either model

(*Continued*)

TABLE 2.1 (*Continued*)
Old Work of Water Quality Parameter

R. No	Author	Title	Publication	Year	Proposal
[25]	H. S. Atta, M. A.-S. Omar, and A. M. Tawfik	Water quality index for assessment of drinking groundwater purpose case study: area surrounding Ismailia canal, Egypt	IEEE	2022	This study highlights the potential threat to the groundwater system due to increasing human activities near and along the Wadi Canal. To determine if the groundwater can still be used as a primary or secondary source of drinking water, the study suggests using the WQI as a measure to assess its fitness for drinking
[21]	S. Hakak, W. Z. Khan, G. A. Gilkar, N. Haider, M. Imran, and M. S. Alkatheiri	Industrial wastewater management using Blockchain technology: architecture, requirements, and future directions	IEEE	2020	This study highlights the threat of industrial effluent to aquatic life and the local ecology and proposes using blockchain-based management to ensure proper treatment of sewage before being released into water bodies. The authors suggest the implementation of a conceptual architecture built on blockchain and provide case studies to demonstrate the need for incorporating blockchain into wastewater management. The study emphasizes the importance of further research in this area
[23]	N. Mandal, S. Mitra, and D. Bandyopadhyay	Paper sensors for point-of-care monitoring of drinking water quality	IEEE	2019	This work describes the successful verification of sensors using real samples for inexpensive spot pollution detection in drinking water. The sensors were developed and calibrated using known concentrations of countermeasures and then illuminated using a light-emitting diode from one side and a light-dependent resistor collecting the transmitted light from the other side. The resulting POCT equipment is accurate, reliable, and user-friendly for detecting pollution in drinking water
[22]	F. Solano, S. Krause, and C. Wollegns	An internet-of-things enabled smart system for wastewater monitoring	IEEE	2022	"Industrial Wastewater Management Using Blockchain Technology: Design, Essentials, and Future Path for an IoT-Enabled Smart System for Wastewater Monitoring" has been written as a part of a project. The essay discusses the use of blockchain technology in managing industrial wastewater and proposes an IoT-enabled smart system for monitoring and managing wastewater. The essay also highlights the importance of effective

(Continued)

TABLE 2.1 (*Continued*)
Old Work of Water Quality Parameter

R. No	Author	Title	Publication	Year	Proposal
					wastewater management and how blockchain technology can be used to ensure transparency, traceability, and accountability in the process. The future path for the implementation of the proposed system is also discussed in the essay
[26]	D. Dheda, L. Cheng, and A. M. Abu-Mahfouz	Long short term memory water quality predictive model discrepancy mitigation through genetic algorithm optimization and ensemble modeling	IEEE	2022	This study aims to reduce disparities in model prediction performance when applying a method to different data sets, specifically focusing on improving the tolerance of the LSTM model. The study successfully predicts the amount of dissolved oxygen present in river water using genetic algorithm optimization, resulting in a significant reduction in RMSE values for the Baffle model. The RMSE values for the average ensemble, weighted ensemble, and GABaffle model also show improvement after optimization
[30]	M. Aktar, M. Al Mamun, M. S. R. Shuvo, and M. A. Hossain	Histogram based water quality assessment in satellite images	IEEE	2015	This study evaluated WQ using histogram comparisons and satellite images. The study selected a water body from the satellite image that met the standards for a typical clean water body. A Euclidean distance separated the histograms of the tested and standard photos, and a tolerance threshold was used to assess the water quality as excellent, better, decent, low, or bad
[31]	R. A. Haq and V. Harigovindan	Water quality prediction for smart aquaculture using hybrid deep learning models	IEEE	2022	This chapter proposes HDL models for predicting aquaculture water quality (WQP) by combining a CNN with a LSTM network and a gated recurrent unit (GRU). The authors found that LSTM and GRU perform better than GRU and CNN in spotting long-term dependencies in time series data to get the characteristics of aquaculture WQ. The hybrid CNN-LSTM model outperformed other models, including attention-based LSTM and attention-based GRU-DL models and baseline LSTM, GRU, and CNN-DL models, in terms of prediction accuracy and processing speed, according to the evaluation results

(*Continued*)

TABLE 2.1 (Continued)
Old Work of Water Quality Parameter

R. No	Author	Title	Publication	Year	Proposal
[33]	Á. F. Gambín, E. Angelats, J. S. González, M. Miozzo, and P. Dini	Sustainable marine ecosystems: Deep learning for water quality assessment and forecasting	IEEE	2021	This study focused on analyzing WQ in marine environments using deep learning (DL) approaches for predicting and calculating water quality. The study reviewed existing literature and categorized it based on the nature of the work, context, and architecture. The study also identified potential future paths for improving WQ analysis, including edge computing, decision-making rules, reinforcement learning, transfer learning, and knowledge fusion. The ultimate goal of the study is to promote the ecological sustainability of marine environments
[36]	C. Qi, S. Huang, and X. Wang	Monitoring water quality parameters of Taihu Lake based on remote sensing images and LSTM-RNN	IEEE	2020	This study emphasizes the importance of LTDM of aquatic resource quality for the effective functioning of human civilization. The study found that shallow neural networks do not perform optimally when monitoring WQ and proposed an LSTM model to invert four critical water parameters, including CODM, pH, DO, and NH_3-H. Additionally, the study used satellite images captured at various intervals to construct an inverted picture of each WQ measure. The proposed LSTM model performed well in the WQ assessment with RMSE, MRE, and R-squared (R^2) values of 0.83, 0.16, and 0.18, respectively. The study suggests that the proposed LSTM model can be used for effective WQ monitoring
[39]	E. V. A. Sylvester, P. Bentzen, I. R. Bradbury, M. Clément, J. Pearce, J. Horne, and R. G. Beiko	Applications of random forest feature selection for fine-scale genetic population assignment	–	2018	This study used a partial mesh network design, based on radio mobile simulations, to collect real-time data on water properties. Three machine learning models, including RF, LR, and SVM, were used to categorize the water samples. The study found that while LR worked better for drinking purposes, SVM was more efficient for agricultural productivity. The results suggest that machine learning models can be useful for categorizing water samples based on their suitability for different purposes

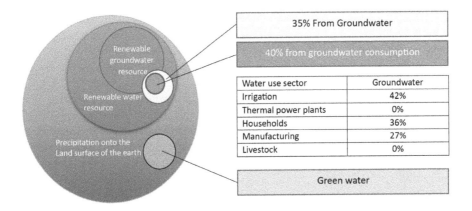

FIGURE 2.1 Water resource with applications and withdrawals.

industrial purposes, etc.). To accurately measure the water's parameters, these devices make use of a variety of sensing technologies. These devices can collect data that can be used to make better decisions and use water more efficiently as shown in Figure 2.1.

2.3.1 DOMESTIC

The infrastructure and source of domestic water supply refer to households. There are many different ways to get water at home: water vendors, a spring, a stream, a hand-dug well, a borehole with a hand pump, a rainwater collecting system, a piped water supply with a tap stand, or a home connection [40]. Water is used in many household activities: drinking, preparing food, washing one's clothes, cleaning one's hands and body, cleaning one's cooking utensils, cleaning the house, watering animals, irrigating one's garden, and frequently participating in commercial activities. It is possible to use various water sources for various activities, and the available water sources may change with the seasons. Because people cannot live without water, they always have access to some kind of source. However, the source may not be sufficient; it might be far away, dangerous, hard to get to, or have little water, making it impossible to get to or unavailable. It might provide low-quality water [41].

2.3.2 IRRIGATION

Water is essential for survival and plays a key role in agricultural productivity. Twenty percent of all agricultural land and 40% of all food produced globally are based on water-based agriculture, which account for typically at least twice as high as rain-fed irrigation per unit of area, enabling increased crop diversification and production intensification [42]. Population growth, industrialization, and climate change are all expected to increase competition for water resources, with an emphasis on agriculture. Whether they reside in cities or the countryside, the predicted global population of approximately 10 billion by 2050 will require food and fiber to meet their basic requirements. By 2050, due to these variables, it is anticipated that agricultural output would be required to expand by almost 70% along with the increase in calorie and complex food consumption that comes with economic growth in emerging nations.

Insufficient policies, severe organizational unsatisfactory performance, and funding constraints are frequently barriers to enhancing water management in agriculture. Public and private organizations, including basin authorities, water agencies, groups of farmers and water consumers, and agricultural and water ministries, typically lack the supportive atmosphere and essential resources to perform their duties [42].

2.3.3 INDUSTRIAL

During the manufacturing process, water is utilized in the industrial and other sectors for the production of goods or to cool the equipment used in production. The use of industrial water includes production, manufacturing, cleaning, dilution, chilling, or transportation of goods, according to the United States Geological Survey (USGS) [43].

Industrial water and wastewater are by-products of commercial activities. Regardless of the food we consume or the products we use, water is needed at nearly every stage of production across various industries. It is essential to manage the resulting effluent effectively. The required level of treatment technology varies based on the product being produced and the quality of the region's raw water. For example, deionized water is a critical component in the processing of food, electronics, and medical supplies. This type of water, also known as liquid or semi-deionized water, has had most minerals, dissolved substances, and dirt particles removed, which eliminates obstacles in the creation of precise and sensitive items such as circuit boards [43]. Meanwhile, feed water is used in cooling systems and burners to maintain performance standards, increase the lifespan of boilers and systems, and ensure efficiency [44].

Industries that have high water consumption and treatment demands include breweries and carbonated beverage manufacturers, dairy producers, sugar plantations and refineries, textile manufacturers, paper producers, oil and natural gas producers, as well as the automotive and aviation industries [44]. Table 2.2 shows parameters defined with their effect and measurement.

2.4   ORGANIZATION FOR WATER QUALITY TESTING

This objective indicator is "safely managed drinking water services," which entails providing access to safe, pollution-free drinking water.

In 2020, 5.8 billion people received improved water that was free of toxins and readily available when needed. These water sources were safely maintained. On the other hand, the remaining two billion people faced difficulties in accessing such services. As a result, they had limited access to clean water from these types of sources.

TABLE 2.2
Real-time Parameters Defined with Effect and Measurement

Parameter	Definition	Effect	Measurement
Chloride	Most frequently found as an element of salt (sodium chloride), chloride is a naturally occurring element that is present in most natural fluids. It can also occasionally be found in conjunction with other elements like potassium or calcium	Injurious to heart or kidney patients	mg/l
Chlorine	To get rid of worms, viruses, and germs, chlorine is added to drinking water. To get drinking water with acceptable amounts of chlorine, many techniques can be utilized	It may prevent plants from growing, provide drinking water with a "salty" flavor, harm home appliances and boilers, and prevent plants from growing if the water is used for irrigation	mg/l
Hardness	The quantity of calcium and magnesium absorbed in the liquid may be used to simply define water hardness. The majority of the dissolved solids in hard water are calcium and magnesium	Scaling, frequent soap use, and artery categorization	mg/l
Dissolved oxygen	The word "dissolved" refers to the amount of air that is dissolved in the water or the level of oxygen that is available to living aquatic organisms. By assessing the amount of dissolved oxygen present, we may learn a lot about the quality of the water in a particular stream or lake	Additionally, oxygen is released into the water as a by-product of aquatic plant photosynthesis, which is essential for fish and other marine species to survive.	mg/l
Total dissolved solution	The entire level of liquid substances in the water supply is referred to as "total dissolved solids" (TDSs). TDSs include organic materials and inorganic salts in varying amounts	For a new user, it could produce intestinal irritability, corrosion, and laxative effects.	mg/l
Sodicity/ SAR	In Sydney's fresh watersheds, soil fertility is a significant factor in the deterioration of the soil. It is brought on by salt in high proportions, which is typically bound to soil's finer particles. As a result, the clay particles in the soil lose their propensity to adhere to one another when wet	Soil deflocculation	mg/l
Temperature	At 32°F (0°C), pure water freezes, while at 212°F (100°C), it boils	At higher temperatures, chemical reactions often happen more quickly	C

(Continued)

TABLE 2.2 (*Continued*)
Real-time Parameters Defined with Effect and Measurement

Parameter	Definition	Effect	Measurement
Turbidity	Turbidity is caused by particles that are dissolved or suspended in water and that reflect light, making the water appear cloudy or murky. Particulate matter includes sediment, especially clay and silt, microscopic inorganic and organic debris, soluble colored chemical molecules, algae, and other microorganisms		NTU
pH	The pH level establishes the acidity or basicity of water. Neutrality is symbolized by 7 on the scale, which ranges from 0 to 14. A pH value of 7 or less denotes acidity, and a pH of 7 or more suggests baseness	Drinking water with a pH lower than 6.5 is risky because it is more likely to contain pollutants	pH
Salinity/EC	Salinity is the measure of how much salt has been dissolved in a body of water. It has a considerable impact on conductivity and affects a variety of biological processes as well as some aspects of the biochemistry of natural waters	In high salinity, plant development is slowed, and fruit is present	Mmhoc/cm

5.8 billion people were able to utilize safe water services, while 2 billion people in 2020 were unable to access well-managed water services.

- 1.2 billion people have access to basic water services.
- 282 million people lack access to basic water services.
- There are 368 million people who obtain their water from unsafe wells and springs.

There are still significant disparities in access to improved water sources between rural and urban areas, as well as among cities and towns. People living in low-income, unregistered, or illegal settlements often have limited access to better water sources compared with other communities due to physical, sociological, and socio-economic factors [45].

Inadequate waste management in urban, industrial, and agricultural contexts may have polluted or chemically poisoned the drinking water of hundreds of millions of people. For example, naturally occurring substances such as arsenic and salt can have potential health effects. Additionally, other substances, such as lead, can leach into the water supply and be present in drinking water in higher amounts [26].

Polluted water can potentially cause several diseases in the human body, depending on the type and level of contamination. Some examples include diarrhea, cholera, typhoid fever, hepatitis A, and giardiasis. Fifteen out of every 100 people worldwide are admitted to the hospital due to water-related illnesses, which is a significant proportion. The rate is much higher in underdeveloped countries.

2.4.1 BUREAU OF INDIAN STANDARDS

To ensure that Indian citizens have access to pure water for drinking, the Bureau of Indian Standards (BIS) has supported certain standards. The aforementioned requirements called for the routine and periodic assessment of possible water sources to make sure they adhered to fundamental standards.

Mineral levels in drinking water should not be too high for human consumption. The stand-alone directive BIS 10500:2012 sets the drinking water standards in India. In light of numerous realities, including groundwater exploitation, the statement is modified appropriately. The directive has supported the minimum and allowed values for hardness, TDS, chlorides, etc. According to BIS, any water sample with a TDS level exceeding 500 mg/l may cause digestive problems and should therefore conform to the permissible contamination limit [46].

2.4.2 THE EUROPEAN UNION (EU)

By 2030, the EU 2030 Biodiversity Plan hopes to have Europe's biodiversity back on track and ensure that all of the world's environments are robust, restored, and properly protected by 2050. One of the goals of the Biodiversity Strategy is the restoration of freshwater ecosystems. The Biodiversity Strategy calls for increased efforts to restore the natural functioning of rivers and to properly implement current freshwater regulations. Moreover, the policy aims to restore floodplains and wetlands and remove inefficient barriers on at least 25,000 km of rivers by 2030 in order to achieve this goal [47].

The Commission has produced a document to help Member States identify and prioritize barriers that can be addressed to support the attainment of the objectives set out in the Biodiversity Strategy, and to identify potential sources of financing, as stated in the Biodiversity Strategy. Although Europe is generally thought to have ample water resources, droughts and water shortages are becoming more prevalent throughout the European Union. The primary overall goal of EU water policy is to guarantee that all Europeans have sufficient access to high-quality water and that all water bodies are in excellent condition.

2.4.3 UNITED STATES ENVIRONMENTAL PROTECTION AGENCY

In December 1970, Richard Nixon issued an executive order that formed the Agency for Environmental Protection (EPA). This government agency works to protect both the environment and people's health. The EPA, which has its headquarters in Washington, D.C., is responsible for creating laws and regulations that enhance both environmental and human health [48].

TABLE 2.3

Real-time Parameters Defined with Effect and Measurement

Parameter	WHO	BIS	EU	USEPA
Chloride	200	250	250	–
Dissolves oxygen	–	250	250	–
Hardness	300	200–600	–	–
Salinity	–	–	2500mus/cm	–
pH	6.5–8.5	6.5–8.5	6.5–8.5	6.5–8.5
Turbidity	2	1–5	4	0.5–1.0
TDS	500	500–2000	500	500

KEY TAKEAWAYS

- Protecting both human health and the environment is the mission of the EPA, a federal government agency in the US.
- The EPA controls the production, transformation, distribution, and use of pollutants and other substances.
- The agency uses penalties, punishments, and other measures to make sure that its conclusions are followed.
- It is responsible for managing initiatives that support clean air and water, sustainable development, environmental stewardship, and energy efficiency.

Various concerns, such as nuclear waste, wetlands, product safety, and wildlife, are not handled by the EPA. Table 2.3 shows real time parameters with effect and measurement unit.

2.5 DATA SETS

This evaluates all the necessary equipment and procedures for collecting data from water sources such as the Ganga, Godavari, Brahmaputra, Bangalore lakes, Hindon, and Yamuna. The process of accurately assessing the WQ of these rivers involves a combination of data collection, measurement, and analysis using DL techniques. The primary objective of this data collection is to determine the impact of human activities on the quality of the river water. The gathered data are available in "Histogram-based WQ assessment in satellite images" [30]. There are two categories of river water data used in this study: a sensory data set collected and a laboratory data set.

2.5.1 SENSORY SET OF DATA

The collection and analysis of sensory data involve incorporating sensor data, setting sensors, and receiving and transmitting data to the waste management system.

These data have been used in the identification process of the canal sources. Waste materials from industries, agriculture, and other sources are mixed with the river water. To measure the values of the key variables in the river water, a boat has been equipped with a Hannah submarine automatic sensor, known as the "HI-9829 multi-parameter" The HI9829 is a compact, waterproof multi-parameter that can track up to 14 distinct aspects of WQ. The microprocessor-based multi-sensor probe can measure a number of significant variables, such as pH, Oxidation-reduction Potential (ORP), conductivity, dissolved oxygen, turbidity, ammonium, chloride, and nitrate, as well as temperature. The data were later time-stamped and pre-processed using various filtering methods.

2.5.2 LAB SET OF DATA

The laboratory data are identified by the process of collecting samples, laboratory analysis, and data posting, similar to the sensory data set. The laboratory receives water samples from designated locations to measure and analyze various parameters including dissolved oxygen, nitrite, pH, chlorine, fluorine, potassium, etc. Lab testing techniques have to be employed to reduce the pollution in the data file, and the calculated values have been tagged with GPS location information.

2.6 METHOD AND MODELS

2.6.1 MACHINE LEARNING MODEL

Machine learning models are used to automatically categorize water sample data.. To run the ML, we selected several widely used water parameters from the information sources, including pH, hardness, chloride, TDS, and EC. Three ML algorithm models, including RF, LR, and support vector classifier (SVC), were taken into consideration. RF is a combination of multiple decision trees [30]. It can be applied to both classification and regression problems. Generally, RF does not suffer from over fitting the training data. To address the issue of the large variance in decision trees, RF also employs techniques such as bagging and random feature selection [39].

LR models the dependent variable, commonly known as the probability of an event occurring, based on one or more independent variables. Since LR does not require a specific relationship between the dependent and independent variables, it is well-suited for determining dual outcome probabilities, such as true or false.

Water evaluation is considered a classification problem, with the main objective of determining whether water samples are "fit for use or not." Although it is prone to outliers, linear regression, when using the sigmoid activation function, is well-suited for binary classification problems. Although it is less affected by outliers than linear regression, support vector classification was also considered, as it is also well suited for two-factor problems, and performs well with smaller data sets. RF was also taken into consideration because it can handle mixed feature sets and data sets of varying sizes, and is typically faster than SVC.

2.6.2 RNN Model

RNNs have been used to handle sequence data, as they can more accurately predict data with time sequences. RNNs are the most logical neural network topology used to deal with time-series-related issues [49]. They are often used in timing analysis, data analysis, translation software, language modeling, and voice recognition.

RNN determines an output, A_d, the current state after receiving an input, X_d, at each instant (d). The state, $A_{(d-1)}$, from the previous moment and the current input, X, are used to compute A_d (as shown in Equation (2.1)). The calculation formula for the output layer is given in Equation (2.2). RNN retains key elements of information from past and present moments and uses these elements to predict future events with a high degree of accuracy. Unlike other networks, RNN only requires an input at all times and does not necessitate an output. Additionally, the network shares parameters across different time intervals.

$$A_d = f\left(U_x X_d + W_x A_{(d-1)}\right) \tag{2.1}$$

When the f activation function is used, the weight matrices for input and memory are, respectively, U and W.

$$Y_i = softmax\left(V_x A_d\right) \tag{2.2}$$

V represents the output weight matrix, SoftMax is the classifier in that context, and Y is the highly probable result.

2.6.3 LSTM Model

The gradient issue has been resolved, and the ability to handle memory material on time series has been accomplished by incorporating memory units into each neuron in the hidden layer of a regular RNN through the use of the modified structure referred to as LSTM.

The advantage of LSTM over RNN is that it is easier to understand. It is clear that an LSTM differs from a standard RNN in that its hidden units are not simply perceptrons; instead, Forget Gate (FG), Input Gate (IG), Cell State (CG), and Output Gate (OG) work together to integrate past and current information. This network topology accomplishes long-term memory functionality for sequential data by addressing the exploding gradient problem and avoiding the vanishing gradient.

Controlling the cell state is essential for the long-term memory of an LSTM network. Only a few simple linear operations are performed as the cell state is transmitted, ensuring that the information remains essentially unchanged. The gate operations use linear manipulation of neurons to control the cell state; $c-1$ represents the cell state at a prior instant and c denotes the current cell state. The cell state is controlled by the FG, IG, and OG in the most basic LSTM network.

First, the data set was split into two parts: 80% used for training and 20% used for testing. The models were created using the training data set. The performance of the created models was then evaluated and compared using the testing data set. The whole flow of the proposed work is shown in Figure 2.2.

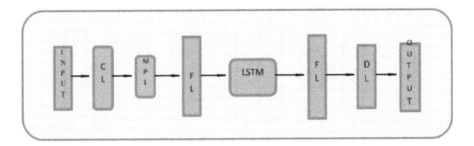

FIGURE 2.2 Proposed LSTM deep learning neural network model. CL, convolution layer with filter; MPL, max pooling layer; FL, flatten layer; DL, dense layer.

2.6.4 CNN Model

CNNs, which are different from fully connected multi-layer networks, are deep neural networks with a feed-forward architecture. They contain one or more convolutional layers, each of which has several weights that are fully connected to the input. This extends the convolution process throughout the input span, using the same weights, or kernel, for all input data. It is important to note that the network connection structure is sparse because the same weights are repeated and each kernel only processes a small part of the input signal. As a result, the computational complexity is significantly reduced when compared to fully connected feed-forward neural networks, providing a benefit [50].

Common layers found in CNN systems include the Linear Transfer Unit (LTU) and Max Pooling. The LTU maintains positional information while decreasing the size of the data. It is employed as an activation map to detect nonlinear correlations. CNNs have been demonstrated to have efficient architectures for DL tasks that need pictures or image-like inputs as a result of important breakthroughs in fields including object recognition, super-resolution, image classification, and computer vision [50].

2.6.5 Blockchain-based Model

The architecture of the blockchain-based industrial wastewater management system consists of four layers: the Layer 2 application, the edge of network systems, cloud computing systems, and data collection. Industrial equipment, including flow meters, level gauges, water meters, water storage tanks, and waste treatment facilities, have been connected with IoT-based smart objects throughout the Layer 1 data gathering process. These objects possess the capability to sense, monitor, process, gather, and communicate information about the water storage level, water consumption, volume of industrial effluents treated by wastewater treatment systems, and the volume of garbage produced [21].

2.6.6 GRU Model

LSTM and GRU neural networks have been found to be comparable in terms of performance; however, GRUs are considered more efficient in terms of processing

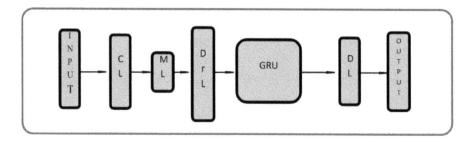

FIGURE 2.3   Proposed GRU deep learning neural network model.

resources. This is due to their simplified architecture, which consists of just two gates: an update gate and a reset gate. This makes GRUs an improvement over traditional RNNs as they do not require additional memory cells. The update gate chooses whether to send $g(d-1)$, the previous output, to the following cell. The reset gate examines the input sequence and discards the prior state if set to zero, making GRUs generally faster than LSTMs with fewer tensor operations. The memory units and architecture [51] of GRUs can be explained as follows:

$$a_t = \sum \left[W_z^* \left(g_{(t-1)x_t} \right) \right]$$

$$b_t = X \left[W_r^* \left(g_{[(t-1),X_t]} \right) \right]$$

$$g_t = \tanh \left[W_* \left(b_{*t} g_{(t-1),x_t} \right) \right]$$

$$g_t = (1 - a_t) \star g_{(t-1)} + a_t g_{-t}$$

In this design, the reset and update gates are labeled a_t and b_t, respectively. The processes of updating the input and hidden layers are labeled g_t and "tilde," respectively.

In Figure 2.3, CL denotes a convolution layer with filters, ML represents a maximum pooling layer, DrL indicates a dropout layer, and DL is represented by a dense layer.

2.7   WORK DISCUSSIONS

In this research, the technology and back-propagation algorithm have been combined, resulting in a substantial improvement compared with conventional techniques. The error curve, which shows the root mean square error (MSE), is used to assess how well the ANN performed while being trained. As the size of the training set increases, the error decreases. The RMSE of the training set (as described in [19]) indicates that the error has been minimized [14].

$$\text{RMSE} = \sqrt{\frac{1}{N \sum (c_i - \hat{c}_i)^2}}$$

N, number of values overall; $\hat{c}_i$, estimation value for i; and c_i, actual value for i.

The system uses the training set and runs through multiple cycles to minimize the error rate. The error rate decreases rapidly as the training process continues, with a noticeable reduction by the end of the performance, as observed by comparing the first and last iterations (as described in [14]). It is important to note, however, that due to the fact that many of the studied dams are located either higher than their respective WWTPs or below sea level, surrounded by hills and mountains, establishing a wireless link between the water parametric sensors and the WWTPs may not always be feasible. Examples of internet connections between the water parametric sensors and the relevant WWTPs of the dams can be found in [37]. For all data inputs, our team computed the WQI and the agriculture WQI in accordance with the instructions in [38]. The WQI ratings, which range from 0 to 100, show whether the water is suitable for irrigation or drinking.

The researcher has created a prototype to demonstrate how the proposed method works. Once this prototype has been tested on a large scale, it can be implemented at water treatment plant outlets to improve water resource management [14].

The author used fictitious data sets that were compiled from actual data sets found on the Internet, as the author expected that WaterNet would provide information on water parameters. The results of the data curation process are presented in this subsection (as described in [37]). To predict variables for the irrigation quality of water, the author evaluated the performance of CNN-LSTM and CNN-GRU HDL models against traditional LSTM, GRU, CNN, attention-based LSTM models, and attention-based DL models (for salinity, pH, DO, and temperature). Using a fixed set of hp on two data sets, the performance of the proposed HDL models was compared to that of baseline learning techniques and attention-based DL algorithms [34].

By comparing how well the DL models performed for various hyper-parameters (such as the number of epochs, measurement unit, learning rate, and batch size) in terms of prediction accuracy and computation time, the hyper-parameters (hp) have been established. The performance of each model was examined through a number of experiments by adjusting the hyper-parameters. In the final experiment, the effectiveness of all learning algorithms was compared, and the optimal hyper-parameters were selected based on prediction accuracy and computation speed [34].

To determine the anticipated values and actual data for the WQ data set, the Agency for the Development of Aquaculture Kerala (ADAK) employed multiple DL models. To train these models, 80% of the approved surface water data set was utilized, with 20% being used for testing. The expected values and actual data were compared. 100 epochs, an activation function of 0.0008, an increased batch size of 32, 30 dropout units, and the Adam optimizer were set as fixed hyper-parameters. During the training and testing phases, the processes leading to the evaluation of the models were done using the metrics of MAE, MSE, RMSE, and MAPE. The calculation time for each model was also determined [34].

In terms of prediction accuracy, the CNN-LSTM model performs better than the CNN model while taking less time to analyze data overall. The hybrid CNN-LSTM model beats attention-based models during training but falls short of them in terms of prediction accuracy. In light of this, it can be said that the CNN-LSTM is the DL model most suited for using data from approved sources to predict WQ. The effectiveness of the conventional ARIMA model was also compared with the various DL models for

TABLE 2.4

WQI Range with Classification Classes and Rating

RANGE	CLASS	RATING
91–100	C-1	Excellent
71–90	C-2	Good
51–70	C-3	Average
26–50	C-4	Below average
0–25	C-5	Poor

the Agency for Development of Aquaculture Kerala data set. The results indicate that all the DL models outperform the ARIMA model for the ADAK data set [34].

In this chapter, the decision tree model was found to be quite suitable for determining WQ. A large database collected from various reliable sources was utilized to improve machine learning capabilities and validate the results of the tested samples. As per Table 2.4, five categories, C-1, C-2, C-3, C-4, and C-5, were used to classify WQ.

After proper training with samples and using these samples for validation, the aforementioned classification was carried out in a decision tree format using software. A decision tree graph was used to classify WQ based on the selected parameters, and accuracy was achieved through the decision tree technique. The results showed that while some cases were incorrectly classified, many cases were accurately identified according to the training data, resulting in an accuracy of 98.28% when classifying WQ using the decision tree method. The average error was 0.0199, with an RMSE of 0.0996 [20].

The author utilized the RF model to maintain stability and achieved the highest accuracy when using an additional 96% of filtered bands, which comprised only 8.4% of the total bands. The algorithm performed better when using the three key ID-CNN frequency clusters as inputs compared with when using the full spectrum of data. With a reduction in input data, the training speed of the models noticeably increased, and the RF method showed greater computational efficiency. By randomly picking a subset of characteristics from the available input features of each internal decision tree to participate in modeling, the RF approach dramatically decreased the complexity of calculations [19].

The findings indicate that both retrieval models rely heavily on a limited subset of crucial wavelength durations. Hence, selecting key wavelengths is critical for enhancing the models. The RF retrieval model benefited significantly from dimensionality reduction, which reduced data redundancy and improved retrieval efficiency. The effects of reducing dimensionality were different for the ID-CNN algorithms. To maintain the robustness of the model, the IDCNN network should maintain a fixed number of variables, as the convolution and pooling techniques significantly decrease the complexity of the data [19].

The ideal input spectral wavelengths for modeling decreased from 1136 to 96 for RF and 484 for ID-CNN when the key wavelength was identified, but the impact of the modification on retrieval was unchanged. According to this study, it is possible to identify the spectral frequency that has the most direct impact on the quality of river water.

The critical wavelength selection method can enhance modeling effectiveness while ensuring forecast accuracy and simplifying the model. Despite the need for further work to find the ideal wavelength combination for input data in the ID-CNN algorithm, this is a promising result for its application to hyperspectral data [19].

The units of the input and output data values of the latent construct are included in the internal connection model of the latent variable (referred to as "This LV"). This LV reflects the variance, and the partial least squares regression method uses linear relationships within the latent space. The cumulative variance is expressed as "Total" in percentage form and is used to select the latent variables. Given that there was no discernible rise in the output's cumulative variance once the second latent variable was attained, the second latent variable was selected for PLS modeling [18].

The results were improved when different wavelengths were combined with an RF of 0.574, compared to when the full-spectrum percentile data were used as the classifier input with 36.6 fewer variables for the ID-CNN algorithm [27]. Models that utilize fuzzy techniques (FPLS-BN and FPLS-DBN) perform better than models that use linear methods (PLS-BN and PLS-DBN). The use of fuzzy rules further enhances the performance of the FPLS-BN versus the FPLS-DBN models. Nevertheless, the RMSE values between the FPLS-BN and FPLS-DBN models differ significantly. This is because actual industrial processes often have time-varying characteristics, which significantly decreases modeling accuracy [18].

Given that the time-varying feature has been considered by the FPLS-BN, it is important to strive to improve the model's performance through a methodology. As a result, after incorporating the dynamic approach into the static model, the FPLS-DBN exhibits an improvement in modeling accuracy. The predicted results of the RMSE model indicate that the RMSE value for the FPLS-DBN (RMSE = 0.71750) is 56.47 lower than that of the FPLS-BN [18].

The results indicate that incorporating fuzzy rules improves the performance of the proposed dynamic model. However, the number of latent variables for the fuzzy rules may negatively impact the performance of the model in different ways. The FPLS-DBN and the cumulative variance of the FPLS were estimated using various numbers of fuzzy systems to assess the efficacy of models with varied numbers of fuzzy rules. Furthermore, the bar graph in [18] displays the cumulative variance and the prediction results of the FPLS-DBN, while the line chart represents the number of latent variables and the complexity of the FPLS models. Table 2.5 shows Statistical Indices Models and RMSE with LV (Latent Variable).

TABLE 2.5
Statistical Indices Models and RMSE with LV (Latent Variable)

Models	RMSE	LV
FPLS-DBN	0.7437	2
FPLS-DBN	0.7175	3
FPLS-DBN	0.7998	4
FPLS-DBN	0.9844	5

2.8　CONCLUSION

In this chapter we studied about wastewater covers various models and technologies, some of which are mentioned in this chapter. Its main aim is to assess the quality and accuracy of the water. The WQ is evaluated using different parameters, including physical, chemical, and biological elements, and these methods have been improved by increasing the range of parameters used in the water model. Moreover, water purification was evaluated using two types of data sets: sensor device sets and laboratory-tested data sets. The quality of the purification process is heavily dependent on the quality of the water. We plan to develop a multi-functional application that incorporates various sensor parameters, methods, and technologies to measure WQ based on specific factors and improve the accuracy of these measurements in the future.

REFERENCES

1. Udeshani, W., Dissanayake, H., Gunatilake, S., and Chandrajith, R., "Assessment of groundwater quality using water quality index (WQI): A case study of a hard rock terrain in Sri Lanka," *Groundwater for Sustainable Development*, vol. 11, p. 100421, 2020.
2. Dong, J., Wang, G., Yan, H., Xu, J., and Zhang, X., "A survey of smart water quality monitoring system," *Environmental Science and Pollution Research*, vol. 22, no. 7, pp. 4893–4906, 2015.
3. Menon, G. S., Ramesh, M. V., and Divya, P., "A low-cost wireless sensor network for water quality monitoring in natural water bodies," in *2017 IEEE Global Humanitarian Technology Conference (GHTC)*, pp. 1–8, IEEE, 2017.
4. Prasad, A., Mamun, K. A., Islam, F., and Haqva, H., "Smart water quality monitoring system," in *2015 2nd Asia-Pacific World Congress on Computer Science and Engineering (APWC on CSE)*, pp. 1–6, IEEE, 2015.
5. Zheng, X., and Nguyen, H., "A novel artificial intelligent model for predicting water treatment efficiency of various biochar systems based on artificial neural network and queuing search algorithm," *Chemosphere*, vol. 287, p. 132251, 2022.
6. Mai, T., Ghosh, B., and Wilson, S., "Short-term traffic-flow forecasting with autoregressive moving average models," in *Proceedings of the Institution of Civil Engineers-Transport*, vol. 167, pp. 232–239, Thomas Telford Ltd, 2014.
7. Maleki, A., Nasseri, S., Aminabad, M. S., and Hadi, M., "Comparison of ARIMA and NNAR models for forecasting water treatment plant's influent characteristics," *KSCE Journal of Civil Engineering*, vol. 22, no. 9, pp. 3233–3245, 2018.
8. Adnan, R. M., Yuan, X., Kisi, O., and Yuan, Y., "Streamflow forecasting of Astore river with seasonal autoregressive integrated moving average model," *European Scientific Journal*, vol. 13, no. 12, pp. 145–156, 2017.
9. Liu, H., Li, C., Shao, Y., Zhang, X., Zhai, Z., Wang, X., Qi, X., Wang, J., Hao, Y., and Wu, Q., *et al.*, "Forecast of the trend in incidence of acute hemorrhagic conjunctivitis in China from 2011–2019 using the seasonal autoregressive integrated moving average (SARIMA) and exponential smoothing (ETS) models," *Journal of Infection and Public Health*, vol. 13, no. 2, pp. 287–294, 2020.
10. Javadinejad, S., Dara, R., Hamed, M. H., Saeed, M. A. H., and Jafary, F., "Analysis of gray water recycling by reuse of industrial waste water for agricultural and irrigation purposes," *Journal of Geographical Research*, vol. 3, no. 2, 2020.
11. Song, C.-M., "Analysis of the effects of local regulations on the preservation of water resources using the CA-Markov model," *Sustainability*, vol. 13, no. 10, p. 5652, 2021.

12. Wenbing, F., and Zhang, Z., "A CNN-SVR hybrid prediction model for wastewater index measurement," in *2020 2nd International Conference on Advances in Computer Technology, Information Science and Communications (CTISC)*, pp. 90–94, IEEE, 2020.

13. Ho, T. K., "Random decision forests," in *Proceedings of 3rd International Conference on Document Analysis and Recognition*, vol. 1, pp. 278–282, IEEE, 1995.

14. Bansal, S., and Ganesan, G., "Advanced evaluation methodology for water quality assessment using artificial neural network approach," *Water Resources Management*, vol. 33, no. 9, pp. 3127–3141, 2019.

15. Yang, Q., Cao, W., Meng, W., and Si, J., "Reinforcement-learning-based tracking control of waste water treatment process under realistic system conditions and control performance requirements," *IEEE Transactions on Systems, Man, and Cybernetics: Systems*, vol. 52, no. 8, pp. 5284–5294, 2021.

16. Li, J.-S., Liu, C.-G., Wu, C.-J., Wu, C.-C., Huang, C.-W., Li, C.-F., and Liu, I.-H., "Design of industrial control system secure communication using moving target defense with legacy infrastructure," *Sensors and Materials*, vol. 33, no. 10, pp. 3415–3424, 2021.

17. Malisa, R., Schwella, E., and Batinge, B., "Augmenting water supplies through urban wastewater recycling (March 2019)," *IEEE Systems Journal*, vol. 14, no. 1, pp. 1523–1530, 2019.

18. Liu, H., Zhang, H., Zhang, Y., Zhang, F., and Huang, M., "Modeling of wastewater treatment processes using dynamic Bayesian networks based on fuzzy PLS," *IEEE Access*, vol. 8, pp. 92129–92140, 2020.

19. Chai, T., and Draxler, R. R., "Root mean square error (RMSE) or mean absolute error (MAE)," *Geoscientific Model Development Discussions*, vol. 7, no. 1, pp. 1525–1534, 2014.

20. Bansal, S., and Geetha, G., "A machine learning approach towards automatic water quality monitoring," *Journal of Water Chemistry and Technology*, vol. 42, no. 5, pp. 321–328, 2020.

21. Hakak, S., Khan, W. Z., Gilkar, G. A., Haider, N., Imran, M., and Alkatheiri, M. S., "Industrial wastewater management using blockchain technology: Architecture, requirements, and future directions," *IEEE Internet of Things Magazine*, vol. 3, no. 2, pp. 38–43, 2020.

22. Solano, F., Krause, S., and Wöllgens, C., "An internet-of-things enabled smart system for wastewater monitoring," *IEEE Access*, vol. 10, pp. 4666–4685, 2022.

23. Mandal, N., Mitra, S., and Bandyopadhyay, D., "Sensors for point-of-care monitoring of drinking water quality," *IEEE Sensors Journal*, vol. 19, no. 18, pp. 7936–7941, 2019.

24. Salem, R. M., Saraya, M. S., and Ali-Eldin, A. M., "An industrial cloud-based iot system for real-time monitoring and controlling of wastewater," *IEEE Access*, vol. 10, pp. 6528–6540, 2022.

25. Atta, H. S., Omar, M. A.-S., and Tawfik, A. M., "Water quality index for assessment of drinking groundwater purpose case study: Area surrounding Ismailia Canal, Egypt," *Journal of Engineering and Applied Science*, vol. 69, no. 1, pp. 1–17, 2022.

26. Dheda, D., Cheng, L., and Abu-Mahfouz, A. M., "Long short term memory water quality predictive model discrepancy mitigation through genetic algorithm optimisation and ensemble modeling," *IEEE Access*, vol. 10, pp. 24638–24658, 2022.

27. Cai, J., Chen, J., Dou, X., and Xing, Q., "Using machine learning algorithms with in situ hyperspectral reflectance data to assess comprehensive water quality of urban rivers," *IEEE Transactions on Geoscience and Remote Sensing*, vol. 60, pp. 1–13, 2022.

28. Kapoor, A. J., Fan, H., and Sardar, M. S., "Intelligent detection using convolutional neural network (ID-CNN)," in *IOP Conference Series: Earth and Environmental Science*, vol. 234, p. 012061, IOP Publishing, 2019.

29. Li, Q., Gao, M., and Li, Z.-L., "Ground hyper-spectral remote-sensing monitoring of wheat water stress during different growing stages," *Agronomy*, vol. 12, no. 10, p. 2267, 2022.

30. Aktar, M., Al Mamun, M., Shuvo, M. S. R., and Hossain, M. A., "Histogram based water quality assessment in satellite images," in *2015 International Conference on Computer and Information Engineering (ICCIE)*, pp. 95–98, IEEE, 2015.

31. Haq, K. R. A., and Harigovindan, V., "Water quality prediction for smart aquaculture using hybrid deep learning models," *IEEE Access*, vol. 10, pp. 60078–60098, 2022.

32. Wang, Y., Sun, L., and Peng, D., "A multihead ConvLSTM for time series classification in ehealth Industry 4.0," *Wireless Communications and Mobile Computing*, vol. 2022, 2022 Article ID 8773900, 7 pages, 2022. https://doi.org/10.1155/2022/8773900

33. Gambín, A. F., Angelats, E., González, J. S., Miozzo, M., and Dini, P., "Sustainable marine ecosystems: Deep learning for water quality assessment and forecasting," *IEEE Access*, vol. 9, pp. 121344–121365, 2021.

34. Chopade, S., Gupta, H. P., Mishra, R., Oswal, A., Kumari, P., and Dutta, T., "A sensors based river water quality assessment system using deep neural network," *IEEE Internet of Things Journal*, vol. 9, no. 16, pp. 14375–14384, 2021.

35. Qi, C., Huang, S., and Wang, X., "Monitoring water quality parameters of Taihu Lake based on remote sensing images and LSTM-RNN," *IEEE Access*, vol. 8, pp. 188068–188081, 2020.

36. Yu, Y., Si, X., Hu, C., and Zhang, J., "A review of recurrent neural networks: LSTM cells and network architectures," *Neural Computation*, vol. 31, no. 7, pp. 1235–1270, 2019.

37. Sylvester, E. V., Bentzen, P., Bradbury, I. R., Clément, M., Pearce, J., Horne, J., and Beiko, R. G., "Applications of random forest feature selection for fine-scale genetic population assignment," *Evolutionary Applications*, vol. 11, no. 2, pp. 153–165, 2018.

38. Szeląga, B., Mehranib, M.-J., Drewnowskib, J., Majewskaa, M., Łagódc, G., Kumarid, S., and Buxd, F., "Assessment of wastewater quality indicators for wastewater treatment influent using an advanced logistic regression model," in *Presented at the 1st International Conference Strategies toward Green Deal Implementation–Water and Raw Materials (ICGreenDeal2020)*, vol. 14, p. 16, 2021.

39. Inoue, J., Yamagata, Y., Chen, Y., Poskitt, C. M., and Sun, J., "Anomaly detection for a water treatment system using unsupervised machine learning," in *2017 IEEE international conference on data mining workshops (ICDMW)*, pp. 1058–1065, IEEE, 2017.

40. Li, P., and Wu, J., "Drinking water quality and public health," *Exposure and Health*, vol. 11, no. 2, pp. 73–79, 2019.

41. Crouch, M. L., Jacobs, H. E., and Speight, V. L., "Defining domestic water consumption based on personal water use activities," *AQUA—Water Infrastructure, Ecosystems and Society*, vol. 70, no. 7, pp. 1002–1011, 2021.

42. Guravaiah, K., and Raju, S. S., "e-Agriculture: Irrigation system based on weather forecasting," in *2020 IEEE 15th International Conference on Industrial and Information Systems (ICIIS)*, pp. 617–622, IEEE, 2020.

43. Rafiq, A., Ikram, M., Ali, S., Niaz, F., Khan, M., Khan, Q., and Maqbool, M., "Photocatalytic degradation of dyes using semiconductor photocatalysts to clean industrial water pollution," *Journal of Industrial and Engineering Chemistry*, vol. 97, pp. 111–128, 2021.

44. Pal, O. K., "The quality of drinkable water using machine learning techniques," *International Journal of Advanced Engineering Research and Science*, vol. 8, p. 5, 2021.

45. World Health Organization and Water, Sanitation and Health Team, *Guidelines for Drinking-Water Quality*, vol. 1. World Health Organization, 2004.

46. Bureau of Indian Standards, "I. S. D. Water-Specification," *New Delhi, India*, pp. 1–12, 2012.

47. Kallis, G., and Butler, D., "The EU water framework directive: Measures and implications," *Water Policy*, vol. 3, no. 2, pp. 125–142, 2001.

48. Kerenhapukh, Y., Fadhila, A., Puteri, H. N., Fadilah, P., and Halim, A., "Effectiveness of waste management in the United States of America," *Frequency of International Relations (FETRIAN)*, vol. 3, no. 1, pp. 33–55, 2021.

49. Jin, L., Li, S., and Hu, B., "RNN models for dynamic matrix inversion: A control-theoretical perspective," *IEEE Transactions on Industrial Informatics*, vol. 14, no. 1, pp. 189–199, 2017.

50. Li, X., Yi, X., Liu, Z., Liu, H., Chen, T., Niu, G., Yan, B., Chen, C., Huang, M., and Ying, G., "Application of novel hybrid deep leaning model for cleaner production in a paper industrial wastewater treatment system," *Journal of Cleaner Production*, vol. 294, p. 126343, 2021.

51. Pan, M., Zhou, H., Cao, J., Liu, Y., Hao, J., Li, S., and Chen, C.-H., "Water level prediction model based on GRU and CNN," *IEEE Access*, vol. 8, pp. 60090–60100, 2020.

3 Design of Tea Ontology for Precision-based Tea Crop Yield Prediction Using Machine Learning

Pallavi Nagpal, Deepika Chaudhary, and Jaiteg Singh

3.1 INTRODUCTION

Ontology plays a crucial role in machine learning by providing a structured representation of knowledge that can be used to facilitate learning and reasoning. Ontology is a formal representation in the form of naming of a domain, which describes the concepts and relationships that exist within that domain. In machine learning, ontology can be used to:

a. **Facilitate data integration:** Ontology can be used to unify and integrate data from different repositories providing a common knowledge base and framework for representing the data.
b. **Improve data quality:** Ontology can help to ensure that data is structured consistently and accurately, which can improve the quality of machine learning models that are trained on the data.
c. **Enhance machine learning algorithms:** Ontology can be used to inform the design of machine learning algorithms by providing a structured representation of the domain knowledge that the algorithm is intended to learn.
d. **Support knowledge transfer:** Ontology can be used to transfer knowledge from one domain to another by providing a structured representation of the relevant concepts and relationships.

The use of ontology in machine learning can help to improve the best ever parameters, i.e., Efficiency and precision, of machine learning models, and facilitate the development of more sophisticated and effective AI systems. There are several examples where the use of ontology has improved the performance of machine learning algorithms. Here are a few:

1. **Medical Diagnosis:** In the field of medical diagnosis, an ontology-based approach has been used to develop a machine learning algorithm for diagnosing rare diseases. The ontology provides a structured representation of

DOI: 10.1201/9781003388845-4

the symptoms, diseases, and relationships between them. This ontology-based approach has been shown to outperform other machine learning algorithms that do not use ontology.

2. **Recommender Systems:** Ontologies have been used to increase the outcomes of recommender systems, which are used to suggest products or services to users based on their preferences. By using ontologies to represent domain knowledge, the recommender system can make more accurate and relevant recommendations to users.

3. **Natural Language Processing:** Ontologies have been used to improve the accuracy of natural language processing (NLP) systems. For example, an ontology-based approach has been used to develop a machine learning algorithm for classifying text into categories such as news, sports, and entertainment. The ontology provides a structured representation of the domain knowledge, which can be used to upgrade the correctness of the classification algorithm.

In general, the use of ontology in machine learning has improved the performance of algorithms in a variety of domains. Below, we present some studies that focus on the role of ontologies in machine learning and recommender systems: The authors in this paper provide a comprehensive survey of the two ontologies by finding the semantic mappings [1, 2]. The authors in the said paper have explored a novel ontology-based approach to user profiling within recommender systems [3]. The authors, through their study on the theme of furnished recommendation, which will serve as a personalized method of knowledge in a heterogeneous environment and by which the users will be able to eliminate repetitive and tedious information [4], carried out a systematic review on the value of an ontology-based recommender system in e-learning. The article successfully suggested the implementation of a comprehensive survey that will detail the research in progress using ontology and thereby be used to achieve personalization in recommender systems in the e-learning domain. Altogether, these studies demonstrate the usefulness of ontologies in machine learning and recommender systems and suggest that the use of ontologies can improve the effectiveness of these systems. The next section presents the different traits of the tea ontology (TO).

3.2. DIFFERENT TRAITS FOR TEA ONTOLOGY

3.2.1 TEA PLANT AND ABIOTIC STRESS

Plants of different types emerged and thereby grew in various seasons based on their climatic conditions in various parts of the world. Also the growth of plants depends upon various factors, which include conditions like temperature, climate and quality and quantity of light, which play a crucial role in plant growth. There are certain plants that require a specific environment and conditions to grow. Such plants require conditions that are favorable to their growth. For such plants, the process

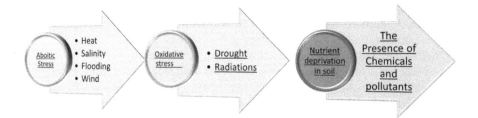

FIGURE 3.1   Causes for different stress levels for tea crop.

of adaptation is quite meaningful because different plants in various geographical regions cannot let go of unfavorable climatic conditions.

Interestingly, it can be stated that all kinds of existing species present and located on earth differentiate themselves genetically in their composition and adaptation. Various plant species depend upon a number of variables and fall under optimum environments. Key abiotic forms of stress factors that affect the productivity and growth of the tea plantation and planning include the following (Figure 3.1).

3.2.2   BIOTIC STRESS

Biotic stress is initiated by different forms of living organisms. The existing and operational tea plants have incorporated various feasible strategies to counter the effects of biotic form of stress. The presence of biotic forms of stress includes the presence of plant diseases and arthropod pests. The tea pests can lead to havoc damage to tea plantations [5]. Also, the involvement of plant diseases is an important factor that creates direct and indirect effects on tea plants. In various scientific research, it was reported that there are almost 400 forms and types of disease-causing pathogens [6]. One of the common problems in tea plantations is the leaf disease.

3.2.3   MORPHOLOGICAL ATTRIBUTES OF TEA

The tea plant falls under the "aceae" family. The leaf of the tea plant has a light green shade. Mature tea plant leaves are bright green in color. The flowers of the tea plant are white in color and incorporate fragrant properties. It involves a range of 2.5–4 cm in diameter. The flowers of the tea plant are composed of numerous stamens. It also involves the yellow anther, which can produce brownish-red capsules [7]. Similarly, the fruit of the tea plant bears a flattened, rounded seed with a small nut [7].

3.2.4   PHONOLOGICAL ATTRIBUTES OF TEA

The primary four important phenophases are mature flower buds, immature flower buds, immature fruits, pen flowers, and mature fruits. Visual observations are carried out on each of different phenophases separately. It employs a nonparametric scale of 0–5 (Table 3.2). The constructs of the scale were based on [8]. Visual observations were also implemented on a monthly basis in five randomly selected healthy trees for three years, from January 2014 to December 2016.

3.2.5 PHYSIOLOGICAL ATTRIBUTES OF TEA

In the past few years, attention has been given to the *Camellia sinensis* L. (tea flower). Amino acids, catechins, and caffeine are the main constituents that exist in both tea flowers and tea leaves. Over a long period of time, the tea flower has been considered as an industrial waste, but past research has revealed that the tea flower has many health benefits with lots of medicinal properties like antitumor, anti-allergic, anti-obesity, antioxidant, immune stimulating, etc.

3.2.6 QUALITY PARAMETERS OF TEA

The significant factors of geography and climate have played an important role in determining whether the conditions of tea plantations are favorable or unfavorable at a particular place. The factors explain the answers to questions like where tea can be grown. How does the tea grow in a particular region? In simplified terms, the technique of plucking can be segmented into fine and coarse. In the first part of the technique of fine plucking, the tender two leaves along with the bud are extracted. Also, in the simultaneous step of coarse plucking, it involves the removal of three to four leaves along with the segregation of buds. However, in comparison, the first technique of fine plucking is seen as superior in relation to the creation of a balance between yield and quality. Some producers use and prefer fewer tender shoots to sense extra biomass production while involving in the exercise of plucking. The limitation of coarse plucking is that it reduces the quality of tea, thereby inhibiting the plucking frequency. The exercise of hand-picking or going through mechanical plucking processes reduces and affects the characteristics and grade of tea. The process of hand plucking produces better quality due to the feature of selective plucking. But the limitation is that the persons and pluckers who lack knowledge create a gap in substantiating a balance between hand pressure and tenderness. The methodology involved in processing the tea leaves is also a critical parameter. The practice of mass-scale mechanical processes cannot be compared and collated with the age-old traditional practice. The step of orthodox processing involves plucking of leaves in batches and thereby treated with a precise amount of withering, rolling, and oxidation. Special care is given to rolling and handling the leaves, as the leaves are delicate and tender and can lead to adulteration and damage. The timing followed in the various processes, including withering, rolling, and fermentation, is considered as an important factor affecting the quality of the tea. In the absence of examination of the above-mentioned factor, the quality of the tea produced can be greatly compromised. Table 3.1 highlights the various traits of crop tea. These traits form the basis for creating tea Ontology.

3.3 LITERATURE REVIEW

As we are creating an ontology of tea yield, we have looked into various sources of information for creating an ideal ontology. A number of sources were gathered for this purpose, and after selecting an appropriate source, we chose crop ontology.org as a

TABLE 3.1

Different Traits of Tea Ontology

Different Traits of Tea Ontology

Abiotic [9]	Agronomic	Biotic [10]	Morphological [11]	Phonological [12]	Physiological [13, 14]	Quality [15]	Weather [15]
Cold (chilling and frost)	Plantation	Bacteria	Height	Immature flower buds	Relative water content (RWC)	Region	Rainfall
Heat (high temperature)	Water supply	Fungi	Width	Mature flower buds	Protein content	Climate	Temperature
Salinity (salt)	Nutrient management	Nematodes	Color	Open flowers	Cell membranes integrity	Elevation	Humidity
Drought (water deficit condition)	Canopy establishment	Arthropod pests	Length	Immature fruits	Sugar content	Cultivators	Sunshine
Excess water (flooding)	Tea garden ecology management	Tea mosquito bug	Type	Mature fruits	Proline content	Plucking process	
Ultraviolet light		Red spider mites	Diameter			Tea making method	
Pollutants and chemicals		Tea geometrid					
Oxidative stress		Shot hole borer					
Dust particles							
Nutrient deprivation in soil							

valuable source. We found that there are various crops that are equipped with ontology creation, but in tea as a crop, there is no such ontology created, which we have considered as research gap, and the necessary actions were taken to fill the gap, i.e. parameters creation, factor analysis, and comparative study on various crop ontologies. Here are some studies that discuss the role of ontologies in the agriculture sector:

- "Ontology Based Approach for Precision Agriculture" by Ngo, Quoc Hung, Nhien-An Le-Khac, and Tahar Kechad [16]. This paper presents an ontology-based approach to data integration in the agriculture sector, which uses an ontology to represent the domain knowledge and guide the integration process.
- "An ontology-based decision support system for the diagnosis of plant diseases" by Lagos-Ortiz, Katty, et al. [17] This paper presents an ontology-based expert system for agriculture decision support, which uses an ontology to represent the domain knowledge and to guide the decision-making process.
- "An Ontology-based Knowledge Mining Model for Effective Exploitation of Agro Information" by Murali, E., and S. Margret Anouncia [18]. This paper presents an ontology-based approach to knowledge management for sustainable agriculture, which uses an ontology to represent the domain knowledge and to support the sharing and reuse of knowledge.

Overall, these papers demonstrate the usefulness of ontologies in the agriculture sector, and suggest that the use of ontologies can improve decision-making, knowledge management, and data integration in agriculture (Table 3.2).

TABLE 3.2
Literature Survey

Year of publication	Citation	Reference	Summary
2009	43	[19]	The major highlight of the paper is that it furnishes a good schematic representation for ontology merging by taking insights from the agricultural domain. The paper attempted to list out a set of ontologies related to agricultural models
2012	111	[20]	The paper elaborated on the development of GCP crop ontology for breeders and simultaneously acknowledged research in the field of agronomic research. The premier agencies that include USDA, Cornell University, and The National Centre for Biotechnology all recognized the concept of GCP Crop Ontology. The CO Development uses the model of Trait Dictionary for the purpose of use in IB field book
2013	35	[21]	The usage of ontology has relevance and impact in many domains of applications in agricultural sciences. Still, there are gray areas where applications of ontology theories are weak. In this particular study, the authors have suggested a modeling tool for representing domain ontology and they have also described a

(Continued)

TABLE 3.2 (*Continued*)
Literature Survey

Year of publication	Citation	Reference	Summary
			V-model system to lay out task ontology, which stands against the background of CSS. The article successfully demonstrated a plant-standardized management system that will boost agriculture knowledge management and innovation
2017	138	[22]	The study explained the significance of Planteome, which is understood as a meritorious resource for plant biology researchers and plant breeders. The strength of the technique of Plantome depends upon an integrated ontology network that can also be traversed computationally. The importance of the technique of Plantome lies in the fact that it can be employed to select ideal traits of interest, identify and locate necessary data, and prove to be crucial in designing hypotheses to test the results
2018	145	[23]	An important article that talks about feasibility and relevance of Agro Portal, which can be understood as a platform for open vocabulary and repository of ontology
2018	22	[24]	In this study, a schematic representation for ontology merging is done. The ideas incorporated in the paper overcome the weaknesses faced by using existing mechanisms for ontology amalgamation
2018	5	[25]	The article successfully recommends a system for cotton crop farmers with the overall objective of detailing improved cotton farming practices. The technological part uses an advanced and strengthened set of web technologies, including type's ontology, resource description framework, and SPARQL to suggest and generate interventions for farmers regarding the best set of practices that can be implemented in cotton crop farming. The system used is helpful to farmers in detailing advice in areas such as elaborating on the appropriate time of sowing seeds and listing out the best set of insecticides and pesticides to cure and prevent diseases in various crops
2021	2	[26]	The article pens down a model for ontology to fulfill the broader objective of crop planning and production processes to enhance crop production. The article also details the C3PO ontology, which has operations in constructing a knowledge base for Elzeard web application data
2021	12	[27]	This paper proposed the framework for the ontology-based model AquaONT. It has significance in boosting knowledge-based systems for crop production and also in bed design at various sites like aquaponics. To analyze the results, parametric modeling is performed
2021	15	[28]	In this study, the authors have proposed a well-designed framework for agricultural ontology. Under this, existing evaluation methods are coupled with certain methods that are specifically evaluated. The applicability of the framework was then determined by taking up the case of pest control ontology

(Continued)

TABLE 3.2 (*Continued*)
Literature Survey

Year of publication	Citation	Reference	Summary
2022	31	[29]	The authors of the study have stated that hybrid machine learning models are better suited for any crop yield prediction and they have explored many machine learning models for crop yield prediction
2022	0	[30]	The authors here have applied ANN for wheat crop yield prediction and they have preferred ANN over multivariate linear regression

3.4   DESIGN AND DEVELOPMENT OF TEA ONTOLOGY

Design and development of TO involve various stages. Below, we present the major steps involved in defining an ontology:

a. **Domain recognition:** The first step is to identify the domain that the ontology will represent. This may involve reviewing existing literature, consulting with domain experts, and conducting a needs analysis.

b. **Define the scope:** Once the domain has been identified, the scope of the ontology needs to be defined. This includes identifying the types of concepts that will be represented, the relationships between these concepts, and any constraints or rules that apply to the domain.

c. **Choose a formal language:** The next step is to choose a formal language for representing the ontology. Commonly used languages include OWL and RDF.

d. **Define the concepts:** The concepts that will be represented in the ontology need to be defined. This involves specifying their properties and relationships to other concepts in the domain.

e. **Define the axioms:** Axioms are statements that are true by definition in the domain. They may be used to specify constraints and rules that apply to the domain.

f. **Create instances:** Instances are specific examples of the concepts represented in the ontology. They may be used to test and validate the ontology.

g. **Test and refine the ontology:** Once the ontology has been created, it needs to be tested and refined to ensure that it accurately represents the domain and is useful for its intended purpose. This may involve evaluating the ontology against a set of test cases, soliciting feedback from domain experts, and making revisions as needed.

h. **Publish and maintain the ontology:** Finally, the ontology needs to be published and maintained so that it can be used by others in the domain. This may involve making the ontology available online, documenting the ontology, and updating it as new knowledge is acquired or changes are made to the domain.

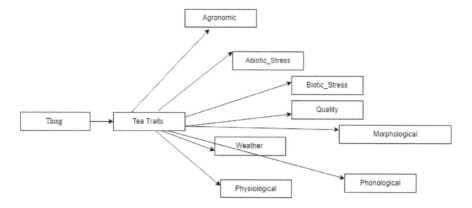

FIGURE 3.2   Tea traits.

These steps may be iterative and may involve revisiting earlier steps as the ontology is developed and refined. Using the tea trait, we have crafted TO using Protégé. This ontology can be used by future researchers for tea-related data integration. Figure 3.2 is a hierarchical representation of how the different traits are related together.

After defining the subclasses using "is-a", a relationship is created between the super and the subclass. This designed ontology will help data scientists to know the important traits pertaining to. This ontology can be used for data curation and integration pertaining to tea crop.

3.5   CONCLUSION AND FUTURE SCOPE

In conclusion, the role of ontologies in machine learning in the agriculture domain is becoming increasingly important. By providing a structured and standardized representation of domain knowledge, ontologies can help machine learning algorithms to better understand and reason about agricultural data. Ontologies can enable more accurate and efficient data classification, clustering, and prediction, leading to better decision-making in agriculture. For example, an ontology-based machine learning system can be used to predict crop yields, detect crop diseases, and optimize crop management practices. In addition, ontologies can help in sharing data and interactivity between different agricultural applications and systems, leading to better collaboration and knowledge exchange among different stakeholders in the agriculture domain. However, developing ontologies for agriculture can be a complex and time-consuming process, requiring domain expertise and careful consideration of the specific needs of the agriculture domain. Nonetheless, the potential benefits of using ontologies in machine learning for agriculture make it a promising avenue for future research and development in this field. This paper summarizes some important traits of tea crops that can be used by data scientists for data integration related to tea crop yield in different parts of the world. Further, in the future, data collection for the prediction of tea crop yield would be based on the classes defined and would be used for precision-based prediction.

REFERENCES

1. Doan, A., Madhavan, J., Domingos, P., & Halevy, A. (2004). Ontology matching: A machine learning approach. In AnHai Doan, Jayant Madhavan, Pedro Domingos & Alon Halevy (Eds.) *Handbook on Ontologies* (pp. 385–403). International Handbooks on Information Systems book series (INFOSYS).

2. Middleton, S. E., De Roure, D., & Shadbolt, N. R. (2004). Ontology-based recommender systems. In *Handbook on Ontologies* (pp. 477–498).

3. Ge, J., Chen, Z., Peng, J., & Li, T. (2012, August). An ontology-based method for personalized recommendation. In *2012 IEEE 11th International Conference on Cognitive Informatics and Cognitive Computing* (pp. 522–526). IEEE.

4. George, G., & Lal, A. M. (2019). Review of ontology-based recommender systems in e-learning. *Computers & Education, 142*, 103642.

5. Borchetia, S., Handique, G., Roy, S., & Wani, S. H. (2018). Genomics approaches for biotic and abiotic stress improvement in tea. In Stress Physiology of Tea in the Face of Climate Change (pp. 289–312).

6. Ponmurugan, P., Baby, U. I., & Rajkumar, R. (2007). Growth, photosynthetic and biochemical responses of tea cultivars infected with various diseases. *Photosynthetica, 45*(1), 143–146.

7. Tariq, M., Naveed, A., & Khan, B. (2010). The morphology, characteristics, and medicinal properties of *Camellia sinensis'* tea. *Journal of Medicinal Plant Research, 4*, 2028–2033. https://doi.org/10.5897/JMPR10.010

8. Ariyarathna, H. A. C. K., Gunasekare, M. T. K., & Kottawa-Arachchige, J. D. *et al.* (2011). Morpho-physiological and phenological attributes of reproductive biology of tea (*Camellia sinensis* (L.) O. Kuntze) in Sri Lanka. *Euphytica, 181*, 203–215. https://doi.org/10.1007/s10681-011-0399-9

9. Van Evert, F. K., Fountas, S., Jakovetic, D., Crnojevic, V., Travlos, I., & Kempenaar, C. (2017). Big data for weed control and crop protection. *Weed Research, 57*(4), 218–233.

10. Jeyaraj, A., Elango, T., Li, X., & Guo, G. (2020). Utilization of microRNAs and their regulatory functions for improving biotic stress tolerance in tea plant [*Camellia sinensis* (L.) O. Kuntze]. *RNA Biology, 17*(10), 1365–1382.

11. Tahmood, T., Akhtar, N., & Khan, B. A. (2010). The morphology, characteristics, and medicinal properties of *Camellia sinensis* tea. *Journal of Medicinal Plants Research, 4*(19), 2028–2033.

12. Piyasundara, J. H. N., Wickramasinghe, I. P., Gunesekara, M. T. K., Wijeratne, M. A., Perera, S. A. C. N., Ranathunga, M. A. B., & Mudalige, A. K. (2018). Reproductive phenology of tea (*Camellia sinensis* (L.) O. Kuntze) cultivars in Sri Lanka. Department of Agricultural Biology, Faculty of Agriculture, University of Peradeniya, Sri Lanka 2 Ministry of Primary Industries, Colombo, Sri Lanka 3 Agronomy Division, Tea Research Institute of Sri Lanka, Thalawakale, Sri Lanka.

13. Chen, D., Chen, G., Sun, Y., Zeng, X., & Ye, H. (2020). Physiological genetics, chemical composition, health benefits and toxicology of tea (*Camellia sinensis* L.) flower: A review. *Food Research International, 137*, 109584.

14. Samarina, L. S., Malyukova, L. S., Efremov, A. M., Simonyan, T. A., Matskiv, A. O., Koninskaya, N. G., … & Hanke, M. V. (2020). Physiological, biochemical and genetic responses of Caucasian tea (*Camellia sinensis* (L.) Kuntze) genotypes under cold and frost stress. *PeerJ, 8*, e9787.

15. Necessary parameters for tea quality (indiatimes.com).

16. Ngo, Q. H., Le-Khac, N. A., & Kechadi, T. (2018). Ontology based approach for precision agriculture. In *Multi-disciplinary Trends in Artificial Intelligence: 12th International Conference, MIWAI 2018, Hanoi, Vietnam, November 18–20, 2018, Proceedings 12* (pp. 175–186). Springer International Publishing.

17. Lagos-Ortiz, K., Medina-Moreira, J., Paredes-Valverde, M. A., Espinoza-Morán, W., & Valencia-García, R. (2017). An ontology-based decision support system for the diagnosis of plant diseases. *Journal of Information Technology Research (JITR)*, *10*(4), 42–55.

18. Murali, E., & Anouncia, S. M. (2022). An ontology-based knowledge mining model for effective exploitation of agro information. *IETE Journal of Research*, *1*, 1–18.

19. Athanasiadis, I. N., Rizzoli, A. E., Janssen, S., Andersen, E., & Villa, F. (2009). Ontology for seamless integration of agricultural data and models. In *Metadata and Semantic Research: Third International Conference, MTSR 2009, Milan, Italy, October 1-2, 2009. Proceedings 3* (pp. 282–293). Springer Berlin Heidelberg.

20. Shrestha, R., Matteis, L., Skofic, M., Portugal, A., McLaren, G., Hyman, G., & Arnaud, E. (2012). Bridging the phenotypic and genetic data useful for integrated breeding through a data annotation using the crop ontology developed by the crop communities of practice. *Frontiers in Physiology*, *3*, 326.

21. Li, D., Kang, L., Cheng, X., Li, D., Ji, L., Wang, K., & Chen, Y. (2013). An ontology-based knowledge representation and implement method for crop cultivation standard. *Mathematical and Computer Modelling*, *58*(3–4), 466–473.

22. Cooper, L., Meier, A., Laporte, M. A., Elser, J. L., Mungall, C., Sinn, B. T., & Jaiswal, P. (2018). The planteome database: An integrated resource for reference ontologies, plant genomics and phenomics. *Nucleic Acids Research*, *46*(D1), D1168–D1180.

23. Jonquet, C., Toulet, A., Arnaud, E., Aubin, S., Yeumo, E. D., Emonet, V., & Larmande, P. (2018). AgroPortal: A vocabulary and ontology repository for agronomy. *Computers and Electronics in Agriculture*, *144*, 126–143.

24. Chatterjee, N., Kaushik, N., Gupta, D., & Bhatia, R. (2018). Ontology merging: A practical perspective. In *Information and Communication Technology for Intelligent Systems (ICTIS 2017)-Volume 2 2* (pp. 136–145). Springer International Publishing.

25. Upadhyaya, H., & Panda, S. K. (2013). Abiotic stress responses in tea [*Camellia sinensis* L (O) Kuntze]: An overview. *Reviews in Agricultural Science*, *1*, 1–10.

26. Darnala, B., Amardeilh, F., Roussey, C., & Jonquet, C. (2021, September). Crop Planning and Production Process Ontology (C3PO), a new model to assist diversified crop production. In *IFOW 2021-Integrated Food Ontology Workshop@ 12th International Conference on Biomedical Ontologies (ICBO)*.

27. Abbasi, R., Martinez, P., & Ahmad, R. (2021). An ontology model to support the automated design of aquaponic grow beds. *Procedia CIRP*, *100*, 55–60.

28. Goldstein, A., Fink, L., & Ravid, G. (2021). A framework for evaluating agricultural ontologies. *Sustainability*, *13*(11), 6387.

29. Bali, N., & Singla, A. (2022). Emerging trends in machine learning to predict crop yield and study its influential factors: A survey. *Archives of Computational Methods in Engineering*, *29*, 1–18.

30. Bali, N., & Singla, A. (2022). ANN-Based Wheat Crop Yield Prediction Technique for Punjab Region. In *Emerging Research in Computing, Information, Communication and Applications: ERCICA 2020, Volume 2* (pp. 207–217). Springer Singapore.

4 Analyzing the Social Media Activities of Users Using Machine Learning and Graph Data Science

Puneet Kaur, Deepika Chaudhary, and Jaiteg Singh

4.1 INTRODUCTION

Social media platforms generate large amounts of data on user activities, including likes, shares, comments, and follows. This data can be analyzed using graph data science techniques to gain insights into user behavior, network structure, and trends. Social media activities generate large amounts of data that can be analyzed using machine learning techniques. Here are some examples of how machine learning can be applied to social media activities:

4.1.1 SENTIMENT ANALYSIS

Sentiment analysis provides insights into how users feel about a particular topic, product, or brand.

4.1.2 PERSONALIZED RECOMMENDATIONS

Machine learning algorithms can be used to analyze users' social media activity data to make personalized recommendations. For example, Netflix uses machine learning to recommend TV shows and movies to users based on their viewing history.

4.1.3 USER PROFILING

Machine learning profiles can be used for targeted advertising and personalized recommendations.

4.1.4 SOCIAL NETWORK ANALYSIS

Machine learning algorithms can be used to analyze social media activity data to identify the structure of social networks. This analysis can provide insights into the relationships between users and help identify influential users and communities.

Machine learning can be a powerful tool for analyzing social media activity data. However, it is important to be aware of ethical considerations around privacy

DOI: 10.1201/9781003388845-5

and data usage when analyzing social media data using machine learning techniques. In the next section, we primarily focus on the application of machine learning, i.e., how various machine learning techniques can be utilized for analyzing social media content.

4.2 STEPS IN ANALYZING SOCIAL MEDIA ACTIVITIES

4.2.1 DATA ACQUISITION

The first step in analyzing social media activities is to collect data from social media platforms. Depending on the platform and the type of analysis you want to perform, you may need to use an API to collect data. Social media platforms such as Twitter and Facebook provide APIs that allow developers to collect data in real time. Once you have collected the data, you need to transform it into a graph database format that can be analyzed using graph data science tools such as Neo4j.

4.2.2 GRAPH MODELING

The second step is to model the data as a graph. In a social media context, this involves creating nodes to represent users, content, interactions, and relationships to represent the connections between them. For example, a node may represent a user, and relationships may represent their followers, likes, retweets, mentions, and comments. By modeling the data as a graph, we can analyze the relationships between users, content, and interactions to gain insights into user behavior, preferences, and trends.

4.2.3 GRAPH ANALYSIS

The third step is to perform graph analysis on the data. Graph analysis allows us to uncover patterns, trends, and insights that are not easily visible using traditional data analysis techniques. Graph analysis techniques such as centrality analysis, community detection, and link prediction can be used to identify key users, content, and interactions, uncover communities of users with similar interests, and predict future interactions between users and content.

4.2.4 SENTIMENT ANALYSIS

Social media activities also contain valuable information about user sentiment. Sentiment analysis can be used to classify the sentiment of user interactions such as likes, comments, and mentions. This involves using natural language processing (NLP) techniques to analyze the text of user interactions and classify them as positive, negative, or neutral. By analyzing the sentiment of user interactions, we can gain insights into user preferences, opinions, and trends. Sentiment analysis is a NLP technique that enables the extraction of emotions, opinions, and attitudes from text data.

4.2.5 VISUALIZATION

Finally, visualization is an important part of social media analysis. Graph visualization tools such as Neo4j Bloom and Graph can be used to visualize the graph data and explore the relationships between users, content, and interactions. Visualization can help uncover patterns and trends that are not easily visible using traditional data analysis techniques. By visualizing the data, we can gain a deeper understanding of user behavior and preferences.

One approach to analyzing social media activities using graph data science is to represent the data as a graph, where users are nodes and their activities are edges. For example, if User A likes a post from User B, this can be represented as an edge between nodes A and B. Once the data is represented as a graph, various graph analysis techniques can be applied to gain insights into the network structure and user behavior. Clustering algorithms such as modularity clustering or the Louvain algorithm can be used to identify communities of users who are more closely connected than users outside their community. Another approach is to use graph-embedding techniques to represent the graph as a lower dimensional space, where nodes are represented as vectors. This can be useful for downstream machine learning tasks, such as predicting user behavior or identifying anomalous activity. Overall, graph data science can provide valuable insights into social media activities and user behavior, helping to identify trends, influential users, and communities within the network. However, it is important to be aware of ethical considerations around privacy and data usage when analyzing social media data. These data contain valuable information about user behavior, preferences, interests, and trends. Graph data science provides an effective way to analyze social media activities by modeling the relationships between users, content, and interactions. Twitter generates a large amount of data that can be analyzed to gain insights into user behavior, network structure, and trends. Neo4j is a graph database that can be used to represent Twitter data as a graph, where users are nodes and their activities are edges. This approach allows for efficient and flexible analysis of Twitter data. In this chapter, we will discuss how to analyze social media activities using graph data science.

In conclusion, analyzing social media activities using graph data science can provide valuable insights into user behavior, preferences, and trends. By modeling the data as a graph and performing graph analysis techniques such as centrality analysis, community detection, and link prediction, we can uncover patterns and trends that are not easily visible using traditional data analysis techniques. Sentiment analysis can be used to classify the sentiment of user interactions, and visualization can help uncover patterns and trends that are not easily visible using traditional data analysis techniques. This chapter uses tweets about mental illness and applies graph data science to analyze the mental health of human beings. In the next section, we discuss data analytics and its various categories, and in the following section, we present how we can perform data analytics on tweets using Neo4j.

4.3   TWITTER DATA ANALYTICS USING Neo4j

Twitter is a powerful social media platform, with millions of users generating a vast amount of data every day. This data includes tweets, retweets, mentions, hashtags, and user profiles, among other things. Analyzing this data can provide valuable insights into user behavior, trends, and sentiments, which can be useful for businesses, researchers, and policymakers. Graph data science provides a powerful toolkit for analyzing Twitter data, as it enables the exploration of complex relationships and patterns among users and their interactions. One of the primary ways in which graph data science can be applied to Twitter data analytics is through network analysis. A network is a set of nodes (users) that are connected by edges (interactions), and network analysis involves examining the structure and properties of these networks. One common type of network analysis is centrality analysis, which measures the importance of nodes in a network based on their degree of connectedness to other nodes. In the context of Twitter, this might involve identifying influential users who have many followers or who are frequently mentioned or retweeted by others. Another important aspect of Twitter data analytics is sentiment analysis, which involves determining the emotional tone of tweets and user interactions. Graph data science can be used to model the sentiment of Twitter conversations as a network, where nodes represent users and edges represent the sentiment of their interactions. This can enable the identification of positive and negative sentiment clusters as well as the tracking of changes in sentiment over time. In the next section, we present the literature survey on the mentioned topic.

4.4 LITERATURE SURVEY

Analyzing tweets using machine learning is a popular research area that has gained significant attention in recent years. In this literature survey, we will review some of the recent studies that have used machine learning techniques to analyze tweets.

4.4.1 SENTIMENT ANALYSIS

Sentiment analysis is one of the most widely studied areas in Twitter data analytics. In a recent study, Bhardwaj et al. [1] used machine learning algorithms to classify the sentiment of tweets. They used a deep learning model to extract features from tweets and achieved an accuracy of 92.1% on the sentiment analysis task.

4.4.2 TOPIC MODELING

Topic modeling is another area of interest in analyzing tweets. In a recent study, Farkhod et al. [2] used a topic modeling approach to identify the topics of discussion in tweets related to COVID-19. They used the Latent Dirichlet Allocation algorithm to extract topics from tweets and identified topics such as lockdown, vaccines, and testing.

4.4.3 USER PROFILING

User profiling is the process of creating user profiles based on their social media activity. In a recent study, Wang et al. [3] used machine learning algorithms to create user profiles based on their tweets. They used a combination of text and network features to create user profiles and achieved an accuracy of 85.7% on the user profiling task.

4.4.4   EVENT DETECTION

Event detection is the process of identifying events from Twitter data. In a recent study, Zhang et al. [4] used a machine learning approach to detect events related to COVID-19. They used a combination of deep learning and rule-based methods to identify events such as lockdowns and vaccine announcements.

4.4.5   FAKE NEWS DETECTION

Fake news is a major issue on social media platforms such as Twitter. In a recent study, Kumar et al. [5, 6] used machine learning algorithms to detect fake news on Twitter. They used a combination of linguistic and network features to classify tweets as real or fake news and achieved an accuracy of 91.2%.

In conclusion, analyzing tweets using machine learning is a rapidly evolving research area with many applications [7, 8], including sentiment analysis, topic modeling, user profiling, event detection, and fake news detection. These studies demonstrate the potential of machine learning techniques for analyzing Twitter data and provide insights into user behavior, opinions, and trends. Below, we present a more detailed analysis of the literature in this direction.

According to A. Brahmananda Reddy, D.N. Vasundhara, and P. Subhash, sentiment analysis deals with dynamically executing functions using Twitter, an online social network. A dataset is produced by the electronic product's tweets on Twitter. Tweets are brief statements filled with slang and typos. Hence, sentiment analysis at the sentence level is carried out. This can be accomplished in seven steps. Data for the first phase is provided. A username or a hashtag is used as the input data in this case. Then, the total number of tweets to be evaluated is determined; this procedure is carried out before feature extraction. The processing process includes deleting stop words and URLs and avoiding misspellings and slang. Commuting continuous characters with two occurrences helps prevent misspellings. Extracting features comes next. A feature vector is created by using pertinent settings.

The idea put forth by Hetu Bhavsar, Richa Manglani, and others is that the emotions expressed by social media users in their tweets might be utilized to analyze and describe them. They categorized emotions using the tweet's polarity, which can be either positive or negative. Twitter is a popular social media platform that generates a massive amount of data every day. Analyzing this data can provide valuable insights into user behavior, preferences, and trends. Graph data science provides an effective way to analyze Twitter data by modeling the relationships between users, content, and interactions [9, 10]. This literature survey presents the viewpoints of various researchers who have used graph data science on Twitter data sets. In the research cited by Kushal et al. [11], an issue of conflicting reviews was identified. Concerning the classification of evaluations that include both positive and negative feelings, the author highlighted his worries. Due to improper categorization, these reviews frequently have the effect of lowering the performance score. They also concluded that because Amazon reviews are often longer than Twitter ones, using the same machine learning algorithm for sentiment prediction for them is likely to provide superior results. Graph data science provides an effective way to analyze Twitter data by modeling the relationships between users, content, and interactions [12, 13]. Recent studies have used graph data science to analyze the dynamics of user attention and communication structure, detect trends, perform community detection and opinion mining, identify influential users, and analyze and visualize trending topics [14–16]. By using graph data science to analyze Twitter data, we can gain valuable insights into user behavior, preferences, and trends.

4.5 RESEARCH METHODOLOGY

In this study, we follow the below-mentioned methodology for analyzing tweets about mental illness and their impact on human health.

4.5.1 EXTRACTING TWEETS BASED ON ONTOLOGICAL STRUCTURE FROM TWITTER API

Extracting tweets based on an ontological structure from the Twitter API involves using a domain-specific ontology to retrieve tweets that are relevant to a particular domain or topic [17–19]. An ontology is a formal representation of knowledge that defines concepts and their relationships. Here are the steps involved in extracting tweets based on an ontological structure:

4.5.1.1 Define the Ontology
The first step is to define an ontology that represents the domain or topic of interest. The ontology should include concepts and relationships that are relevant to the domain or topic. For example, if the domain is healthcare, the ontology might include concepts such as diseases, treatments, and symptoms, as well as relationships such as causes and treatments.

4.5.1.2 Map the Ontology to the Twitter API
The next step is to map the ontology to the Twitter API. This involves identifying Twitter search queries that are relevant to the concepts and relationships in the ontology. For example, for the concept of diseases, search queries might include the names of specific diseases or related keywords such as symptoms and treatments.

4.5.1.3 Query the Twitter API
Once the ontology has been mapped to the Twitter API, queries can be submitted to retrieve relevant tweets. The queries should be constructed based on the search queries identified in Step 2.

4.5.1.4 Extract Relevant Tweets

The final step is to extract relevant tweets from the results of the Twitter API queries. This can be done by filtering tweets based on their content, such as the presence of specific keywords or the use of domain-specific terminology. In addition, tweets can be analyzed using NLP techniques to extract relevant information such as named entities (e.g., disease names) and relationships (e.g., causes and treatments). Based on an already created ontology (Figure 4.1), the tweets were extracted using Python code and loaded into neo4j.

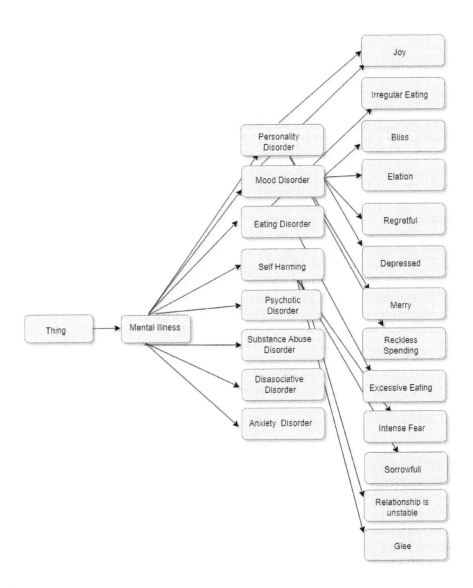

FIGURE 4.1 Ontological structure for selecting tweets.

In conclusion, extracting tweets based on an ontological structure involves using a domain-specific ontology to retrieve relevant tweets from the Twitter API. By mapping the ontology to the Twitter API and querying for relevant tweets, it is possible to extract valuable insights and information about a particular domain or topic.

4.5.2 LOADING CSV INTO Neo4j

Loading CSV files into Neo4j is a common practice in graph database management. Here are the steps to load a CSV file into Neo4j: Prepare the CSV file: The first step is to prepare the CSV file to be loaded into Neo4j. The file should be in tabular format, with columns and rows. The first row should contain column headers. Each row in the file represents a node or relationship in the graph. Create a new database in Neo4j: If you don't have an existing Neo4j database, you will need to create a new one. This can be done by downloading and installing Neo4j on your local machine and then running the Neo4j Desktop application to create a new project. Open the Neo4j Browser: Once you have created a new database, open the Neo4j Browser. This is a web-based interface that allows you to interact with your Neo4j database. Create constraints (optional): If you want to enforce constraints on your data, such as unique values for a particular property, you can create constraints in Neo4j. This can be done using the Cypher query language. For example, to create a constraint on a "name" property, you can use the following query:

CREATE CONSTRAINT ON (n: Node) ASSERT n.name IS UNIQUE

Load the CSV file: To load the CSV file into Neo4j, you will need to use the LOAD CSV command in Cypher. This command allows you to specify the location of the CSV file and the columns to be loaded into the graph. For example, to load a CSV file with columns "id," "name," and "age," you can use the following query:

The collected tweets were first loaded into Neo4j using the below-mentioned query: LOAD CSV WITH HEADERS FROM 'FILE:///Mental_Illness_Tweets.CSV' AS row MERGE (t:tweets{user_name:row.user_name,user_location:coalesce(row.user_location,"unkownn"),user_verified:coalesce(row.user_verified,"unknown"),text:row.text,source:row.source})

Check the data: Once you have loaded the CSV file into Neo4j, you can use the Neo4j Browser to check the data in the graph. You can run queries to retrieve nodes and relationships and use the visualization tools in the browser to explore the graph. As shown in Figure 4.1, almost 1966 nodes with 9830 properties were created in just 13691 ms.

In conclusion, loading CSV files into Neo4j is a straightforward process that involves preparing the file, creating a database, opening the Neo4j Browser, creating constraints (optional), and using the LOAD CSV command in Cypher to load the data into the graph. By following these steps, you can easily load your data into Neo4j and start exploring and analyzing your graph (Figure 4.2).

FIGURE 4.2 Loaded CSV into the Neo4j database.

4.5.3 CREATING RELATIONSHIPS BETWEEN NODES

Creating relationships between nodes in Neo4j involves using the Cypher query language to specify the type of relationship, the direction of the relationship, and the nodes that are connected by the relationship. Here are the steps to create relationships between nodes in Neo4j:

> Identify the nodes: The first step is to identify the nodes that you want to connect with a relationship. These nodes may already exist in your database or may need to be created using a Cypher query. Define the relationship type: The next step is to define the type of relationship that you want to create between the nodes. Relationship types are defined using a string value enclosed in square brackets, such as [: FOLLOWS] or [: LIKES].

Specify the direction of the relationship: Relationships in Neo4j can be directed, meaning that they have a specific direction. You can specify the direction of the relationship using either the "->" or "<-" operator. The "->" operator indicates that the relationship flows from the first node to the second node, while the "<-" operator indicates that the relationship flows from the second node to the first node. You can also use the "-" operator to indicate an undirected relationship.

Connect the nodes with the relationship: Once you have defined the relationship type and direction, you can use the Cypher query language to connect the nodes to the relationship. For example, to create a "FOLLOWS" relationship from a node with the "User" label to another node with the "User" label, you can use the following query:

> MATCH (a:User {username: 'user1'}), (b:User {username: 'user2'}) CREATE (a)-[:FOLLOWS]->(b)

This query matches two nodes with the "User" label and specific usernames and creates a directed "FOLLOWS" relationship from the first node to the second node.

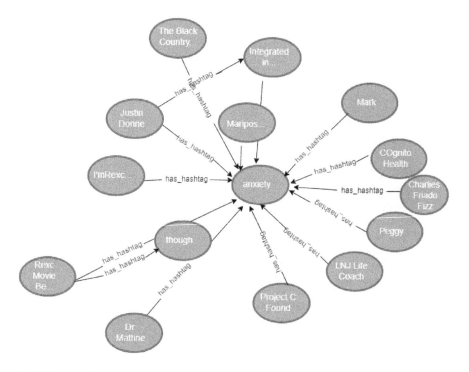

FIGURE 4.3   Representation of tweets based on hashtags.

Check the relationships: Once you have created relationships between nodes, you can use the Neo4j Browser to check the relationships. You can run queries to retrieve nodes and relationships and use the visualization tools in the Browser to explore the graph. For this application, the following data were created: After loading the file in the Neo4j database, relationships 'has_hashtag' were created (Figure 4.3).

In conclusion, creating relationships between nodes in Neo4j involves identifying the nodes, defining the relationship type and direction, and using the Cypher query language to connect the nodes with the relationship. By following these steps, you can easily create relationships in your Neo4j graph and model complex relationships between entities in your data (Figure 4.4).

4.5.4   CLUSTERING TERMS RELATED TO MENTAL ILLNESS

Clustering terms related to mental illness is an important task in NLP and data analysis. Clustering helps to group similar terms and identify patterns in the data that might not be apparent at first glance. In this section, we will discuss a few methods that can be used to cluster terms related to mental illness. After creating the nodes and relationships, the nodes were clustered as shown in Figure 4.3 based on hashtags and relationships between them. In the first part, we analyzed that some users are really happy, and while they are tweeting, the maximum number of times they make use of the words joy, happiness, etc.

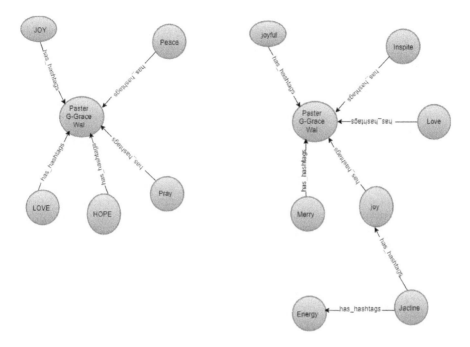

FIGURE 4.4 Relationships among Nodes.

4.6 CONCLUSION

In conclusion, this study aimed to extract and analyze tweets related to mental illness using graph data science. Tweets were extracted from the Twitter API and loaded into a graph database, and relationships were created between the nodes. The tweets were then clustered based on mental illness categories using K-means clustering. The analysis revealed that individuals who express peaceful and joyful sentiments tend to use mental illness-related terms more frequently. In the future, more advanced machine learning algorithms could be applied to determine centrality and other parameters, which could provide a deeper understanding of mental health trends and behaviors on social media platforms. Overall, this study provides insights into the potential of graph data science and machine learning in analyzing social media data related to mental illness.

REFERENCES

1. Bhardwaj, A., & Srivastava, P. (2021). A machine learning approach to sentiment analysis on web-based feedback. In *Applications of Artificial Intelligence and Machine Learning: Select Proceedings of ICAAAIML 2020* (pp. 127–139). Springer Singapore.
2. Farkhod, A., Abdusalomov, A., Makhmudov, F., & Cho, Y. I. (2021). LDA-based topic modeling sentiment analysis using topic/document/sentence (TDS) model. *Applied Sciences, 11*(23), 11091.
3. Sinnott, R., & Wang, Z. (2021, December). Linking user accounts across social media platforms. In *2021 IEEE/ACM 8th International Conference on Big Data Computing, Applications and Technologies (BDCAT'21)* (pp. 18–27).

4. Chen, J., Wu, L., Zhang, J., Zhang, L., Gong, D., Zhao, Y., ... & Yu, H. (2020). Deep learning-based model for detecting 2019 novel coronavirus pneumonia on high-resolution computed tomography. *Scientific Reports, 10*(1), 19196.

5. Kumar, S., Asthana, R., Upadhyay, S., Upreti, N., & Akbar, M. (2020). Fake news detection using deep learning models: A novel approach. *Transactions on Emerging Telecommunications Technologies, 31*(2), e3767.

6. Annamoradnejad, I., & Habibi, J. (2019, April). A comprehensive analysis of twitter trending topics. In *2019 5th International Conference on Web Research (ICWR)* (pp. 22–27). IEEE.

7. Amati, G., Angelini, S., Gambosi, G., Rossi, G., & Vocca, P. (2019). Influential users in Twitter: Detection and evolution analysis. *Multimedia Tools and Applications, 78,* 3395–3407.

8. Li, C., Bai, J., Zhang, L., Tang, H., & Luo, Y. (2019). Opinion community detection and opinion leader detection based on text information and network topology in cloud environment. *Information Sciences, 504,* 61–83.

9. Zhai, Q., Rahardjo, H., Satyanaga, A., Zhu, Y., Dai, G., & Zhao, X. (2021). Estimation of wetting hydraulic conductivity function for unsaturated sandy soil. *Engineering Geology, 285,* 106034.

10. Eom, Y. H., Puliga, M., Smailović, J., Mozetič, I., & Caldarelli, G. (2015). Twitter-based analysis of the dynamics of collective attention to political parties. *PLoS One, 10*(7), e0131184.

11. Sharma, K., & Kumar, A. (2022, December). A Graph Database-Based Method for Network Log File Analysis. In *2022 11th International Conference on System Modeling & Advancement in Research Trends (SMART)* (pp. 545–550). IEEE.

12. Mittal, R., Ahmed, W., Mittal, A., & Aggarwal, I. (2021). Twitter users' coping behaviors during the COVID-19 lockdown: An analysis of tweets using mixed methods. *Information Discovery and Delivery, 49*(3), 193–202.

13. Lavanya, B., & Princy, A. A. (2018). A survey on contribution of data mining techniques and graph reading algorithms in concept map generation. *Journal on Today's Ideas-Tomorrow's Technologies, 6*(2), 99–105.

14. Lavanya, B., & Madhumitha, T. (2018). A survey on identification of motifs and ontology in medical database. *Journal on Today's Ideas-Tomorrow's Technologies, 6*(1), 29–34.

15. Singh, S., Singh, J., Shah, B., Sehra, S. S., & Ali, F. (2022). Augmented reality and GPS-based resource efficient navigation system for outdoor environments: Integrating device camera, sensors, and storage. *Sustainability, 14*(19), 12720.

16. Kumar, N., Panda, S. N., & Pradhan, P. (2017). Hybrid approach for automatic drug dispensing and control. *Journal of Multidisciplinary Research in Healthcare, 3*(2), 69–77.

17. Kamal, P., & Ahuja, S. (2017). A review on prediction of academic performance of students at-risk using data mining techniques. *Journal on Today's Ideas-Tomorrow's Technologies, 5*(1), 30–39.

18. Agarwal, A. K., Tiwari, R. G., Khullar, V., & Kaushal, R. K. (2021, August). Transfer learning inspired fish species classification. In *2021 8th International Conference on Signal Processing and Integrated Networks (SPIN)* (pp. 1154–1159). IEEE.

19. Mahajan, N., Kaur, S., Kaur, M., & Kaur, D. (2021). Enhanced Optimized MSVM Classification of Lung Cancer in Biomedical CT Image Database. IRJET, 2021, 728–737.

Part II

AI and ML in Healthcare

5 Deep Learning-Based Multiple Myeloma Identification Using Micro-imaging Technique

Shamama Anwar

5.1 INTRODUCTION

Blood, being one of the most vital body fluids, essentially has four components: red blood cells (RBC), white blood cells (WBC), plasma and, platelets. A plasma cell or plasmacyte is a kind of immune cell that produces antibodies. The bone marrow produces a type of WBC known as B lymphocytes (B cells), which are precursors to plasma cells. These B cells transform into plasma cells when some external virus or bacteria invade the body. Abnormal growth in the plasma cells may lead to the development of tumor cells in the bones or soft tissues known as myeloma cells. An antibody protein known as *M* protein is also produced by the plasma cells. This antibody protein is an inessential component and does not aid in immunity against infections. These antibody proteins accumulate in the bone marrow, causing neoplasms that may be benign (not cancerous) or malignant (cancerous) [1].

Multiple myeloma (MM) develops in the plasma cells of WBC. They develop as cancerous plasma cells, multiply in the bone marrow, and throng out the good blood cells, producing abnormal proteins that can cause complications [2]. MM cells can spread in the body and can damage and weaken bones and many other organs in the body, including the nerves, heart, kidneys, and digestive tract, thereby resulting in severe health issues [3]. The diagnosis of MM is based on the $\beta2$ microglobulin test and is divided into three stages [4]:

Stage 1: The $\beta2$ microglobulin level is less than 3.5 mg/L.
Stage 2: The $\beta2$ microglobulin levels range from 3.5 to 5.4 mg/L.
Stage 3: The $\beta2$ microglobulin levels in the blood are 5.5 mg/L or higher in stage III multiple myeloma.

MM, however, is also an incurable condition, and it normally recurs after a period of remission while on treatment [5]. Prompt identification and routine monitoring are essential for delaying the progression of the disease. Thus, computer-aided diagnostic (CAD) was created to help radiologists improve diagnosis accuracy, speed, and reliability [6]. Various CAD schemes have evolved for detecting and characterizing various lesions in medical imaging from different modalities, including magnetic

DOI: 10.1201/9781003388845-7

resonance imaging (MRI), computed tomography (CT), conventional projection radiography, and ultrasound imaging. These CAD systems slowly evolved to work efficiently with different data modalities, including images [7]. The initial implementation of CAD revolved around radiology diagnosis [8], but with the advent of modern medical imaging technologies, the scope expanded. CAD is now capable of assisting clinicians in diagnosis of various diseases through interactions with a wide range of medical image modalities [9]. Recent implementation of CAD methods is driven by artificial intelligence and machine learning/deep learning to be more specific, which is creating a shift towards precision medicine [10].

The work reported in this chapter aims at taking the CAD method a step further in assisting in the early diagnosis of MM using deep learning techniques. The remainder of this chapter contains a brief overview of the literature that helped to identify the potential application of the proposed idea (Section 5.2), followed by a detailed description of the proposed model's architecture (Section 5.3). The results and discussion section follows (Section 5.4).

5.2 LITERATURE REVIEW

In the context of applying automation to cancer detection, employing handcrafted features with conventional classifiers can be found in [11–15]. The systems so developed may not be reliable in a practical situation where massive amounts of data come in as input, as these data have large-scale heterogeneity. Besides the usual limitations of using hand-crafted features, such systems also tend to be time-consuming [16]. With the advent of deep learning techniques, the requirement of explicitly extracting features diminished, paving the way for the new concept of implicit feature extraction through learning. This characteristic of deep learning techniques led to an expeditious rise in its use in medical imaging. Interestingly, the application varied among different imaging techniques like X-rays, CT scans, MRI scans, and even microimaging. Convolutional neural network (CNN)-based techniques have been found to work fairly well with unbalanced X-ray images and have been profoundly used for classifying multiple TB manifestations [17], intervertebral disc labeling [18], and pneumonia detection [19] using X-ray images. Recently, an upsurge in literature pertaining to the identification of Covid-19 using CNN-based techniques can be seen [20–22].

CT imaging has also been profoundly used in deep learning-based identification/ classification tasks. Other than Covid-19 detection [23–25], prior work can be seen for lung cancer detection [26], hemorrhage detection [27], automated detection of critical findings in head trauma CT [28], and diagnosis of pancreatic diseases [29] using CT images. Similar applications of deep learning in the MRI imaging modality can also be found for cardiac segmentation and abnormality detection [30], brain tumor segmentation [31, 32], neurodegenerative disease [33], liver tumor diagnosis [34, 35], and many more.

This chapter explores the application of micro-imaging data (microscopic) for automatic disease identification. A notable contribution in this regard using deep learning techniques can be found in the diagnosis of acute lymphoblastic leukemia [36, 37], malaria disease identification from blood smear images [38, 39], and WBC segmentation [40, 41]. The majority of literature found on deep learning-based applications on micro-imaging data revolves around the above-mentioned diseases. Identification of multiple myeloma based on blood smear microscopic imaging is very minuscule. The most dominant method for the detection of myeloma cells is bone marrow aspiration using aspirate slide images [42]. These images (micro-images) are either studied visually or digitally to identify MM cells. Predominantly, the available literature in this context employs imaging mechanisms like PET/CT scans [43, 44] and MRI [45, 46]. These studies employed pre-trained CNN models like U-net, V-net, W-net, etc. A deep learning-based model for MM identification using micro-imaging is still a work less explored. Some contributions in this domain can be found in [47], which aimed at segmentation of plasma cells. A transfer learning-based model combining different ensemble techniques has also been applied to MM micro-imaging data [16]. These classification models are pre-trained on the ImageNet dataset, which is a non-medical dataset. In such networks, the input micro-images (medical images) are matched with the input image size that these pre-trained networks are trained on. This requires pre-processing of the micro-images with suitable scaling to match the pre-trained networks' size. Furthermore, these networks may be unpleasantly enormous for medical applications, and in general, the medical domain does not have as many classes as available in the ImageNet dataset [48].

For this reason, this chapter proposes a deep learning-based model that has been trained from scratch on medical imaging data to better suit its applicability. As the proposed approach is trained from the beginning, a large dataset is required. To obtain this dataset, a variety of augmentation techniques are applied. Specifically, the original dataset contained 450 microscopic images (84 MM cells and 366 normal). After augmentation, the dataset size increased to 820 micro-images (384 for MM and 436 for normal), which are then split into training and test data, i.e., 574 images (70%) are used for testing and 246 (30%) are used for testing. The model is tested for 10 trails by altering the data selection randomly to observe its performance, which has been documented in the Results section. The notable contributions of this works are listed as follows:

1. The available work on MM detection uses images from MRI, PET, or CT scans; the proposed work uses micro-imaging techniques obtained through microscopic blood smear images for identification.
2. The proposed model does not use a pre-trained model, as the majority of these models are trained on the ImageNet dataset, are capable of multi-class classification, and are hence more complex. The proposed model employs a simple architecture capable of performing binary classification into MM and normal cells.
3. As with traditional machine learning techniques, no explicit hand-crafted feature extraction is needed. The features are automatically extracted from the raw (unprocessed) image using the feature extractor unit.

5.3   DATASET DESCRIPTION AND PREPARATION

In the proposed study, the MM dataset has been obtained from the Laboratory of Biomedical Engineering, Faculty of Technology, University of Tlemcen, Algeria,

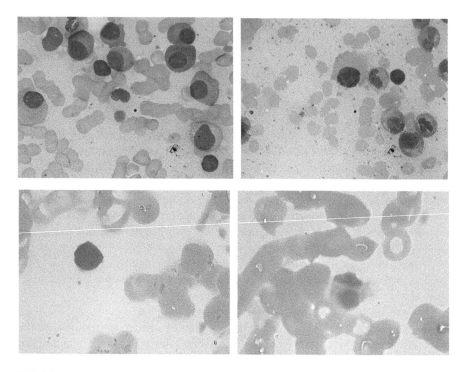

FIGURE 5.1   Dataset images: (a–b) MM-infected cells; (c–d) normal cells.

and the Hematology Department, University Hospital of Tlemcen, Algeria [49]. There are imaging data available for MM and normal subjects. There are 84 microscopic images in the MM class gathered between 2008 and 2019 from 200 patients. The normal class consists of a set of 366 microscopic images. Figure 5.1(a–b) and (c–d) depicts samples of the blood micro-image taken from the dataset for MM and normal subjects, respectively. As mentioned, the dataset consists of 450 images in all for both MM-infected and normal subjects; data augmentation is needed to enhance the size of the dataset. Data augmentation includes operations on the training dataset using different tools to increase its size.

Deep learning techniques are known to perform better when trained on a large dataset, introducing variability in the model and enhancing its capability to correctly classify new input samples. It also addresses the issue of overfitting, which occurs when there are fewer training data. A variety of data augmentation techniques have been used to enhance the dataset size (Figure 5.2) such as:

- **Shear:** Shear shifts every pixel in an image with a constant distance either in the x or y direction.
- **Flipping:** Flipping just inverts the image along the horizontal or vertical axis and is one of the simplest augmentation techniques.
- **Rotation:** This operation rotates the image on an axis between 1 and 359 either to the right or left.

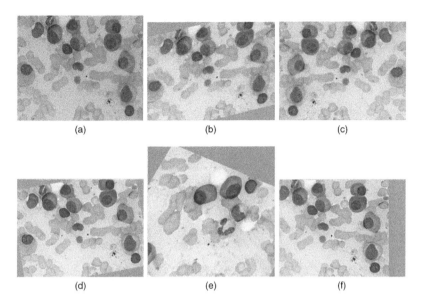

FIGURE 5.2   Images obtained after augmentation: (a) original image; (b) shear; (c) flipping; (d) rotation; (e) translation; and (f) cropping.

- **Translation:** It includes shifting the image in either of the four directions and is known to be helpful in avoiding positional bias in data [50].
- **Color space:** Color images are represented using three channel space: R, G, and B. Alterations in these channels lead to a variety of techniques for generating new images. Isolating a single-color channel can split the image into three instances, thereby increasing the image dataset size. Additionally, the RGB values can be conveniently adjusted to increase or decrease the image's brightness using simple matrix operations.
- **Cropping:** Random cropping of an image can drastically increase the dataset size, and it can be used to produce a similar effect as translation but different in spatial dimension.

As discussed, the dataset consists of 450 images, out of which 84 are of MM-infected subjects and the remaining 366 are of normal subjects. Due to this imbalance in the dataset, augmentation techniques applied in this work are more focused on increasing the size of the MM-infected class to create a balance between both classes. Augmentation artificially increased the size of the dataset from 450 images to a total of 820 images, i.e., an additional 370 images were added after augmentation. The dataset now contains 384 images for the MM class and 436 images for the normal class. The dataset is further split into training and testing data, where 574 (70%) images are used for training and 246 (30%) images are used for testing. The detailed description of the dataset is provided in Table 5.1.

TABLE 5.1

Dataset Description in Terms of Data Split

	Subjects	Training Split	
		Original dataset	Augmented dataset
Number of images	MM	58	268
	Normal	256	306
Total images in training		315	574
		Testing Split	
	Subjects	Original dataset	Augmented dataset
Number of images	MM	26	116
	Normal	110	130
Total images in testing		135	246

5.4 PROPOSED CONVOLUTION NEURAL NETWORK MODEL

Successful application of automated techniques in medical imaging requires advanced technology combined with different image modalities [51]. The emergence of machine learning and, more specifically, deep learning, in the medical imaging domain has the capability to supplement the overall CAD scenario. Traditional machine learning techniques like regression, decision trees, support vector machines, etc. depend on handcrafted feature extraction for accurate implementation. Such models may be better suited for textual data, but in terms of medical imaging, feature extraction manually from these data is cumbersome and, at the same time, time -consuming. Deep learning is well known to exhibit finer performance than the customary machine learning for processing massive amounts of images. CNNs are capable of combining multi-layer perceptrons and are known to exhibit better results with very little or sometimes no pre-processing. CNN is further capable of extracting features efficiently in each convolution layer as it learns a new feature from the image and produces a high activation.

In the proposed work, a simple yet robust automated method for identifying MM cells from micro-image data using CNN is presented. The proposed model essentially has two broadly categorized components: the feature extractor and the classifier. In the feature extractor, convolution layers extract and distinguish the different features of the micro-image for analysis. And further, the dense or fully connected layers are used to classify the image's class or label using the features extracted through the feature extractor unit.

5.4.1 THE FEATURE EXTRACTOR

The CNN model's initial part caters to automatic feature extraction from the input image. This is attained by a set of five units, each consisting of convolution layers of different dimensions and a pooling layer. The final feature vector then passes through the flatten layer to be reduced to a feature vector. Figure 5.3 represents the overall structure of the feature extractor unit.

In general, the convolution layer extracts various features from input images by performing a mathematical (convolution) operation using a filter of a specific size. Smaller portions of the image are selected by sliding a window over the entire image,

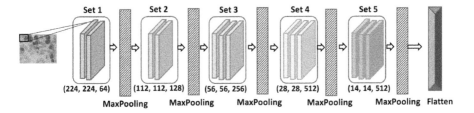

FIGURE 5.3 Feature extractor unit.

starting from top to bottom and from left to right. The dot product between the filter and the selected portion of the input image is taken for the convolution process. The proposed model's feature extractor unit consists of a set of 5 convolution units, each comprising 1 or 2 convolution layers. The exact dimensions of each set can be observed in Figure 5.3. In between each convolution set, a pooling layer is applied. The addition of a pooling layer (here maxpooling is considered) reduces the size of the feature map and also reduces computational costs. In maxpooling, the largest value from the function map is retained to be used in the next layer. At the end of the extractor unit, a flatten layer is incorporated to transform the feature map into a one-dimensional feature vector representation of 25,088 units. Table 5.2 highlights the details of each unit in the feature extractor unit. The filters used in these convolution and max pooling layers are 3×3. After each convolution layer, a 1-pixel padding (same padding) is applied to prevent the image's spatial attribute from being lost.

TABLE 5.2
Proposed CNN-Based Feature Extractor Unit Details

Set	Layers (Type)	Output Shape	No. of Parameters Used
1	Convolution	(224,244,64)	1792
	Convolution	(224,224,64)	36928
	Maxpooling	(112,112,64)	0
2	Convolution	(112,112,128)	73856
	Convolution	(112,112,128)	147584
	Maxpooling	(56,56,128)	0
3	Convolution	(56,56,256)	295168
	Convolution	(56,56,256)	590080
	Convolution	(56,56,256)	590080
	Maxpooling	(28,28,256)	0
4	Convolution	(28,28,512)	1180160
	Convolution	(28,28,512)	2359808
	Convolution	(28,28,512)	2359808
	Maxpooling	(14,14,512)	0
5	Convolution	(14,14,512)	2359808
	Convolution	(14,14,512)	2359808
	Convolution	(14,14,512)	2359808
	Maxpooling	(7,7,512)	0
	Flatten	25088	0

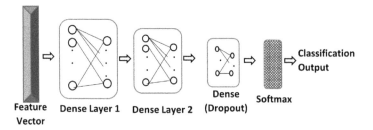

FIGURE 5.4 Classifier unit.

5.4.2 THE CLASSIFIER UNIT

The classifier unit consists of three fully connected or dense layers, which are made up of neurons that are trained by adjusting their bias and weight to minimize error. The feature extractor's output was a single 1D flattened feature vector, which was then used as input for the dense layer. The neurons in this layer are governed by an activation function. It determines which information should be sent forward and which information should not. The neurons in the dense layer use an activation function that controls which neurons transmit information further. ReLU, tanH, sigmoid, and softmax are some of the functions most widely used as activation functions. Each of these functions has a distinct application. The implemented model uses the ReLU (Rectified Linear Unit) activation function at the first two dense layers to prevent negative values from being passed on to the next layer. The final two-unit dense layer uses softmax activation, followed by the output layer, which employs cross-entropy and the Adam optimizer. Another layer that is embedded in the final dense layer is the dropout layer. Overfitting occurs when a model performs admirably on training data but has a drastic opposite effect on its functioning when tested on new data. To solve this issue, a dropout layer is implemented where a few neurons are dropped (removed) from the neural network during the training phase, resulting in a smaller but more efficient model. After reaching a dropout of 0.3, 30% of the nodes in the neural network are dropped out at random [52]. Figure 5.4 depicts the model of the classifier unit, and Table 5.3 depicts the details.

5.5　RESULTS AND DISCUSSION

The model proposed in this chapter is segmented into two different stages: the feature extractors and the classifier units. The model eliminates the requirement of any explicit segmentation or feature extraction technique, as seen in most of the

TABLE 5.3

Proposed CNN-Based Classifier Unit Details

Layers (Type)	Output Shape	No. of Parameters Used
Dense 1	256	6422784
Dense 2	256	65792
Dense 3	2	514
Softmax	2	-

implementations on micro-imaging data. The acquired, unprocessed micro-image can be directly used as input to the feature extractor unit. As discussed previously in Section 5.3, an augmentation technique is needed to enhance the dataset size. The dataset initially consisted of 450 images (84 MM and 366 normal), which escalated to 820 images, which are classified as MM-infected cells (384 images) and normal cells (436 images) after successful augmentation. This escalation in the dataset size avoids the chances of overtraining the model and makes the dataset more balanced in terms of having a comparable number of samples in each class. The images were further split into the training and testing sets (Table 5.1). The architecture of both the feature extractor and classification unit has been discussed in the foregoing section. The choice of ReLU as the activation function prevents the training operation from lingering in a negative gradient and also stops the weight updation in the learning stage by yielding values below zero, eventually letting the training process stop.

Figure 5.5 visualizes the accuracy and loss values obtained during the training process by means of a plot. An accuracy of 92.8% was achieved in 25 epochs during the training process. The loss plot also shows a good fit. A good fit is the goal

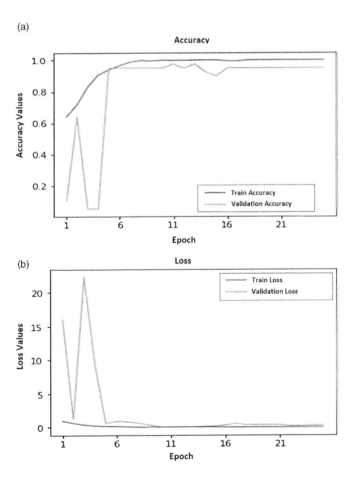

FIGURE 5.5 Performance evaluation: (a) Accuracy plot; (b) Loss plot.

TABLE 5.4
Accuracy of Different Trial Runs of the Proposed Model

Trail No.	Accuracy Achieved	Trail No.	Accuracy Achieved
1	91%	6	92%
2	92%	7	92%
3	94%	8	94 %
4	94%	9	95%
5	93%	10	91%

of the learning algorithm and exists between an overfit and an underfit model. The model was evaluated for 10 different trials by changing the data selection to prove its robustness. Table 5.4 shows the accuracy achieved during the various trial runs of the model. It can be concluded from the table that the average accuracy of the model remains at 92.8%.

5.6   CONCLUSION

This chapter describes a deep learning method focused on CNNs for detecting multiple myeloma in microscopic blood samples. There were 450 microscopic blood sample images in the dataset, which were labeled as normal blood cells or MM cells. The dataset was augmented using a data augmentation method, resulting in a sample size of 820 images. The aim of augmentation is to give the model enough samples for an efficient training process, to increase the variety of data available for training models, and to avoid overtraining. Without any further preprocessing, the data obtained can be used directly as an input to the model. The proposed CNN model employs 5 sets of convolution layers with pooling operations embedded between them for feature extraction. For classification, there are three FC (fully connected layers) or dense layers, followed by a softmax for output. The average accuracy obtained after ten trials was around 92.8%. This automated CAD method will assist the pathologist in accurately diagnosing and treating this disease. A potential path for this research may be to retrain the model to diagnose other diseases with minimal effort.

CONFLICT OF INTEREST

The authors declare that they have no conflict of interest.

REFERENCES

1. Kumar S, Kimlinger T, Morice W (2010) Immunophenotyping in multiple myeloma and related plasma cell disorders. *Best Practice & Research Clinical Hematology* 23(3):433–451
2. Vyshnav M, Sowmya V, Gopalakrishnan E, Menon VK, Soman K (2020) Deep learning based approach for multiple myeloma detection. In: 2020 11th International Conference on Computing, Communication and Net- working Technologies (ICCCNT), IEEE, pp 1–7

3. Ramani P (2019) Prevalence of multiple myeloma and its complication in a tertiary medical college at Calicut district, India. *International Journal of Research in Medical Sciences* 7(8):3138

4. Collins CD (2010) Multiple myeloma. *Cancer Imaging: The Official Publication of the International Cancer Imaging Society* 10(1):20–31

5. Munshi NC, Anderson KC (2013) New strategies in the treatment of multiple myeloma. *Clinical Cancer Research* 19(13):3337–3344

6. Doi K (2007) Computer-aided diagnosis in medical imaging: Historical review, current status and future potential. *Computerized Medical Imaging and Graphics* 31(4–5):198–211

7. Doi K (2009) Computer-aided diagnosis in medical imaging: achievements and challenges. In: World Congress on Medical Physics and Biomedical Engineering, September 7–12, 2009, Munich, Germany, Springer, pp 96–96

8. MacMahon H, Vyborny C, Sabeti V, Metz C, Doi K (1985) The effect of digital unsharp masking on the detectability of interstitial infiltrates and pneumothoraxes. In: Medical Imaging and Instrumentation'85, International Society for Optics and Photonics, vol 555, pp 246–252

9. Halalli B, Makandar A (2018) Computer aided diagnosis-medical image analysis techniques. *Breast Imaging* 85, pp 85–109.

10. Santos MK, Ferreira JR, Wada DT, Tenório APM, Barbosa MHN, Marques PMA (2019) Artificial intelligence, machine learning, computer-aided diagnosis, and radiomics: Advances in imaging towards to precision medicine. *Radiologia Brasileira* 52:387–396

11. Mohapatra S, Patra D, Satpathy S (2014) An ensemble classifier system for early diagnosis of acute lymphoblastic leukemia in blood microscopic images. *Neural Computing and Applications* 24(7):1887–1904

12. Reta C, Altamirano L, Gonzalez JA, Diaz-Hernandez R, Peregrina H, Olmos I, Alonso JE, Lobato R (2015) Segmentation and classification of bone marrow cells images using contextual information for medical diagnosis of acute leukemias. *PloS One* 10(6):e0130805

13. Mishra S, Majhi B, Sa PK (2019) Texture feature based classification on microscopic blood smear for acute lymphoblastic leukemia detection. *Biomedical Signal Processing and Control* 47:303–311

14. Rawat J, Singh A, Bhadauria H, Virmani J, Devgun JS (2017) Computer assisted classification framework for prediction of acute lymphoblastic and acute myeloblastic leukemia. *Biocybernetics and Biomedical Engineering* 37(4):637–654

15. Mishra S, Majhi B, Sa PK, Sharma L (2017) Gray level co-occurrence matrix and random forest based acute lymphoblastic leukemia detection. *Biomedical Signal Processing and Control* 33:272–280

16. Gehlot S, Gupta A, Gupta R (2021) A CNN-based unified framework utilizing projection loss in unison with label noise handling for multiple myeloma cancer diagnosis. *Medical Image Analysis* 72:102099

17. Liu C, Cao Y, Alcantara M, Liu B, Brunette M, Peinado J, Curioso W (2017) TX-CNN: Detecting tuberculosis in chest X-ray images using convolutional neural network. In: 2017 IEEE international conference on image processing (ICIP), IEEE, pp 2314–2318

18. Sa R, Owens W, Wiegand R, Studin M, Capoferri D, Barooha K, Greaux A, Rattray R, Hutton A, Cintineo J, et al (2017) Intervertebral disc detection in X-ray images using faster R-CNN. In: 2017 39th Annual International Conference of the IEEE Engineering in Medicine and Biology Society (EMBC), IEEE, pp 564–567

19. Rahman T, Chowdhury ME, Khandakar A, Islam KR, Islam KF, Mahbub ZB, Kadir MA, Kashem S (2020) Transfer learning with deep convolutional neural network (CNN) for pneumonia detection using chest X-ray. *Applied Sciences* 10(9):3233

20. Heidari M, Mirniaharikandehei S, Khuzani AZ, Danala G, Qiu Y, Zheng B (2020) Improving the performance of CNN to predict the likelihood of COVID-19 using chest X-ray images with preprocessing algorithms. *International Journal of Medical Informatics* 144:104284

21. Abraham B, Nair MS (2020) Computer-aided detection of COVID-19 from X-ray images using multi-CNN and bayesnet classifier. *Biocybernetics and Biomedical Engineering* 40(4):1436–1445

22. Hira S, Bai A, Hira S (2021) An automatic approach based on CNN architecture to detect covid-19 disease from chest X-ray images. *Applied Intelligence* 51(5):2864–2889

23. Thakur S, Kumar A (2021) X-ray and CT-scan-based automated detection and classification of covid-19 using convolutional neural networks (CNN). *Biomedical Signal Processing and Control* 69:102920

24. Polsinelli M, Cinque L, Placidi G (2020) A light CNN for detecting COVID-19 from CT scans of the chest. *Pattern Recognition Letters* 140:95–100

25. Kundu R, Singh PK, Mirjalili S, Sarkar R (2021) COVID-19 detection from lung CT-scans using a fuzzy integral-based CNN ensemble. *Computers in Biology and Medicine* 138:104895

26. Alakwaa W, Nassef M, Badr A (2017) Lung cancer detection and classification with 3D convolutional neural network (3D-CNN). *Lung Cancer* 8(8):409

27. Grewal M, Srivastava MM, Kumar P, Varadarajan S (2018) Radnet: Radiologist level accuracy using deep learning for haemorrhage detection in CT scans. In: 2018 IEEE 15th International Symposium on Biomedical Imaging (ISBI 2018), IEEE, pp 281–284

28. Chilamkurthy S, Ghosh R, Tanamala S, Biviji M, Campeau NG, Venugopal VK, Mahajan V, Rao P, Warier P (2018) Deep learning algorithms for detection of critical findings in head CT scans: A retrospective study. *The Lancet* 392(10162):2388–2396

29. Sekaran K, Chandana P, Krishna NM, Kadry S (2020) Deep learning convolutional neural network (CNN) with Gaussian mixture model for predicting pancreatic cancer. *Multimedia Tools and Applications* 79(15):10233—10247

30. Bernard O, Lalande A, Zotti C, Cervenansky F, Yang X, Heng PA, Cetin I, Lekadir K, Camara O, Ballester MAG, et al (2018) Deep learning techniques for automatic MRI cardiac multi-structures segmentation and diagnosis: Is the problem solved? *IEEE Transactions on Medical Imaging* 37(11):2514–2525

31. Işın A, Direkoğlu C, Şah M (2016) Review of MRI-based brain tumor image segmentation using deep learning methods. *Procedia Computer Science* 102:317–324

32. Bermudez C, Plassard AJ, Davis LT, Newton AT, Resnick SM, Landman BA (2018) Learning implicit brain MRI manifolds with deep learning. In: Medical Imaging 2018: Image Processing, International Society for Optics and Photonics, vol 10574, p 105741L

33. Noor MBT, Zenia NZ, Kaiser MS, Mahmud M, Mamun SA (2019) Detecting neurodegenerative disease from MRI: a brief review on a deep learning perspective. In: International conference on brain informatics, Springer, pp 115–125

34. Trivizakis E, Manikis GC, Nikiforaki K, Drevelegas K, Constantinides M, Drevelegas A, Marias K (2018) Extending 2-D convolutional neural networks to 3-D for advancing deep learning cancer classification with application to MRI liver tumor differentiation. *IEEE Journal of Biomedical and Health Informatics* 23(3):923–930

35. Hamm CA, Wang CJ, Savic LJ, Ferrante M, Schobert I, Schlachter T, Lin M, Duncan JS, Weinreb JC, Chapiro J, et al (2019) Deep learning for liver tumor diagnosis part I: Development of a convolutional neural network classifier for multi-phasic MRI. *European Radiology* 29(7):3338–3347

36. Anwar S, Alam A (2020) A convolutional neural network–based learning approach to acute lymphoblastic leukaemia detection with automated feature extraction. *Medical & Biological Engineering & Computing* 58(12):3113–3121

37. Rastogi P, Khanna K, Singh V (2022) LeuFeatx: Deep learning-based feature extractor for the diagnosis of acute leukemia from microscopic images of peripheral blood smear. *Computers in Biology and Medicine* 142:105236

38. Fuhad K, Tuba JF, Sarker M, Ali R, Momen S, Mohammed N, Rahman T (2020) Deep learning based automatic malaria parasite detection from blood smear and its smartphone based application. *Diagnostics* 10(5):329

39. Pattanaik PA, Mittal M, Khan MZ (2020) Unsupervised deep learning cad scheme for the detection of malaria in blood smear microscopic images. *IEEE Access* 8:94936–94946

40. Khan S, Sajjad M, Hussain T, Ullah A, Imran AS (2020) A review on traditional machine learning and deep learning models for WBCs classification in blood smear images. *IEEE Access* 9:10657–10673

41. Hegde RB, Prasad K, Hebbar H, Singh BMK (2019) Comparison of traditional image processing and deep learning approaches for classification of white blood cells in peripheral blood smear images. *Biocybernetics and Biomedical Engineering* 39(2):382–392

42. Lee BH, Park Y, Kim JH, Kang KW, Lee SJ, Kim SJ, Kim BS (2020) PDL1 expression in bone marrow plasma cells as a biomarker to predict multiple myeloma prognosis: Developing a nomogram-based prognostic model. *Scientific Reports* 10(1):1–12

43. Xu L, Tetteh G, Lipkova J, Zhao Y, Li H, Christ P, Piraud M, Buck A, Shi K, Menze BH (2018) Automated whole-body bone lesion detection for multiple myeloma on 68Ga-pentixafor PET/CT imaging using deep learning methods. *Contrast Media & Molecular Imaging* 2018:2391925

44. Wang J, Shi X, Yao X, Ren J, Du X (2021) Deep learning-based CT imaging in diagnosing myeloma and its prognosis evaluation. *Journal of Healthcare Engineering* 2021:5436793

45. Zhou C, Chan HP, Dong Q, Hadjiiski LM (2021) Deep learning based risk stratification for treatment management of multiple myeloma with sequential MRI scans. In: Medical Imaging 2021: Computer-Aided Diagnosis, International Society for Optics and Photonics, vol 11597, p 1159716

46. Licandro R, Hofmanninger J, Perkonigg M, Röhrich S, Weber MA, Wennmann M, Kintzele L, Piraud M, Menze B, Langs G (2019) Asymmetric cascade networks for focal bone lesion prediction in multiple myeloma. arXiv preprint arXiv:190713539

47. Bozorgpour A, Azad R, Showkatian E, Sulaiman A (2021) Multi-scale regional attention deeplab3+: Multiple myeloma plasma cells segmentation in microscopic images. arXiv preprint arXiv:210506238

48. Wong KC, Syeda-Mahmood T, Moradi M (2018) Building medical image classifiers with very limited data using segmentation networks. *Medical Image Analysis* 49:105–116

49. Mendeley data (2019) Multiple myeloma dataset (MM-dataset), https://data.mendeley.com/datasets/7wpcv7kp6f/1

50. Shorten C, Khoshgoftaar TM (2019) A survey on image data augmentation for deep learning. *Journal of Big Data* 6(1):1–48

51. Currie G, Hawk KE, Rohren E, Vial A, Klein R (2019) Machine learning and deep learning in medical imaging: Intelligent imaging. *Journal of Medical Imaging and Radiation Sciences* 50(4):477–487

52. Mishra R, Tripathi SP (2021) Deep learning based search engine for biomedical images using convolutional neural networks. *Multimedia Tools and Applications* 80(10):15057–15065

6 Artificial Intelligence (AI) on a Rise in Healthcare

Ritwik Dalmia, Sarika Jain, and Atef Shalan

6.1 INTRODUCTION

Delays in healthcare directly delineate life and death. Artificial intelligence (AI) is transforming the healthcare industry, offering a wide range of advantages that fill us with hope and optimism. The use of artificial intelligence (AI) in healthcare has the potential to assist healthcare providers in many aspects, some of which are as follows:

1. **Disease diagnosis and prediction:** AI can analyze medical images and other patient data to help diagnose diseases such as cancer, heart disease, and neurological disorders. It can also be used to predict a patient's likelihood of developing a disease.
2. **Administrative tasks:** By automating administrative activities like scheduling and accounting, AI can free up healthcare professionals to concentrate on patient care.
3. **Virtual assistants:** Patients are given medical information and support by AI-powered virtual assistants, which enables them to better manage their health.
4. **Mental Health:** By examining social media data, patient studies, and other sources to spot trends and foresee the likelihood of mental health disorders, AI can enhance mental health. This may make it possible to treat and take the appropriate actions in cases of illnesses like depression and anxiety.
5. **Quality assurance and fraud prevention:** AI can be used to examine medical data and spot fraud, inconsistencies, and errors. By identifying and fixing problems in billing, diagnosis, and treatment, this can help increase the quality of care and lower costs.

AI has the ability to transform illness diagnosis and monitoring by providing various benefits, including:

- **Increased accuracy:** AI systems can evaluate huge volumes of medical data with rapid speed and accuracy. This can lead to more accurate diagnostics and earlier illness identification.
- **Improved efficiency:** Routine operations, such as evaluating medical imaging or processing laboratory tests, may be automated by AI, freeing up medical practitioners to focus on more difficult duties.
- **Better resource utilization:** AI can help healthcare workers manage resources more effectively and prioritize treatment for those who need it the most by identifying people at high risk of getting certain diseases.

DOI: 10.1201/9781003388845-8

- **Reduced healthcare costs:** By optimizing treatment plans, eliminating the need for unnecessary testing and procedures, and increasing overall patient outcomes, AI can help lower healthcare expenses.

Thanks to machine learning, medical professionals can accurately predict disease outbreaks, detect cancer earlier, and save lives. Here are some of the key applications of AI in this field:

1. **Medical Imaging Analysis [1]:** Medical imaging data from X-rays, MRIs, CT scans, and ultrasounds may be analyzed by AI algorithms to aid in the detection and diagnosis of illnesses including cancer, heart disease, and neurological problems. AI is a useful tool for early detection and diagnosis because it can spot patterns and anomalies in pictures that may not be evident to the human eye.

2. **Electronic Health Records (EHRs):** In Figure 6.1, The large quantity of information in EHRs, like patient histories, test findings, and diagnostic

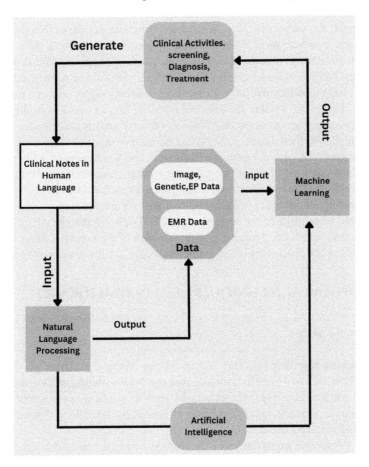

FIGURE 6.1 Diagnosis of disease with the help of AI.

imaging, may be analyzed and interpreted using AI. AI may use this data to analyze patterns and trends that might indicate an illness, helping clinicians diagnose patients more accurately and create more efficient treatment plans.

3. **Remote Patient Monitoring:** AI can be used to monitor patients from a distance while simultaneously gathering information on their vital signs, symptoms, and other health parameters.

4. **Drug Discovery and Development:** Massive amounts of data on molecular structures, drug interactions, and other aspects of drug research and development can be analyzed using AI. AI can aid researchers in more swiftly and accurately developing novel medications and therapies by spotting patterns and links in this data.

5. **Personalized Medicine:** A patient's genetic information and other health data can be analyzed using AI to create individualized treatment programs that are catered to their unique requirements and traits. This strategy can lessen the possibility of negative side effects while enhancing the efficacy of treatments.

But many others are still unsure. What does AI indicate for the healthcare industry, and what are its advantages? What role will AI play in healthcare in the future, and how is it now used? Will it eventually take the place of people in critical operations and medical care? This serves as a brief introduction to the use of AI in healthcare, but in order to truly understand it fully, we must dig as deeply as possible into the subject.

In this chapter, we explore the role and potential impact of AI in healthcare. We begin by providing an overview of AI and its subsets, such as machine learning and deep learning. We then discuss how AI can be used in disease diagnosis and monitoring. However, we also consider the challenges and limitations of AI in this field, including the need for high-quality data and ethical considerations around its use. Finally, we look at future directions and opportunities for AI in disease diagnosis and monitoring, including the development of new algorithms and technologies and how India's AI reinforced the response to COVID-19. By the end of this chapter, readers should have a comprehensive understanding of the potential of AI in healthcare as well as the challenges that must be overcome to fully realize its benefits.

6.2 POPULAR AI TECHNIQUES USED IN HEALTHCARE

There are several AI techniques that are being used in healthcare, see Figure 6.2. Here are some of them:

1. **Machine learning [2]:** This is a technique where algorithms are used to analyze data and identify patterns that can help with diagnosis, treatment, and patient care. The ML techniques used in medical applications try to group the characteristics of patients or predict the likelihood that a disease would manifest itself.
   - **Predictive analytics [3]:** This method helps clinicians deliver preventative treatment and enhance patient outcomes by identifying individuals who are at high risk of acquiring specific illnesses or consequences.

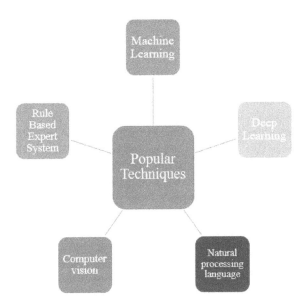

FIGURE 6.2   Popular AI techniques.

- **Deep Learning:** Deep learning has been used for a variety of health-care-related tasks, such as the interpretation of medical images, clinical decision support, drug development, and customized medicine. To help with diagnosis and treatment planning, deep learning has been used, for instance, in the analysis of medical images such as CT scans, MRI scans, and X-rays. In order to find new treatments and forecast patient outcomes, deep learning has also been applied to examine medical literature and patient information.

Have you ever wondered how machine learning helps online doctor consultants treat patients better? According to the researchers, online doctor consultants will see tremendous growth in the upcoming years. Therefore, here is an answer:

2. **Natural Language Processing (NLP) [4]:** This technique is used to analyze and understand human language, allowing computers to understand and respond to patient queries and electronic health records.

   Using NLP techniques, organized medical data may be enhanced and supplemented by information gleaned from unstructured sources like clinical notes and medical journals. The NLP approaches are designed to convert texts into structured data that is machine-readable and can be analyzed by ML techniques.

3. **Robotics and autonomous mobile robotics [5]:** Robots are used in healthcare to assist with surgeries and other medical procedures, allowing doctors to perform complex procedures with greater precision and accuracy.

Robotics has played a significant role in India's fight against COVID-19. Here are some ways in which robotics has helped:

- **Disinfection:** Robots have been used for disinfecting hospitals, public spaces, and airports. They use ultraviolet (UV) light to kill the virus and are controlled remotely, which reduces the risk of exposure for healthcare workers.
- **Remote Consultations:** With the help of telepresence robots, doctors have been able to consult with patients remotely. These robots can move around a hospital and allow doctors to communicate with patients and other healthcare providers while maintaining social distance.
- **Delivery of Medical Supplies:** Autonomous delivery robots have been used to deliver medicines, food, and other essential supplies to COVID-19 patients in hospitals and quarantine centers. These robots can help reduce human-to-human contact and minimize the risk of infection.
- **Screening:** AI-enabled robots have been used for temperature screening and to check whether people are wearing masks. These robots can help identify potential COVID-19 cases and prevent the spread of the virus.
- **Testing:** Robots have been used for COVID-19 testing in India. Some robots can collect samples from patients, while others can perform the tests themselves. This helps increase the number of tests conducted and reduces the risk of infection for healthcare workers.

4. **Computer Vision:** Cameras and sensors are used in this method to interpret visual data. Computer vision may be used in the healthcare industry to examine medical pictures like X-rays and MRIs to find anomalies and identify illnesses.

5. **Rule-based Expert System** [6]: For tasks like diagnosis or treatment suggestions in the healthcare industry, rule-based expert systems can be used. For instance, based on a patient's medical background and present symptoms, a rule-based expert system could be utilized to assist in making a diagnosis. In order to direct the diagnostic procedure and generate recommendations based on the supplied data, the system would need a set of rules. Rule-based expert systems can be effective when analyzing vast amounts of complex data and making decisions based on a set of rules or standards.

6.3   PIONEER AI SYSTEMS AND THEIR SUCCESS STORIES IN HEALTHCARE

In the healthcare sector, AI has completely changed the game by opening up a number of prospects for better patient outcomes, resource management, and simplified clinical procedures. Pioneering AI systems have significantly improved the diagnosis of diseases, the discovery of drugs, and the management of patient care, among other facets of healthcare. These technologies, including IBM Watson and Google DeepMind, have improved patient experiences and provided better treatment to millions of people globally, thus revolutionizing the healthcare industry.

6.3.1   IBM WATSON HEALTH [7]

IBM Watson Health is a cognitive computing system that analyzes and interprets complicated medical data using natural language processing and machine learning methods. It has been applied in several medical fields, including cancer therapy, genetics, and drug development.

By utilizing AI to assist physicians in creating customized treatment regimens for specific patients, IBM Watson Health has significantly improved the way that cancer is treated.

The goal of IBM Watson Health is to assist healthcare organizations and professionals in improving patient outcomes and lowering costs. It makes use of modern technologies like machine learning, natural language processing, and others to evaluate massive amounts of organized and unstructured data from a variety of sources, such as medical records, clinical trials, and research articles.

Cancer therapy is one of IBM Watson Health's most well-known uses. In the field of customized medicine, IBM Watson Health has been heavily utilized in the treatment of cancer. The system uses machine learning and AI to evaluate vast volumes of organized and unstructured data from a variety of sources, such as medical records, clinical trials, and academic publications. As a result, physicians may create custom treatment strategies for each patient based on their unique ailment, genetic makeup, and medical background.

Through genetic analysis, IBM Watson has made a significant contribution to the fight against cancer. The technology may find genetic alterations that might be fueling a patient's cancer by examining the patient's genomic data. Following that, it can suggest targeted medicines that are customized for the patient's unique genetic profile, thereby enhancing treatment efficacy and lowering the likelihood of adverse effects.

IBM Watson may also help physicians by giving them access to the most recent medical research, clinical recommendations, and treatment methods. Moreover, it may review a patient's medical data and make therapy recommendations based on the patient's medical background, present state, and other pertinent criteria.

6.3.2   GOOGLE DEEPMIND [8]

Google DeepMind has created an AI system called AlphaFold that can precisely anticipate the 3D structure of proteins, which is important for the development of new drugs and the comprehension of disease causes. Also, it has created an AI tool called Streams that assists physicians in identifying and prioritizing patients who are at risk for acute renal damage.

Another illustration of how AI may be used to enhance healthcare is the AI tool called Streams from DeepMind. The goal of Streams is to assist doctors in identifying and prioritizing patients who are at risk for acute kidney injury (AKI), a disease that can result in renal failure and is linked to a high death rate. When it discovers an AKI risk, Streams examines patient medical information and sends physicians immediate notifications. This enables medical professionals to step in early and stop the disease from getting worse.

Some hospitals in the UK, notably the Royal Free Hospital in London, where Streams was first created in conjunction with physicians, have successfully adopted it. In the first year of its usage, Streams helped reduce AKI-related mortality by 24%, according to a 2019 research that was published in the *British Medical Journal*. This illustrates how AI has the ability to enhance patient outcomes and prevent fatalities in actual healthcare settings.

6.3.3 BABYLON HEALTH [9]

Based on a patient's symptoms, a chatbot powered by AI created by Babylon Health may offer medical advice and prioritize patients. Also, it has created an AI system that can identify eye conditions and gauge the likelihood of developing cardiovascular disease.

One of Babylon's standout products is an AI-powered chatbot that assists users in evaluating their symptoms and receiving medical advice. Natural language processing is used by the chatbot to comprehend patients' inquiries and offer tailored advice depending on their symptoms. Also, Babylon offers online doctor consultations that let consumers get medicines and medical advice from a distance.

6.3.4 PATHAI

A diagnostic tool that uses AI to evaluate medical photos and deliver precise diagnoses for conditions like cancer. It has been applied to the creation of breast and lung cancer diagnostic tools.

6.3.5 ZEBRA MEDICAL VISION

Zebra Medical Vision is a company that has created an AI system that can analyze medical photos and spot anomalies, including breast cancer, lung nodules, and fractures. Also, it has created an AI tool that can forecast the dangers of cardiovascular illness.

6.4 HURDLES AND ISSUES IN REAL LIFE: IMPLEMENTATION OF AI IN HEALTHCARE

By increasing the precision of diagnoses, the effectiveness of treatments, and the general quality of patient outcomes, AI has the potential to transform healthcare. Yet, before the broad use of AI in healthcare can become a reality, there are considerable obstacles and problems that must be resolved.

1. **Data quality:** AI algorithms rely on high-quality data to make accurate predictions. However, medical data can be incomplete, inconsistent, or biased, which can limit the effectiveness of AI models. For example, imaging studies may be of poor quality, or medical records may be incomplete or inaccurate.
2. **Data privacy and security:** The use of AI in disease diagnosis and monitoring requires access to sensitive patient data. Ensuring data privacy and security is a significant challenge, as medical data are subject to strict regulations regarding their collection, storage, and sharing.
3. **Interpretability:** AI models are often referred to as "black boxes" because they are complex and difficult to interpret. The confidence and acceptance of AI systems by physicians may be constrained as a result of this lack of

interpretability, which might make it difficult to grasp how an AI algorithm arrived at a certain diagnosis or prognosis.

4. **Generalizability:** AI models are often trained on specific patient populations, which may limit their ability to generalize to other populations. For example, an AI model trained on data from a particular geographic region may not be effective in another region with different demographics.

5. **Integration with clinical workflows:** The integration of AI models into clinical workflows can be challenging. Clinicians may be hesitant to adopt new technologies or may not have the necessary training to use AI effectively.

6. **Protection of human genetic resources** [10]: While this information is useful for medical diagnosis and treatment, there is a concern that genetic resources may be utilized to construct bioweapons or discriminate against specific groups of individuals. As a result, safeguarding human genetic resources is critical.

7. **Data can be daunting:** There is a huge amount of data generated every day, including patient data, medical records, test results, and research findings. However, the sheer volume of data can also be a barrier to adoption, as it requires significant investment in data management and processing infrastructure.

8. **Ethical considerations and potential for misuse of AI in healthcare**

   1. **Software security** [11]: It reveals that, despite AI algorithms' good performance during the first design examination, they are vulnerable to assaults at all phases of the algorithm generation process. Someone with comprehensive knowledge of the built neural network model, including the training data, model architecture, hyperparameters, number of layers, activation function, and model weights, may perform these attacks. Attacks can be conducted even if the attacker is not aware of the structure, parameters, or training data set of the target model. Additionally, due to modifications in illness patterns, missing data, and autonomous update mistakes, flaws in the system can develop without external influence. This means that even if the AI system was initially well designed, it might gradually divert from the correct path as the environment changes.

   2. **Ethical considerations:** The use of AI in disease diagnosis and monitoring raises ethical concerns, such as the potential for algorithmic bias and the impact of AI on the doctor–patient relationship.

   3. **Legal issues** [12]: Despite an increase in the utilization of AI in healthcare, there are no global rules or regulations to control its application. This might lead to new sorts of criminal activities involving AI. As a result, it is critical to define precise AI laws with input from parties involved in AI development. It is also critical to establish who is to blame when AI medical therapy fails. Despite the introduction of new legislation to govern AI data protection, liability determination, and supervision, there is presently no clear regulatory entity to monitor AI usage in healthcare. One example is the NHS 111 app, which was classified as a medical device despite a lack of proof.

The biggest issue facing AI in healthcare is not whether the technology will be effective, but rather how to get it accepted into routine clinical practice.

The concern for liability is one justification for this care. Who is responsible if an AI system commits a mistake that results in an incorrect diagnosis or course of treatment? This is a legal and moral issue that has not been fully answered. The requirement to integrate AI technologies into current healthcare procedures is another difficulty. The quantity of data that many healthcare practitioners must handle each day may be overwhelming, so implementing a new technology that creates even more data might be intimidating.

Likewise, healthcare practitioners may be hesitant to employ AI if they do not completely understand how it works or how it may assist their practice.

Diagnostic and monitoring tools for diseases now include AI, which is a potent technology. Medical records, imaging investigations, and genetic sequencing are just a few examples of the massive volumes of data that AI systems can examine to find patterns and generate predictions that might help guide clinical decision-making. However, there are several challenges and limitations to the use of AI in healthcare, as we discussed above.

6.5. FUTURE DIRECTIONS AND OPPORTUNITIES

- **What AI-based algorithm is applied to the diagnosis of diseases?**
  AI-powered disease detection algorithms have proven to be a highly effective method for identifying patients with underdiagnosed, unclassified, and uncommon diseases. In order to help patients in need of an earlier diagnosis and to help pharmaceutical companies with highly improved, focused diagnostics so that these patients can be accurately identified and treated earlier in the course of their disease, AI disease detection models have great potential. Both machine and deep learning models for detecting diseases such as cancer, diabetes, chronic heart disease, Alzheimer's disease, liver disease, arrhythmia disease, and many more will be the subject of study work. In Figure 6.3, machine learning

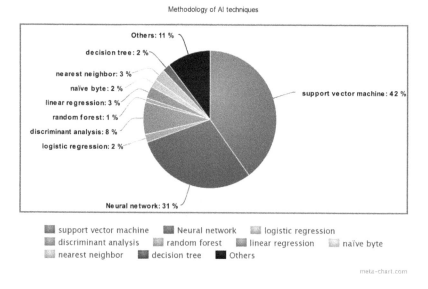

FIGURE 6.3 Methodology of AI techniques for arrhythmia.

models like Random Forest Classifier, Logistic Regression, Decision Tree, KNN, SVM, and CNN are the most commonly utilized deep learning models for illness diagnosis.

- **How are methods based on artificial intelligence assisting doctors in the diagnosis of diseases?** By doing tasks that would often be performed by humans in a small fraction of the time and money, AI enhances the lives of patients, doctors, and hospital administrators. In order to enhance health outcomes and, ultimately, preserve the patient's life, AI, for instance, assists physicians in making suggestions by evaluating vast amounts of healthcare data, such as EHR symptom data and physician reports. Additionally, by using AI-based approaches, these data help to improve and accelerate decision-making when identifying and treating patients' illnesses. Moreover, AI helps clinicians diagnose diseases by utilizing complex algorithms and thousands of doctor's notes. This improves diagnostic accuracy [13].

6.6 INDIA'S AI-REINFORCED RESPONSE TO COVID-19

Are you curious about how we fought back against the pandemic? Well, you'll be amazed to know that artificial intelligence played a critical role in our success! From speeding up vaccine development to analyzing data, AI proved to be an incredible tool in our fight against COVID-19. India has made significant efforts to leverage AI in its response to the COVID-19 pandemic:

1. **COVID-19 diagnosis:** India has developed an AI-powered COVID-19 diagnosis system called "CovidxNet" that can detect the virus from chest X-rays. This system has been used to help diagnose patients more quickly and accurately.
2. **Contact tracing:** The Aarogya Setu contact tracing app was created by the Indian government and uses AI to identify individuals who may have come into contact with COVID-19 patients. The app has been downloaded by millions of people in India and has helped identify potential hotspots for the virus.
3. **Predictive modeling:** Indian researchers have used AI to develop predictive models of the spread of the virus, which have helped public health officials plan for the pandemic and allocate resources more effectively.
4. **Telemedicine:** India has used AI-powered telemedicine platforms to provide remote consultations to patients during the pandemic. This has helped reduce the risk of transmission of the virus and has made healthcare more accessible to patients in remote areas.

Overall, India has made significant efforts to leverage AI in its response to the COVID-19 pandemic, with a focus on improving diagnosis, contact tracing, drug discovery, predictive modeling, and telemedicine. These efforts have helped India respond to the pandemic more effectively and efficiently and have demonstrated the potential of AI to transform healthcare.

6.7 FUTURE OF AI IN HEALTHCARE

Massive amounts of data, including patient records and medical imaging, can be analyzed using AI-powered technologies to find trends and spot anomalies that might otherwise go undetected. This may result in earlier and more precise diagnoses as well as better treatment strategies. By 2030, the healthcare sector should continue to develop and expand in a number of sectors based on current trends and technological breakthroughs.

Developments in genomic sequencing and AI will enable more precise and individualized treatments that are based on a patient's genetic profile, way of life, and medical history. Patients will have increased access to healthcare services and can monitor their health more effectively as telemedicine, mobile health applications, and wearable gadgets expand in popularity. The use of virtual and augmented reality technologies in medical education will increase as they give medical professionals access to practical training in a secure setting.

Clinical professionals will be able to create personalized treatments and therapies based on unique patient characteristics with the help of machine learning and AI, leading to better outcomes.

In general, we may expect that healthcare will become more patient-centric, individualized, and technologically enabled by 2030. These developments will give people greater influence over their medical treatment, resulting in more precise diagnoses, and ultimately enhancing patient outcomes.

At last, AI can help with creating new drugs and making existing drugs work better. Although AI is not widely used in healthcare yet, it has many benefits that can improve healthcare and save money. Healthcare businesses can use AI to stay competitive in expensive sectors. AI can also help with other aspects of healthcare delivery. Collaboration between government and industry is crucial to realizing the potential of AI. The cost of healthcare is increasing due to longer lifespans and more chronic diseases, and AI could be a solution. However, we need to be careful about how we use AI in healthcare and make sure it does not reinforce existing discrimination or biases. There should be a proper database system and a responsible authority to work on the data security and privacy of the patient's data. One of the major issues we find is that we need a lot of data to train machine learning and deep learning models to ensure high precision and accuracy. From my perspective, AI needs to improve more; we can't use AI and machine learning models for every disease diagnosis.

6.8 SUMMARY

Disease diagnosis and monitoring are essential components of healthcare, as they enable early detection, timely treatment, and improved patient outcomes. The study of intelligent computers that can carry out tasks that traditionally require human cognition, such as learning, reasoning, and problem-solving, is known as AI. AI has shown great promise in healthcare, particularly in disease diagnosis and monitoring.

We discussed how the use of AI in healthcare is driven by the need for more accurate, efficient, and personalized diagnoses and treatments. We also discussed different AI techniques, such as machine learning and deep learning, that allow for the analysis of large amounts of data from diverse sources, including medical images, genomic data, electronic health records, and patient-generated data. We also discussed how AI can identify patterns and relationships that may be difficult for humans to detect, leading to more accurate diagnoses, earlier detection, and better treatment outcomes.

We also discussed several applications of AI in disease diagnosis and monitoring, including cancer, heart disease, and infectious diseases. In cancer diagnosis, AI can analyze medical images to identify tumors and predict their growth and spread.

We also discussed the benefits of using AI for disease diagnosis and monitoring, including increased accuracy, speed, and efficiency, as well as improved patient outcomes. However, there are also challenges and limitations to the use of AI in healthcare. These include the need for high-quality data, the risk of bias in AI algorithms, and ethical considerations, such as privacy, security, and the potential for misuse.

The potential impact of AI on healthcare delivery and patient outcomes is significant, and continued research and innovation in this field are likely to lead to further improvements in disease diagnosis and monitoring.

REFERENCES

1. Vial, A., Stirling, D., & Field, M., et al. (2018). The role of deep learning and radiomic feature extraction in cancer-specific predictive modeling: A review. Translational Cancer Research, 7, 803–816.
2. https://www.foreseemed.com/artificial-intelligence-in-healthcare by Steve Barth (accessed on 6 June 2023).
3. Mohanty, S. N., Chatterjee, J. M., Jain, S., Elngar, A. A., & Gupta, P. (Eds.). (2020). Recommender System With Machine Learning and Artificial Intelligence: Practical Tools and Applications in Medical, Agricultural and Other Industries. John Wiley & Sons.
4. Kar, S. "Robotics in HealthCare," 2019 2nd International Conference on Power Energy, Environment and Intelligent Control (PEEIC), Greater Noida, India, 2019, pp. 78–83, https://doi.org/10.1109/PEEIC47157.2019.8976668.
5. https://www.foreseemed.com/artificial-intelligence-in-healthcare by Steve Barth accessed on 06/06/2023.
6. Davenport, T., & Kalakota, R. (2019). The potential for artificial intelligence in healthcare. Future Healthcare Journal, 6(2), 94–98. https://doi.org/10.7861/futurehosp.6-2-94.
7. https://www.ibm.com/common/ssi/cgi-bin/ssialias?appname=skmwww&htmlfid=897%2 FENUS5725-W51&infotype=DD&subtype=SM&mhsrc=ibmsearch_a&mhq=IBM%20 WATSON%20ONcology
8. https://deepmind.google/discover/blog/using-ai-to-give-doctors-a-48-hour-head-start-on-life-threatening-illness/ by Mustafa Suleyman, Dominic King, published on July 31, 2019, accessed on 6 June 2023.
9. Baker, A., Perov, Y., Middleton, K., Baxter, J., Mullarkey, D., Sangar, D., Butt, M., Rosario, A., & Johri, S. (2020). A comparison of artificial intelligence and human doctors for the purpose of triage and diagnosis. Frontiers in Artificial Intelligence, 3, 543405. https://doi.org/10.3389/frai.2020.543405.

10. Jain, S., Jain, V., & Balas, V. E. (Eds.). (2021). Web Semantics: Cutting Edge and Future Directions in Healthcare. Academic Press.

11. Tiwari, S. M., Jain, S., Abraham, A., & Shandilya, S. (2018). Secure semantic smart healthcare (S3HC). Journal of Web Engineering, 17, 8, 617–646.

12. Jiang, L., Wu, Z., Xu, X., Zhan, Y., Jin, X., Wang, L., & Qiu, Y. (2021). Opportunities and challenges of artificial intelligence in the medical field: Current application, emerging problems, and problem-solving strategies. Journal of International Medical Research, 49(3), 3000605211000157. https://doi.org/10.1177/03000605211000157.

13. Gruenwald, L., Jain, S., & Groppe, S. (Eds.). (2021). Leveraging Artificial Intelligence in Global Epidemics. Academic Press.

7 Applications of Multitarget Regression Models in Healthcare

Kirti Jain, Sharanjit Kaur, and Gunjan Rani

7.1 INTRODUCTION

Regression is a supervised machine learning technique used to predict the continuous target variable(s) while considering the impact of explanatory variables. Earlier in the 1950s, regression was commonly used for univariate studies to understand the dependency of a target variable on an independent variable. Since data related to healthcare, medicine, and disease consist of multiple features, it is essential to incorporate their combined relationship in the prediction of the target variable(s), for which multivariate analysis is employed [1–4]. The multivariate regression analysis has been extensively used in medical/healthcare applications such as estimation of systolic or diastolic blood pressure, given a variety of individuals characteristics [1], identification of chronic kidney disease level based on health parameters [5], revelation of anomalies on the heart surface using ECG [6], hospital cost and stay estimation for patients using different health statistics [4], and many more.

This chapter demonstrates the performance of multitarget regression over single-target regression. We begin with a brief categorization of regression models for multivariate and multitarget analysis, followed by the description of nonlinear regression algorithms. We also present a case study using a healthcare dataset to demonstrate the applicability of different approaches for predicting multiple targets.

7.2 CATEGORIZATION OF REGRESSION MODELS

The regression model captures the collective effect of *mp* features ($X : x_1 \ldots x_m$) on the target variable (y). Selected m features are also called explanatory or independent variables [7]. The target variable y is also referred to as the response or dependent variable. Both explanatory and response variables can be of continuous, binary, or categorical type. In cases where the target variable is categorical or binary, the supervised learning is referred to as classification; otherwise; it is called regression. We briefly explain the categorization of regression models based on the number of features used, the interrelationship between predictors and the outcome(s), and the count of predicted variables in the following sections.

DOI: 10.1201/9781003388845-9

7.2.1   UNIVARIATE VS MULTIVARIATE REGRESSION

The simplest univariate regression predicts the target variable using one independent feature ($m = 1$). However, the results predicted based on a single feature are not reliable. On the other hand, multivariate regression (MVR) uses relationships among multiple independent variables ($m > 1$) to predict the outcome of a target variable [1, 2]. MVR is the most commonly used machine learning algorithm for predicting a response variable that exploits correlations between each independent and dependent variable while generating a model.

7.2.2   LINEAR VS NONLINEAR REGRESSION

Regression, being a supervised learning method, takes an input X along with an output y to learn the mapping between the independent feature(s) and the target. This section describes regression analysis methods depending upon the kind of relationship between variables X and y.

7.2.2.1   Linear Regression

It is the most common statistical and machine learning algorithm [8]. Such a model is best suited for problems where a linear relationship is shared between the dependent variable(s) and independent variable(s). *Simple Linear Regression* and *Multiple Linear Regression*, respectively, are the terms used to describe the types of linear regression employed in univariate and multivariate analysis.

   i. **Simple Linear Regression (SLR):** This model captures the linear relationship between one independent feature (x) and a single outcome (y), which is represented using the straight line equation (Eq. 7.1).

$$y = \beta_0 + \beta_1 x + \varepsilon \tag{7.1}$$

where β_0 and β_1 are the y-intercept and slope of the line, respectively, and ε represents an erroneous value due to omitted variables and the nonlinearity effect [9]. While training the model, those values of β_0 and β_1 are used, for which the cost function is minimum, where the cost function is the estimated difference between the true and predicted target. The coefficient estimation and hypothesis testing are done using the least squares method [10].

Example 2.1

Consider a hypothetical situation where a patient's overall healthcare expenditure and pharmacy expenditure are taken as the dependent and independent variables, respectively. Figure 7.1 shows the fitted regression line $y = 3611 + 5.1x$ for the considered sample. In such a scenario, if the pharmacy expenditure of the patient is 0, then his overall health expenditure will be 3611. For any other value of pharmacy expenditure, the patient's overall expenditure will increase by 5.1 times the pharmacy expenditure.

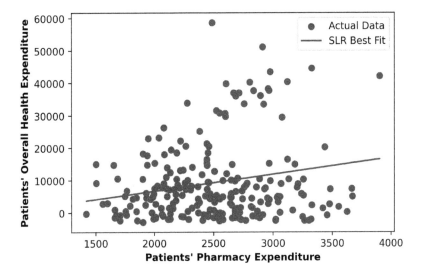

FIGURE 7.1 Simple linear regression, where patients' overall healthcare expenditure, on the y-axis, is taken as the dependent variable and patients' pharmacy expenditure, on the x-axis, is taken as the independent variable. Both variables are measured in dollars. The blue line shows the fitted regression line.

ii. **Multiple Linear Regression (MLR):** The working of this method, also called multilinear regression, is similar to that of SLR, but the target variable is predicted by the linear combination of the independent variables (Eq. 7.2). The MLR model is also called the empirical model or approximation function, where the actual relationship between target y and m predictors $x_1, x_2, \ldots x_m$ is unknown [10].

$$y = \beta_0 + \beta_1 x_1 + \beta_2 x_2 \ldots \beta_m x_m + \varepsilon \qquad (7.2)$$

Here β_0 is the y-intercept, $\beta_1, \beta_2, \ldots, \beta_m$ are coefficients of independent variable $x_1, x_2, \ldots, x_m$ respectively. The term ε, a random error component, has its usual meaning. The value β_i is set depending on the importance of the independent variable x_i in predicting the outcome y. An independent variable with a higher coefficient value is more vital for determining the correct predicted value compared to variables with a lower coefficient value.

Example 2.2

Multiple factors like sugar, blood pressure, sodium, etc. affect chronic kidney disease (CKD), and their collective impact needs to be considered while predicting the level of the disease for any patient. Figure 7.2 shows the 12 most critical independent factors identified for determining the influence of CKD [5].

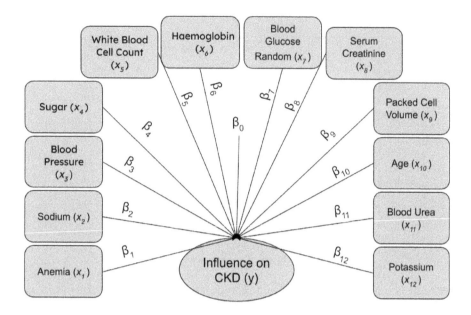

FIGURE 7.2 Independent variables $x_1, x_2, \ldots x_{12}$ that are critical for determining the influence on chronic kidney disease (CKD), the dependent variable. β_0 is the bias and $\beta_1, \beta_2, \ldots, \beta_{12}$ are the coefficients of multiple linear regression.

7.2.2.2 Nonlinear Regression

It is required when the predictors and predicted variables do not exhibit a linear relationship. Most of the regression models for natural processes are nonlinear in their parameters (coefficients) [11]. If we try to fit such cases using MLR, then the obtained model may be underfit and may not perform well both on training and testing data. Also, the presence of noise or outliers in real data deteriorates the performance of the linear regression model more than that of nonlinear regression [1]. Different machine learning models, such as random forest (RF), decision tree (DT), support vector machines, and eXtreme Gradient Boosting (XGBoost (XGB)), are proposed in the literature for capturing the nonlinearity effect between independent and dependent variables [9].

7.2.3 Single-Target vs Multitarget Regression

As the name indicates, single-target regression is used to predict one outcome at a time. However, single-target regression fails to handle noise/outliers, and the impact of multiple features on targets in real data [12]. In contrast, multitarget regression is concerned with predicting multiple and continuous type targets using multiple input variables. Multioutput regression models are employed for predicting more than one outcome, like the characteristics of plants/crops in ecological modeling [13], stock price forecasting for more than one company, and healthcare system for projecting expenditure and total stay of the patient in any hospital based on disease-related factors, and many more.

There are two main approaches that leverage single-target baseline methods to handle multitarget regression. The first is the problem transformation method, where a separate regression model is built for each output value to be predicted and baseline methods are employed directly. However, such an approach requires user assistance in deciding the order for predicting target variables but with the flexibility to the user. The second approach, the algorithm adaptation method, is an extension of the first method that adapts the prevailing univariate target methods to predict all the target variables at the same time. Such an approach not only captures dependencies among targets but has also improved predictive generalization [14].

We briefly explain here two problem transformation approaches, specifically the regression chain and stacking regression models used in the case study given in Section 7.4.

i. **Regression Chain Model:** Targets in a regression chain model are organized into a chain [12]. The regressor chain mechanism makes the prediction in the order specified by the chain using the input features and the predicted outcomes ($\hat{y}_i$) of all prior models. The predicted outcomes $\left\{ \hat{y}_1,...,\hat{y}_{i-1} \right\}$ by all the prior models are used in the subsequent i^{th} regressor, where $i > 1$, as input along with the features of the test record, and the process of output-to-input dependency repeats along the chain of models. Figure 7.3 shows the framework for the regression chain mechanism, in which, for example, Regressor 2 for the y_2 target does training with the initial target y_1 along with y_2, and predicts the target y_2 using the predicted outcome along with the features of the test record.

ii. **Stacking Regression Model:** This model consists of two steps [12]. The first step comprises n regression models, whereby the predicted value

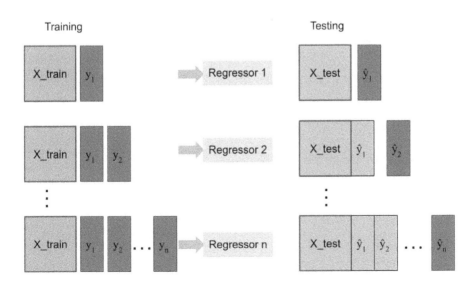

FIGURE 7.3 Regression chain framework for multitarget prediction.

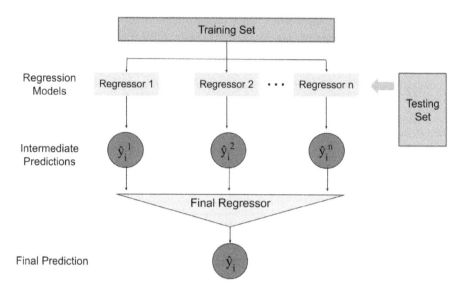

FIGURE 7.4 Stacking regression framework to combine multiple regression models.

$\left(\hat{y}_i^j, j \in \{1,n\}\right)$ of each target variable y_i by n regressors is termed an intermediate prediction. These predictions are used in the second training step, where the final regressor is learned to obtain the final prediction, as shown in Figure 7.4. Hence, the multi-output problem is transformed into n single-target regression problem, where the initial model predictions are corrected by the models built in the next step.

It is to be noted that the advantages of regression chain and regression stacking are uniquely dependent upon the ensemble models and the randomization process for ordering targets [12].

7.3 NONLINEAR REGRESSION MODELS AND THEIR EVALUATION

We detail here three popular nonlinear regression models, followed by two performance metrics for the evaluation of the predictions made by the studied models.

7.3.1 BASELINE ALGORITHMS

We begin with a brief explanation of the regression models used for the case study presented in Section 7.4. A brief enlisting of the strengths and limitations of the baseline algorithms, viz., DT, RF, and XGB, is given in Table 7.1.

7.3.1.1 Decision Tree (DT)

Regression trees are quite effective with public healthcare data, as such data are often unbalanced with missing values and are complex in nature. The determinants and outcome variables involved in public healthcare data often share a nonlinear

TABLE 7.1

Comparing Baseline Algorithms, viz. DT: Decision Tree, RF: Random Forest, and XGB: XGBoost Regression Model

Baseline Algorithms	Strength	Limitations
DT	Interpretable outputs	Unstable outputs
	Easy and fast to build model	Prone to data overfitting
RF	High accuracy of the output	Cannot extrapolate the data
	Stable output because of majority voting	High training time if not parallelized
XGB	Suitable for enormous data	Sensitive to noise
	In-built regularization with better performance	Computationally expensive

relationship [15]. To build the DT, recursive partitioning and multiple regressions are performed on the data [16]. From the root node, the data are continuously partitioned into internal nodes, and the process is repeated until the specified condition is met. The tree splitting across internal nodes is done to obtain a purer tree. There are the many impurity measures, but the most popularly used are Gini Index for Classification and Regression Tree (CART) and Entropy for Iterative Dichotomiser 3 (ID3) [17]. For each node, the tree's impurity is measured before and after splitting the tree. The attribute that gives the maximum impurity reduction is chosen as the splitting criterion. The nodes that are not split further are leaf nodes, and a simple regression model is attached to each such node. The construction of a DT may be followed by its pruning to reduce its complexity and get an optimal tree. Figure 7.5 shows a diagrammatic representation of a DT.

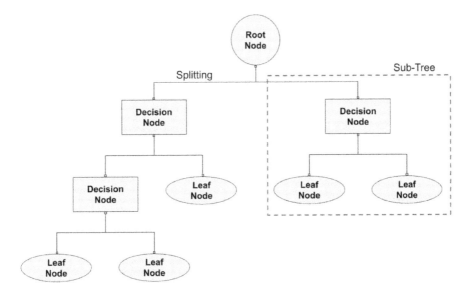

FIGURE 7.5   General structure of a decision tree.

7.3.1.2 Random Forest (RF)

Being an extension of the CART technique [18], RF is one of the most widely used MVR algorithms because of its applicability to both regression and classification. It amalgamates multiple DTs, the weak learners, to predict only one outcome. During training, multiple de-correlated DTs are constructed using random samples of the predictors (Figure 7.6). These trees are further combined using Bootstrap/Bagging Aggregation algorithms [18]. The process of generating a RF by constructing multiple DTs on a random sample of training data is called Bootstrap, where a sample of k observations is selected from a set of N observations with replacement. The bagging algorithm selects different bootstrap samples for creating DTs that constitute an RF. The final outcome is computed by aggregating the predicted outcomes from the underlying DTs.

7.3.1.3 XGBoost (XGB)

XGB is a DT-based method proposed by Chen and Guestrin [19]. XGB, a highly scalable machine learning technique for tree boosting, is widely used in machine learning and data mining challenges [19].

In the algorithm, DTs are built sequentially such that the new tree is trained on the residuals (difference between actual and predicted outcomes) of the previous one (Figure 7.7). In other words, the new tree is the optimized version of the previous one that corrects the errors to predict the optimal outcome [20]. The primary distinction between the RF and XGB techniques is that the trees are built independently in the

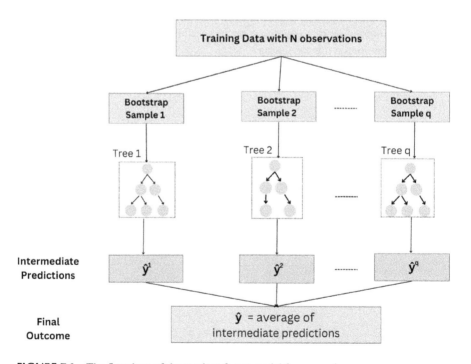

FIGURE 7.6   The flowchart of the random forest model for regression.

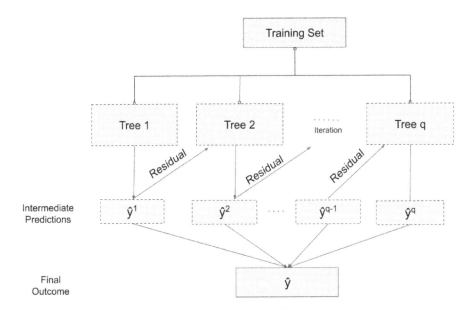

FIGURE 7.7   Basic structure of the XGBoost regression model.

RF technique, whereas the subsequent trees are added in complement to the previous ones in XGB.

7.3.2   PERFORMANCE METRICS

We describe below two important and commonly used standard metrics to determine the efficacy of the built model.

  i. **Root Mean Squared Error (RMSE):** It is a statistical metric that evaluates the quality of predictions by taking the square root of the average squared error between the actual and predicted values (Eq. 7.3). It uses Euclidean distance to calculate how far predictions are from actual values and gives an error in the same unit as that of the predicted variable [21].

$$\text{RMSE} = \sqrt{\frac{\sum_{i=1}^{n}(y_i - \hat{y}_i)^2}{N}} \qquad (7.3)$$

  where N is the number of records, y_i and $\hat{y}_i$ represent the actual and predicted values, respectively, of the target variable y for the ith record. The model with the lowest error value is the best performer.
  ii. **Coefficient of Determination (R^2):** It captures the descriptive power of the underlying model by measuring the proportion of variation in the dependent attributes (y) having a nonlinear relationship with multiple but significant independent variables (X). For multiple targets, the coefficient of determination R^2 score is computed as an average of R^2 scores across all

target variables, where R^2 is the correlation coefficient [22]. The higher value of R^2 depicts the effectiveness of the built model. However, the score R^2 includes all variables while capturing variation in the dependent variable, which may result in overfitting the data. As a few of the variables may be insignificant and do not contribute toward building the regression models, we compute the Adjusted R^2 score (R^2_{adj}) [4] as given below:

$$R^2_{adj} = 1 - (1 - R^2) \frac{N - 1}{N - m - 1} \tag{7.4}$$

where N and m represent the total sample size and the count of features, respectively. The high value of the R^2_{adj} score signifies the good performance of the model.

7.4 APPLICATION OF REGRESSION IN HEALTHCARE: CASE STUDY

Regression models are being extensively used in healthcare studies, but none has compared different types of regression techniques for predicting multiple targets. We investigate three main techniques, viz., single-target regression, regression chain, and stacking regression, and analyze their performance using a healthcare dataset. The code is written in Python for implementing the regression models available in the Scikit-learn library. Programs are executed on an Intel(R) Core(TM) i7 with a CPU speed 1.80GHz and 16GB RAM. We have used the default parameter settings for all the regression models in our experimentation.

7.4.1 DATASET AND PREPROCESSING

This retrospective case study is conducted using a publicly available dataset from the Statewide Planning and Research Cooperative System (SPARCS) of New York (NY) State [23]. It includes de-identified in-patient discharge data with details of disease diagnoses and expenses for different hospitals in New York in 2015. The data set contains 37 attributes/features with 2.35 million records of patients.

The effectiveness of the built model relies upon the training data that is preprocessed to remove ambiguous values, redundant and non-relevant attributes, etc. Therefore, we removed attributes, as done in [24]. Also, we retained attribute codes only and removed attributes related to their descriptions. Since the Age Group attribute has categorical values in the form of *L-H*, where L and H denote the lowest and highest age, respectively, of that group, we use the mean age of the group. For example, the mean age of patients in groups 0 to 17 is 8.5. Out of 37 attributes, we selected 6 attributes as explanatory variables for predicting two target variables, viz., Length of Stay (LOS) and Total Charges (TC) with a sample size of 50,000. We also normalized attribute TC to have a comparable range of values as LOS. Table 7.2 shows the selected variables and their description, along with their categorization.

We compute the correlation coefficient between each of the six explanatory and two target variables (Figure 7.8) to find out the dependencies between them. We find

TABLE 7.2

Description of Selected Variables from the Hospital Inpatient Discharges (SPARCS) Dataset

	Variables	Description
Explanatory Variables	Age Group	Age of the patient at the time of discharge
	CCS Diagnosis Code	Tool to classify patients' diagnoses and procedures
	APR DRG Code	Classification of patients based on their reason for admission
	APR MDC Code	All Patient-Refined Major Diagnostic Category Code
	APRS	Classification of patients based on their APR severity of illness
	APRR	Classification of patients based on their APR risk of mortality
Target Variables	Length of Stay (LOS)	The duration of a patient's hospital stay
	Total Charges (TC)	Total payment made by the patient on discharge

that only two independent variables, APRS and APRR, are monotonically associated with these two target variables. Hence, we omit multivariant linear regression models in the experimental studies and compare the performance of multivariant nonlinear regression models for predicting two target variables.

7.4.2 COMPARATIVE ANALYSIS OF NONLINEAR REGRESSION MODELS

In order to understand the difference between the regression models based on single target and multitarget, we deploy three model classes for training: single-target regression model, regression chain model, and stacking regression model. We use

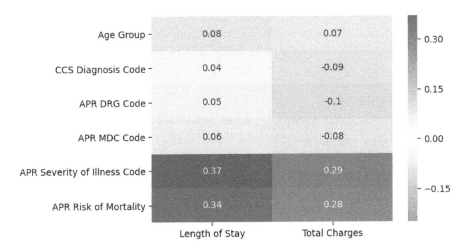

FIGURE 7.8 Correlation values for six selected explanatory variables from the SPARCS dataset with two target variables, viz., LOS and TC.

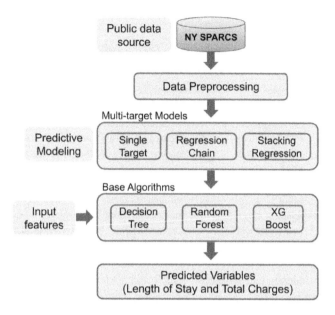

FIGURE 7.9 Steps followed for predicting target variables using multitarget regression models.

three base algorithms, viz. DT, RF, and XGB, which are described in Section 7.1. Figure 7.9 lists the steps followed for predicting the target variables given the dataset. We test the generalization ability of all models employing the cross-validation process with 20 folds and compare their performance using two performance metrics adjusted R^2 score (R^2_{adj}) and root mean squared error (RMSE).

For each of the two target variables, viz. LOS and TC, three single-target models using DT, RF, and XGB, respectively, are trained individually using cross-validation with 20 folds. Table 7.3 shows the performance of three single-target models for both

TABLE 7.3

Performance Metrics R^2_{adj} Score and RMSE for a Single-Target Model Using Three Base Estimators, viz. DT: Decision Tree, RF: Random Forest, and XGB: XGBoost Regression Model

Baseline Algorithms	Length of Stay (LOS)		Total Charges (TC)	
	RMSE	R^2_{adj}	RMSE	R^2_{adj}
DT	6.670	0.2605	4.976	0.3198
RF	6.041	0.3938	4.199	0.5219
XGB	5.911	0.4188	4.449	0.4776

target variables. Results show that the LOS target variable is best predicted using the XGB regression model, followed by the RF model with R^2_{adj} 0.4188 and 0.3938, respectively, whereas the RF model predicts the TC attribute with high accuracy. Although the error is small, the low efficacy of all the algorithms requires deep data analysis before building the model.

Further, we employ the regression chain model using three base estimators for predicting two target variables, LOS and TC. Two chain orders, viz., LOS-TC and TC-LOS, are possible because of two target variables. It is to be noted that the number of possible chains is proportional to the number of target variables. Figure 7.10(a and b) shows the

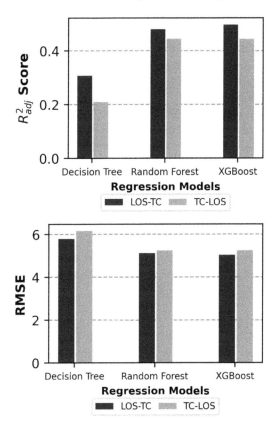

FIGURE 7.10 Performance metrics R^2_{adj} score and RMSE for regressor chain model with two chaining representations, namely LOS-TC and TC-LOS using three estimators viz., decision tree (DT), random forest (RF), and XGBoost (XGB) algorithms. LOS: Length of Stay, TC: Total Charges. We use the third type of regression model, i.e., stacking regression method, considering three base estimators, viz. DT, RF, and XGB, in the first stage and one final estimator. We create two stacking models termed "DT-RF-XGB-RF" and "DT-RF-XGB-XGB" with the final estimators being RF and XGB, respectively. Table 7.4 delineates the computed metrics of the regressor stacking model for both target variables. We observe that performance is worst affected in this class model and should be used cautiously if the dependency between explanatory and target variables is clearly defined.

TABLE 7.4

Performance Metrics R^2_{adj} Score and RMSE for Regressor Stacking Model

Baseline Algorithms	Length of Stay (LOS)		Total Charges (TC)	
	RMSE	R^2_{adj}	RMSE	R^2_{adj}
DT-RF-XGB-RF	6.321	0.3373	4.310	0.459
DT-RF-XGB-XGB	6.408	0.3197	4.476	0.4038

performance metrics, R^2_{adj} and RMSE of the regression chain model for two chaining representations of the targets. We observe that the prediction accuracy increases when the LOS variable is used to predict the total charges attribute, ie., LOS-TC chain order, for all three base regression models. Moreover, RMSE is also comparatively low for the LOS-TC chaining, indicating high performance. It is observed that the chosen base regression algorithm also impacts the performance of the regression chain model. The performance of the XGB algorithm is also best compared to the other two algorithms, as observed in the single-target model, due to the inclusion of weak learners while optimizing the cost function.

Results show that the chaining method boosts the efficacy of the regression models on the used healthcare data. It outperforms the single-target models built separately for each variable as well as the stacking regressor for multitargets. As the applicability and usability of the multitarget regressions depend upon the baseline methods, underlying dataset, and relationships between features and targets, it is recommended to understand the data properly before deciding on the model strategy.

7.5 CONCLUSION

Nonlinear regression techniques have been employed in medical/healthcare applications for predicting a single objective. However, there is an increasing requirement to anticipate multiple targets based on the interdependence of multivariate variables. Motivated by this, we demonstrate the performance of multitarget regression over single-target regression using a case study. It is observed that the accuracy of multitarget regression models is directly related to the underlying base models, the mechanism used for the ensemble, and the dependencies between targets.

REFERENCES

1. Mark Tranmer and Mark Elliot. Multiple linear regression. *The Cathie Marsh Centre for Census and Survey Research (CCSR)*, 5(5):1–5, 2008.
2. Barbara G. Tabachnick and Linda S. Fidell. *Using Multivariate Statistics*. Allyn and Bacon/Pearson Education, New York, 5th edition, 2007.

3. Timothy P Hanrahan, Georgina Harlow, James Hutchinson, M Joel, Jeffrey Dulhunty, Tony Lipman, Jason A Whitehouse and Roberts. Vancomycin-associated nephrotoxicity in the critically ill: A retrospective multivariate regression analysis. *Critical Care Medicine*, 42(12):2527–2536, 2014.

4. Teresa Angela Trunfio, Arianna Scala, Cristiana Giglio, Giovanni Rossi, Anna Borrelli, Maria Romano and Giovanni Improta. Multiple regression model to analyze the total LOS for patients undergoing laparoscopic appendectomy. *BMC Medical Informatics and Decision Making*, 22(1):1–8, 2022.

5. Ahmed Abdelaziz, Mohamed Elhoseny, Ahmed S Salama and AM Riad. A machine learning model for improving healthcare services on cloud computing environment. *Measurement*, 119:117–128, 2018.

6. Shijie Zhou, Abdel Amir, John L Wahab, James W Sapp, B Milan Warren and Horáček. Localization of ventricular activation origin from the 12-lead ECG: A comparison of linear regression with non-linear methods of machine learning. *Annals of Biomedical Engineering*, 47(2):403–412, 2019.

7. Ludwig Fahrmeir, Thomas Kneib, Stefan Lang and Brian Marx. *Regression: Models, Methods and Applications*. Springer, Berlin, Heidelberg, 2013.

8. Dastan Maulud and Adnan M Abdulazeez. A review on linear regression comprehensive in machine learning. *Journal of Applied Science and Technology Trends*, 1(4):140–147, 2020.

9. Alpaydin Ethem. *Introduction to Machine Learning*. PHI Learning, Delhi, India, 3rd edition, 2015.

10. Douglas C Montgomery, Elizabeth A Peck and G Geoffrey Vining. *Introduction to Linear Regression Analysis*. John Wiley & Sons, Hoboken, New Jersey, 2021.

11. David A Ratkowsky. Principles of nonlinear regression modeling. *Journal of Industrial Microbiology*, 12(3–5):195–199, 1993.

12. Hanen Borchani, Gherardo Varando, Concha Bielza and Pedro Larranaga. A survey on multi-output regression. *Wiley Interdisciplinary Reviews: Data Mining and Knowledge Discovery*, 5(5):216–233, 2015.

13. Dragi Kocev, Sašo Džeroski, Matt D. White, Graeme R. Newell and Peter Griffioen. Using single- and multi-target regression trees and ensembles to model a compound index of vegetation condition. *Ecological Modelling*, 220(8):1159–1168, 2009.

14. Liwen Cui, Xiaolei Xie, Zuojun Shen, Rui Lu and Haibo Wang. Prediction of the healthcare resource utilization using multi-output regression models. *IISE Transactions on Healthcare Systems Engineering*, 8(4):291–302, 2018.

15. Niko Speybroeck. Classification and regression trees. *International Journal of Public Health*, 57:243–246, 2012.

16. V Rodriguez-Galiano, M Sanchez-Castillo, M Chica-Olmo and MJOGR Chica-Rivas. Machine learning predictive models for mineral prospectivity: An evaluation of neural networks, random forest, regression trees and support vector machines. *Ore Geology Reviews*, 71:804–818, 2015.

17. Don Coppersmith, Se June Hong and Jonathan RM Hosking. Partitioning Nominal attributes in decision trees. *Data Mining and Knowledge Discovery*, 3:197–217, 1999.

18. Yi Li, Changfu Zou, Maitane Berecibar, Elise Nanini-Maury, Jonathan C-W Chan, Peter Van den Bossche, Joeri Van Mierlo and Noshin Omar. Random forest regression for online capacity estimation of lithium-ion batteries. *Applied Energy*, 232:197–210, 2018.

19. Tianqi Chen and Carlos Guestrin. Xgboost: A scalable tree boosting system. In *Proceedings of the 22nd acm sigkdd international conference on knowledge discovery and data mining*, pages 785–794, 2016.

20. Jessica Pesantez-Narvaez, Montserrat Guillen and Manuela Alcañiz. Predicting motor insurance claims using telematics data—XGBoost versus logistic regression. *Risks*, 7(2):70, 2019.

21. T. Chai and R. R. Draxler. Root mean square error (RMSE) or mean absolute error (MAE)? – Arguments against avoiding RMSE in the literature. *Geoscientific Model Development*, 7(3):1247–1250, 2014.

22. Bruce Ratner. The correlation coefficient: Its values range between +1/-1, or do they? *Journal of Targeting, Measurement and Analysis for Marketing*, 17(2):139–142, 2009.

23. Hospital Inpatient Discharges Dataset New York State Department of Health. *Statewide Planning and Research Cooperative System (SPARCS)*, 2015. Available: https://health.data.ny.gov/Health/Hospital-Inpatient-Discharges-SPARCS-De-Identified/82xm-y6g8

24. Xiangrui Zeng. Length of stay prediction model of indoor patients based on light gradient boosting machine. *Computational Intelligence and Neuroscience*, 2022, 2022.

8 XAI-based Autoimmune Disorders Detection Using Transfer Learning

R.S.M. Lakshmi Patibandla, B. Tarakeswara Rao, Ramakrishna Murthy M, and Hemantha Kumar Bhuyan

8.1 INTRODUCTION

An umbrella term for a set of diseases known as autoimmune illnesses is autoimmunity, in which the immune system unintentionally targets the body's own cells and organs, causing inflammation, harm, and dysfunction. Normally, the immune system defends the body from outside invaders, including bacteria, viruses, and other diseases. However, in autoimmune disorders, the immune system becomes confused and targets the body's own cells, tissues, and organs as if they were foreign invaders [1].

Of the more than 80 different types of autoimmune disorders, rheumatoid arthritis, lupus, multiple sclerosis, type 1 diabetes, and psoriasis are just a few examples. These illnesses can affect the joints, skin, muscles, nerves, liver, kidneys, and lungs, among other regions of the body [2]. Symptoms of autoimmune disorders can vary widely depending on the specific condition and the affected area of the body, but common symptoms include fatigue, joint pain and stiffness, skin rashes, muscle weakness, and fever [3].

A combination of genetic, environmental, and behavioral elements is thought to play a role in the emergence of autoimmune diseases. Treatment for autoimmune disorders often involves medications to suppress the immune system, as well as other therapies to manage symptoms and prevent complications [4]. While there is currently no cure for autoimmune disorders, advances in research are helping to improve our understanding of these conditions and develop new treatments to better manage and ultimately prevent them [5].

Autoimmune diseases are a group of complex diseases that ensue when the immune system erroneously attacks and injures tissues in the body. The diagnosis and treatment of autoimmune diseases can be challenging, as they often present with a wide range of symptoms and can mimic other conditions [6].

Machine learning has emerged as a useful method for the accuracy and efficacy of autoimmune disease identification in recent years [7]. The use of machine learning algorithms, particularly deep learning models, has drawn criticism for being difficult to understand or explain which makes it difficult for doctors to trust and understand the decisions made by these models [8].

DOI: 10.1201/9781003388845-10

Transfer learning, which uses previously trained deep learning models to enhance performance on new [9] related tasks, has been used by researchers to address this problem [10]. By fine-tuning these pre-trained models on a dataset of autoimmune disease patient data [11], researchers can create more accurate and interpretable models for disease detection [12].

One of the methods put forth to assess the data gathered, such as vibration signals, and provide a diagnosis of the asset's operational state is artificial intelligence (AI) [13]. Despite the fact that models trained with labeled data (supervised) are known to produce excellent results, their application in production processes is challenging due to two main issues: (i) it is challenging to collect a sample of all operational conditions or takes a long time [14] (since errors rarely occur), and (ii) it is expensive for experts to label all acquired data [15]. Another impediment to the deployment of AI technologies in this setting is the models' lack of interpretability (i.e., they are "black boxes"), which reduces the accuracy of the diagnosis and user adoption/trust [14]. The authors [15] suggest the Fault Diagnosis using eXplainable AI (FaultD-XAI) method to address these problems. It is a new generic and interpretable method for classifying faults in rotating machinery based on transfer learning from augmented synthetic data to actual rotating machinery FaultD-XAI. Synthetic vibration signals that match the typical behavior of operational failures are developed in order to enable scalability using transfer learning [16]. Grad-CAM (Gradient-weighted Class Activation Mapping; Sekeroglu and Ozsahin, 2020 and 1D CNN [17] are used to interpret the data, assisting the user in making decisions and boosting diagnostic confidence.

Explainable AI (XAI) is a growing field that focuses on developing machine learning models that are transparent and explainable [18], allowing clinicians to understand how the model arrived at its decisions [19]. In the context of autoimmune disease detection [20], XAI techniques can be used to identify the key features or biomarkers that the model is using to make its predictions, providing insight into the underlying biological processes that contribute to these diseases [21].

Overall, the combination of transfer learning and XAI has the prospective to significantly expand the accuracy and interpretability of machine learning replicas for autoimmune disease detection, leading to better analysis and cure outcomes for patients [22].

8.2   TRANSFER LEARNING MODELS

There are several transfer learning models that can be used for XAI related autoimmune diseases detection using transfer learning. Visual Geometry Group (VGG) is a widely used deep convolutional neural network (CNN) architecture for image classification tasks. The VGG model has shown good performance in identifying patterns in medical images, making it a suitable candidate for autoimmune disease detection [23].

The Inception architecture is known for its ability to learn highly abstract features from images, making it an ideal candidate for detecting subtle changes in medical images [24]. ResNet (Residual Network) is a deep CNN that can efficiently train very deep neural networks. It has been shown to perform well in various medical image analysis tasks and is a popular choice for transfer learning in medical image analysis. With the feed-forward neural network design known as DenseNet, each layer is connected to every other layer. It has been shown to perform well in medical image analysis tasks and is suitable for transfer learning [25]. A family of CNNs called EfficientNet has attained cutting-edge performance on numerous image categorization tasks. It has been shown to be effective in medical image analysis and is a promising candidate for transfer learning in autoimmune disease detection [26]. The quantity and complexity of the dataset, the available computational resources, and the interpretability of the model's predictions are all important considerations when choosing a transfer learning model for autoimmune disease detection.

Several datasets can be used for XAI-related autoimmune diseases detection using transfer learning [27]. The National Institutes of Health (NIH) Clinical Center provides a large dataset of medical images and patient data that can be used for autoimmune disease detection. The dataset includes images from a variety of modalities, including MRI, CT, and PET. The Cancer Imaging Archive provides a huge pool of medical images and patient data for various types of cancer. This dataset includes a variety of imaging modalities, including CT, MRI, and PET, and can be used for autoimmune disease detection. The Open Access Series of Imaging Studies (OASIS) dataset provides a large collection of MRI scans and patient data for various neurological disorders. This dataset can be used to detect autoimmune diseases that affect the nervous system. Patients with systemic lupus erythematosus (SLE) can access a database of clinical information called the SLE database. Machine learning models for the detection and diagnosis of autoimmune diseases can be created using this dataset. The multiple sclerosis lesion segmentation challenge (MSLSC) provides a dataset of MRI scans and patient data for patients with multiple sclerosis. The development of machine learning models for the detection and segmentation of multiple sclerosis lesions can be done using this dataset. When selecting a dataset for XAI-related autoimmune disease detection using transfer learning, the size and quality of the dataset, the availability of annotations, and the diversity of the patient population represented in the dataset are key factors.

8.3   LITERATURE SURVEY

Healy et al.'s work, "Automated Diagnosis of Multiple Sclerosis through Transfer Learning and XAI," puts forth a transfer learning-based strategy for multiple sclerosis diagnosis automation. CNNs were employed by the authors to extract features from brain MRI images. They employed transfer learning to categorize the MRI images as either normal or multiple sclerosis by fine-tuning a pre-trained CNN model (VGG16).The authors also employed an XAI approach to explain the predictions of the model [24]. They used the LIME (Local Interpretable Model-Agnostic Explanations) method to generate heatmaps to visualize the areas of the brain that contributed the most to the predictions.

The authors evaluated their model on a dataset of 1,508 brain MRI scans, including 755 scans of patients with multiple sclerosis and 753 scans of healthy controls. The model was 96.3% accurate, 96.3% sensitive, and 96.2% specific in differentiating between healthy and multiple sclerosis MRI scans. The LIME method was also used by the authors to test the model's predictions for interpretability. They found that the heatmaps generated by LIME accurately highlighted the areas of the brain that were most affected by multiple sclerosis.

The study demonstrated that the transfer learning-based approach can be effective for the automated diagnosis of multiple sclerosis. The XAI approach employed in the study also provided interpretability for the predictions, which can help clinicians make more informed decisions and provide better care to patients. The authors indicated that radiologists and neurologists could use the presented technology as a decision assistance tool.

The study's use of a small dataset of MRI images is one of its limitations. Despite the positive results, it is not apparent how well the model would function on larger and more varied datasets. However, the study did not assess how well the proposed method performed in comparison to other cutting-edge techniques for automating multiple sclerosis diagnosis. It would be interesting to compare the proposed method's accuracy and interpretability to those of other approaches. Finally, the study's use of the LIME approach has several drawbacks and might not fully explain the model's predictions. To increase the predictability of the model, future research may investigate more XAI methods.

A deep learning-based strategy for the classification of autoimmune diseases was proposed in the research "A Deep Learning Method to Classification of Autoimmune Diseases Using Transfer Learning and XAI" by Sadhu et al. To extract features from photos of skin lesions, the scientists employed a CNN model (Inception-v3) that had already been trained. They then fine-tuned the model for the classification of six different autoimmune diseases: psoriasis, atopic dermatitis, alopecia areata, vitiligo, pemphigus, and bullous pemphigoid. The authors used an XAI technique as well to explain the model's predictions. They used the SHAP (SHapley Additive Explanations) method to generate feature importance scores to explain the model's predictions.

The authors evaluated their model on a dataset of 4,039 skin lesion images, including 616 images of psoriasis, 756 images of atopic dermatitis, 544 images of alopecia areata, 553 images of vitiligo, 576 images of pemphigus, and 994 images of bullous pemphigoid. In classifying the skin lesions into the six different autoimmune illnesses, the model had an accuracy of 86.5%. The interpretability of the model's predictions was also tested experimentally using the SHAP approach by the authors. They found that the feature importance scores generated by SHAP accurately highlighted the areas of the skin lesions that were most indicative of each disease.

The study showed that the deep learning-based strategy suggested for categorizing autoimmune disorders can be successful. The XAI approach employed in the study also provided interpretability of the predictions, which can help clinicians make more informed decisions and provide better care to patients. The new method may be used by dermatologists as a decision-support tool, according to the authors.

The study's use of a tiny collection of skin lesion photographs is one of its limitations. Despite the positive results, it is not apparent how well the model would function on larger and more varied datasets. The study also limited its evaluation of the model's performance to six distinct autoimmune disorders. It would be intriguing to examine how the suggested approach fares when applied to a larger variety of autoimmune conditions. Finally, the SHAP method used in the study has some limitations and may not provide a complete understanding of the model's predictions. To increase the predictability of the model, future research may investigate more XAI methods.

A deep learning-based strategy for the automated diagnosis of rheumatoid arthritis was proposed in the research "Explainable Deep Learning for Automated Diagnosis of Rheumatoid Arthritis Using Transfer Learning" by Shaban et al (RA). The authors extracted features from hand radiographs using a pre-trained CNN network (ResNet50). They then fine-tuned the model for binary classification of the radiographs as either normal or showing signs of RA. The authors used an XAI technique as well to explain the model's predictions. They created heatmaps to show the areas of the hand that contributed the most to the predictions using the Grad-CAM (Gradient-weighted Class Activation Mapping) approach.

The authors evaluated their model on a dataset of 5,400 hand radiographs, including 3,600 normal radiographs and 1,800 radiographs showing signs of RA. In distinguishing between normal and RA radiographs, the model attained an accuracy of 97.2%, a sensitivity of 97.2%, and a specificity of 97.1%. The Grad-CAM approach was also used by the authors to test the model's predictions for interpretability. They found that the heatmaps generated by Grad-CAM accurately highlighted the joints and bones in the hand that were most affected by RA.

The study proved that the suggested deep learning-based strategy can work well for RA diagnosis automation. The XAI approach employed in the study also provided interpretability of the predictions, which can help clinicians make more informed decisions and provide better care to patients. The authors indicated that radiologists and rheumatologists could use the presented technology as a decision assistance tool.

One of the study's constraints is the use of a small dataset of hand radiographs. Although the results are encouraging, it is unclear how well the model would perform on larger and more diversified datasets. The effectiveness of the suggested method in comparison to other state-of-the-art methods for the automated diagnosis of RA was not also evaluated by the study. The accuracy and interpretability of the suggested method compared to other methods would be interesting to compare. The Grad-CAM technique, meanwhile, has some limitations and falls short of providing a complete explanation for the model's outcomes. Future studies might look into further XAI techniques to make the model more predictable.

Hu and colleagues presented a deep learning-based method for the automated diagnosis of lupus erythematosus in their work, "Interpretable Deep Learning for Automated Diagnosis of Lupus Erythematosus Using Transfer Learning" (LE). To extract features from photos of skin lesions, the scientists employed a CNN model (Inception-v3) that had already been trained. They then fine-tuned the model for the binary classification of the lesions as either LE or non-LE. The authors used an XAI technique as well to explain the model's predictions. They used the LRP (Layer-wise

Relevance Propagation) method to generate heatmaps to visualize the regions of the skin lesions that contributed the most to the predictions.

The authors evaluated their model on a dataset of 7,440 skin lesion images, including 3,720 LE lesions and 3,720 non-LE lesions. The model successfully distinguished between LE and non-LE lesions with an accuracy of 91.2%, a sensitivity of 91.1%, and a specificity of 91.4%. The LRP approach was also used by the authors to test the interpretability of the model's predictions. They found that the heatmaps generated by LRP accurately highlighted the regions of the skin lesions that were most indicative of LE.

The study showed that the deep learning-based approach that was suggested can be useful for LE automated diagnosis. The XAI approach employed in the study also provided interpretability of the predictions, which can help clinicians make more informed decisions and provide better care to patients. The new method may be used by dermatologists as a decision-support tool, according to the authors.

The survey's use of a tiny collection of skin lesion photographs is one of its limitations. Despite the positive results, it is not apparent how well the model would function on larger and more varied datasets. In addition, the study only assessed how well the model performed on LE and non-LE lesions. The effectiveness of the suggested approach on a broader spectrum of autoimmune skin conditions would be fascinating to observe. Finally, the LRP method used in the study has some limitations and may not provide a complete understanding of the model's predictions. To increase the predictability of the model, future research may investigate more XAI methods.

A deep learning-based technique for the automated diagnosis of Sjogren's syndrome was proposed in the research "Transfer Learning and Explainable AI for Automated Diagnosis of Sjogren's Syndrome" by Zhang et al (SS). The scientists employed a pre-trained CNN model (DenseNet-121) to extract features from ultrasound images of the salivary glands. They then fine-tuned the model for binary classification of the images as either showing signs of SS or not. The authors used an XAI technique as well to explain the model's predictions. To determine the areas of the photos that contributed the most to the predictions, they generated feature importance scores using the SHAP approach.

The researchers tested their model using a dataset of 690 ultrasound pictures of the salivary glands, 345 of which contained symptoms of SS and 345 of which did not. The model distinguished between SS and non-SS photos with an accuracy of 96.8%, a sensitivity of 96.1%, and a specificity of 97.6%. The interpretability of the model's predictions was also tested experimentally using the SHAP approach by the authors. They found that the method accurately highlighted the regions of the salivary gland that were most indicative of SS.

The study showed that the deep learning-based technique that was suggested can be successful for the automated diagnosis of SS. The XAI approach employed in the study also provided interpretability for the predictions, which can help clinicians make more informed decisions and provide better care to patients. The authors indicated that radiologists and rheumatologists could use the presented technology as a decision assistance tool.

The survey's use of a tiny dataset of salivary gland ultrasound pictures is one of its limitations. Despite the positive results, it is not apparent how well the model would function on larger and more varied datasets. Furthermore, the study did not assess how well the proposed method performed in comparison to other cutting-edge techniques for the automated diagnosis of SS. It would be interesting to compare the proposed method's accuracy and interpretability to those of other approaches. Finally, the SHAP method used in the study has some limitations and may not provide a complete understanding of the model's predictions. Future studies may explore other XAI approaches to improve the interpretability of the model's predictions.

Overall, these studies demonstrate the potential of transfer learning and XAI techniques for the automated diagnosis of autoimmune disorders. These approaches can improve the accuracy of the model and provide interpretability for the predictions, which can help clinicians make more informed decisions and provide better care to patients.

8.4   PROPOSED MODEL

This proposed model outlines the steps involved in building an XAI-based autoimmune disease detection model using transfer learning, including data preprocessing, pre-training on large medical image datasets, fine-tuning on the autoimmune disease dataset, and incorporating XAI techniques such as saliency maps and feature visualization.

Figure 8.1 is a proposed model architecture for XAI-related autoimmune diseases detection using transfer learning:

- **Preprocessing:** The first step is to preprocess the input data. This includes standardizing the image sizes, converting images to grayscale, and normalizing the pixel values.
- **Transfer Learning:** As a foundation model for feature extraction, researchers can utilize a pre-trained CNN, such as VGG16, ResNet50, InceptionV3,

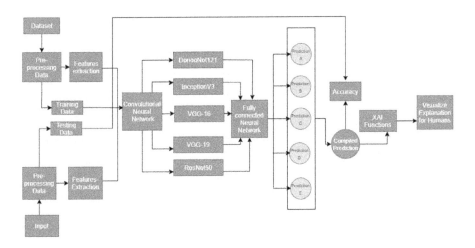

FIGURE 8.1   Proposed architecture.

and Densenet121. The original model's final few levels can then be removed so that we can add our own categorization layers.

- **Attention Mechanism:** To make our model explainable, we can incorporate an attention mechanism that highlights the areas of the image that are most important for classification. Researchers can do this by adding an attention layer on top of the convolutional layers that learns to weight the feature maps based on their importance for classification.
- **Explanation Generation:** To generate explanations for our model's predictions, we can use a technique such as Grad-CAM or LIME. Grad-CAM generates heatmaps that highlight areas of the image where the model used to make its prediction, while LIME generates explanations in the form of text that describe which features of the image were most important for the model's decision.
- **Training:** Researchers can train the model using a supervised learning approach, where they provide labeled images of autoimmune diseases as input to the model. Researchers can use techniques such as data augmentation and dropout to prevent overfitting.
- **Evaluation:** The performance of the model may be evaluated using metrics like accuracy, precision, recall, and F1-score. Researchers can also evaluate the model's explainability using metrics such as explanation fidelity, which measures how well the generated explanations match the model's predictions.
- **Deployment:** Finally, researchers can deploy the model through a web-based interface where users can upload their own images of autoimmune diseases and receive predictions and explanations from the model. Researchers can also make the model available as an API for integration with other healthcare systems.

During training, researchers can use a supervised learning approach where they provide labeled images of autoimmune diseases as input to the model. To avoid overfitting, researchers can employ strategies like dropout and data augmentation. The performance of the model may be evaluated using metrics like accuracy, precision, recall, and F1-score. Researchers can also evaluate the model's explainability using metrics such as explanation fidelity, which measures how well the generated explanations match the model's predictions. Finally, researchers can deploy the model through a web-based interface where users can upload their own images of autoimmune diseases and receive predictions and explanations from the model.

8.5 EXPERIMENTAL RESULTS

The RestNet50 design, which is our suggested model, is shown in Figure 8.2. But for our analysis, we used the VGG-16, VGG-19, DenseNet121, InceptionV3, and ResNet50 models, which were put together utilizing the Adam optimizer across 50 iterations with a learning rate of 1e-5. RestNet50 succeeded in outperforming the other models after 50 iterations, with a validation accuracy of 95.2%.

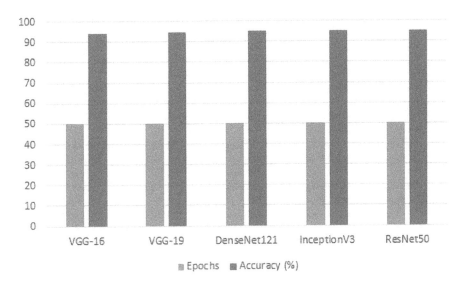

FIGURE 8.2 Transfer learning model's accuracy and loss curve.

8.6 CONCLUSION

XAI is an emerging field that focuses on creating transparent and interpretable AI models. In the context of medical diagnosis, XAI can help clinicians understand the reasoning behind AI predictions, which is particularly important in cases where human lives are at stake.

By using the knowledge gained from one task to another that is closely related, a machine learning model can benefit from transfer learning. Transfer learning can help decrease the quantity of training data needed and increase the model's accuracy in the detection of autoimmune illnesses. Detecting autoimmune disorders using XAI and transfer learning has the potential to increase diagnostic precision and aid physicians in comprehending the logic behind AI predictions. This can lead to earlier and more accurate diagnoses, which in turn can improve patient outcomes and reduce healthcare costs.

However, it is important to note that AI models are not a replacement for clinical expertise, and XAI can only provide explanations for what the model has learned from the data. Therefore, any AI-based diagnostic system should be combined with patient care and expertise.

REFERENCES

1. Akter, S., Shamrat, F. M. J. M., Chakraborty, S., Karim, A., & Azam, S. (2021). Covid-19 detection using deep learning algorithm on chest X-ray images. Biology, 10(11). https://doi.org/10.3390/biology10111174
2. Alrefai, N., & Ibrahim, O. (2021). Deep learning for COVID-19 diagnosis based on chest X-ray images. International Journal of Electrical and Computer Engineering, 11(5), 4531–4541. https://doi.org/10.11591/ijece.v11i5.pp4531-4541

3. Calderon-Ramirez, S., Yang, S., Moemeni, A., Colreavy-Donnelly, S., Elizondo, D. A., Oala, L., Rodríguez-Capitán, J., Jiménez-Navarro, M., Lopez-Rubio, E., & Molina-Cabello, M. A. (2021). Improving uncertainty estimation with semi-supervised deep learning for COVID19 detection using chest X-ray images. IEEE Access, 9, 85442–85454. https://doi.org/10.1109/ACCESS.2021.3085418

4. Degerli, A., Ahishali, M., Kiranyaz, S., Chowdhury, M. E. H., & Gabbouj, M. (2021). Reliable Covid-19 Detection Using Chest X-Ray Images. Proceedings - International Conference on Image Processing, ICIP, 2021-Septe, 185–189. https://doi.org/10.1109/ICIP42928.2021.9506442

5. Hariyani, Y. S., Hadiyoso, S., & Siadari, T. S. (2020). Deteksi Penyakit Covid-19 Berdasarkan Citra X-Ray Menggunakan deep residual network. ELKOMIKA: Jurnal Teknik Energi Elektrik, Teknik Telekomunikasi, & Teknik Elektronika, 8(2), 443. https://doi.org/10.26760/elkomika.v8i2.443

6. Hussain, E., Hasan, M., Rahman, M. A., Lee, I., Tamanna, T., & Parvez, M. Z. (2021). CoroDet: A deep learning based classification for COVID-19 detection using chest X-ray images. Chaos, Solitons and Fractals, 142. https://doi.org/10.1016/j.chaos.2020.110495

7. Iyer, M. (2021). Multimedia Classifiers: Behind the Scenes. MM 2021 - Proceedings of the 29th ACM International Conference on Multimedia, 5670–5672. https://doi.org/10.1145/3474085.3478872

8. Khattak, M. I., Al-Hasan, M., Jan, A., Saleem, N., Verdú, E., & Khurshid, N. (2021). Automated detection of Covid-19 using chest X-ray images and CT scans through multilayer-spatial convolutional neural networks. International Journal of Interactive Multimedia and Artificial Intelligence, 6(6), 15–24. https://doi.org/10.9781/ijimai.2021.04.002

9. Kumar, N., Gupta, M., Gupta, D., & Tiwari, S. (2021). Novel deep transfer learning model for COVID-19 patient detection using X-ray chest images. Journal of Ambient Intelligence and Humanized Computing. https://doi.org/10.1007/s12652-021-03306-6

10. Mahmud, T., Rahman, M. A., & Fattah, S. A. (2020). CovXNet: A multi-dilation convolutional neural network for automatic COVID-19 and other pneumonia detection from chest X-ray images with transferable multi-receptive feature optimization. Computers in Biology and Medicine, 122. https://doi.org/10.1016/j.compbiomed.2020.103869

11. Mousavi, Z., Shahini, N., Sheykhivand, S., Mojtahedi, S., & Arshadi, A. (2022). COVID-19 detection using chest X-ray images based on a developed deep neural network. SLAS Technology, 27(1), 63–75. https://doi.org/10.1016/j.slast.2021.10.011

12. Muhammad, U., Hoque, M. Z., Oussalah, M., Keskinarkaus, A., Seppänen, T., & Sarder, P. (2022). SAM: Self-augmentation mechanism for COVID-19 detection using chest X-ray images. Knowledge-Based Systems, 241. https://doi.org/10.1016/j.knosys.2022.108207

13. Nayak, S. R., Nayak, D. R., Sinha, U., Arora, V., & Pachori, R. B. (2021). Application of deep learning techniques for detection of COVID-19 cases using chest X-ray images: A comprehensive study. Biomedical Signal Processing and Control, 64. https://doi.org/10.1016/j.bspc.2020.102365

14. Nur-a-alam, Ahsan, M., Based, M. A., Haider, J., & Kowalski, M. (2021). COVID-19 detection from chest X-ray images using feature fusion and deep learning. Sensors, 21(4), 1–30. https://doi.org/10.3390/s21041480

15. Ohata, E. F., Bezerra, G. M., Chagas, J. V. S. D., Lira Neto, A. V., Albuquerque, A. B., Albuquerque, V. H. C. D., & Reboucas Filho, P. P. (2021). Automatic detection of COVID-19 infection using chest X-ray images through transfer learning. IEEE/CAA Journal of Automatica Sinica, 8(1), 239–248. https://doi.org/10.1109/JAS.2020.1003393

16. Ozturk, T., Talo, M., Yildirim, E. A., Baloglu, U. B., Yildirim, O., & Rajendra Acharya, U. (2020). Automated detection of COVID-19 cases using deep neural networks with X-ray. Computers in Biology and Medicine, 121, 103792. https://doi.org/10.1016/j.compbiomed.2020.103792

17. Panwar, H., Gupta, P. K., Siddiqui, M. K., Morales-Menendez, R., Bhardwaj, P., & Singh, V. (2020). A deep learning and grad-CAM based color visualization approach for fast detection of COVID-19 cases using chest X-ray and CT-scan images. Chaos, Solitons and Fractals, 140. https://doi.org/10.1016/j.chaos.2020.110190

18. Polat, Ç, Karaman, O., Karaman, C., Korkmaz, G., Balci, M. C., & Kelek, S. E. (2021). COVID-19 diagnosis from chest X-ray images using transfer learning: Enhanced performance by debiasing dataloader. Journal of X-Ray Science and Technology, 29(1), 19–36. https://doi.org/10.3233/XST-200757

19. Qjidaa, M., Ben-Fares, A., Amakdouf, H., El Mallahi, M., Alami, B., Maaroufi, M., Lakhssassi, A., & Qjidaa, H. (2022). Recognizing COVID-19 from chest X-ray images for people in rural and remote areas based on deep transfer learning model. Multimedia Tools and Applications, 81(9), 13115–13135. https://doi.org/10.1007/s11042-022-12030-y

20. Rahman, T., Khandakar, A., Qiblawey, Y., Tahir, A., Kiranyaz, S., Abul Kashem, S., Bin, Islam, M. T., Al Maadeed, S., Zughaier, S. M., Khan, M. S., & Chowdhury, M. E. H. (2021). Exploring the effect of image enhancement techniques on COVID-19 detection using chest X-ray images. Computers in Biology and Medicine, 132. https://doi.org/10.1016/j.compbiomed.2021.104319

21. Raj, R. (2020). CoviDecode : Detection of COVID-19 from chest X-ray images using convolutional neural networks. International Journal for Modern Trends in Science and Technology, 6(12), 436–439. https://doi.org/10.46501/ijmtst061283

22. Salih, S. Q., Abdulla, H. K., Ahmed, Z. S., Surameery, N. M. S., & Rashid, R. D. (2020). Modified AlexNet convolution neural network for Covid-19 detection using chest X-ray images. Kurdistan Journal of Applied Research, 119–130. https://doi.org/10.24017/covid.14

23. Shankar, K., Perumal, E., Díaz, V. G., Tiwari, P., Gupta, D., Saudagar, A. K. J., & Muhammad, K. (2021). An optimal cascaded recurrent neural network for intelligent COVID-19 detection using chest X-ray images. Applied Soft Computing, 113. https://doi.org/10.1016/j.asoc.2021.107878

24. Shorfuzzaman, M., & Masud, M. (2020). On the detection of Covid-19 from chest X-ray images using CNN-based transfer learning. Computers, Materials and Continua, 64(3), 1359–1381. https://doi.org/10.32604/cmc.2020.011326

25. Singh, M., Bansal, S., Ahuja, S., Dubey, R. K., Panigrahi, B. K., & Dey, N. (2021). Transfer learning–based ensemble support vector machine model for automated COVID-19 detection using lung computerized tomography scan data. Medical and Biological Engineering and Computing, 59(4), 825–839. https://doi.org/10.1007/s11517-020-02299-2

26. Tang, G. S., Chow, L. S., Solihin, M. I., Ramli, N., Gowdh, N. F., & Rahmat, K. (2021). Detection of Covid-19 Using Deep Convolutional Neural Network on Chest X-Ray (CXR) Images. Canadian Conference on Electrical and Computer Engineering, 2021-Septe. https://doi.org/10.1109/CCECE53047.2021.9569064

27. Zhao, W., Jiang, W., & Qiu, X. (2021). Fine-tuning convolutional neural networks for Covid-19 detection from chest X-ray images. Diagnostics, 11(10). https://doi.org/10.3390/diagnostics11101887

9 Wearable Smart Technologies
Changing the Future of Healthcare

Shalini Mahato, Laxmi Kumari Pathak, Soni Sweta, and Dilip Kumar Choubey

9.1 INTRODUCTION

Internet of Things (IoT) is contributing in the area of healthcare observation by using wearable devices. A network of physical objects that is backed up by ingrained technology for transmission of data and necessary sensors to connect with inner and outer states of objects and surroundings is called Internet of Things [1].

Today, every IoTs-related discussion necessarily includes the wearable devices. The self-health observation and precautionary medicines are the present need because of the huge growth in the number of old-age people until the year 2020. To decrease the total expense and observation costs, high-end technologies are required. The wearable devices are used to continuously observe the health-related indicators in many areas. The new trend of Medical IoTs is achievable by integrating the wearable devices as well as apps in tele-health and tele-medicine efficiency [2].

The health-care systems are facing the speedy hike in aging population globally, so chronic diseases patients are also increasing in number, and the expense over medical treatment is also rising [3]. The biggest problem is that aging people are less conscious about routine medical check-ups and regular observation of their health condition is required. Some smarter solutions are needed to decrease the economic burden as well as to achieve regular health checks. Sensor-enabled remote biomedical devices are aiding in early diagnosis and control of some major chronic diseases and it is the rapidly growing interdisciplinary research domain. Some of the hybrid wearable devices are designed to help elderly people with persistent diseases such as diabetes, increased blood pressure, chronic kidney disease, and cardiovascular diseases. These kinds of devices will change the future of healthcare instrumentation and future research in the artificial intelligence domain. The data being stored in the warehouse from various sensors will contribute to a great extent to exploring and expanding the area of healthcare science [3].

DOI: 10.1201/9781003388845-11

9.2 BACKGROUND

The healthcare and biomedical sector is transforming into a progressed, digitally improved, high-tech, consumer-oriented sector. Despite numerous challenges, day-by-day this industry is becoming more innovative and generating new solutions for enhancing the way of patient's care. The medical sector is openly adopting the unruly digital processes. The statistics show that more than 1800 hospitals in the U.S. use mobile apps, and 92% of the hospitals have adopted a portal solution for patients.

Patients these days also want to have convenient medical support that must provide first-grade service and also be within budget. The definitive healthcare study shows that 70% of people don't like to personally go to their primary healthcare point but rather prefer an online video conference appointment with the healthcare professional. Now, hospitals are also upgrading themselves as per this requirement. Tele-health services are being provided by 50% hospitals in the U.S. This virtual monitoring of patients has now grown into a $31.3 billion industry. This outpouring is giving a hike to the wearable market, which has grown by 15.3% in the last year to 198.5 million units by the year 2019.

Smart wearable technologies in healthcare are now not just a fitness tracking device but have become real-time healthcare monitors. This innovative shift in technology is predicted to result in an annual industry-wide outlay of $20 billion on fitness tracking and remote patient observation gadgets by 2023.

9.2.1 IoT in Healthcare

Healthcare has become the most important and attractive application area for the IoTs. So many medical services are now possible remotely, such as fitness sessions, chronic disease risk monitoring, remote observation of health conditions, and care of elderly people [4].

The IoTs connect apps, sensors, devices, and network connectivity that improves these entities to acquire and interchange data. In a healthcare system, various parameters can be checked, and a patient can be kept under rigorous observation. This continuous monitoring can give amazing results. There are various devices available in the ICUs today that can even send an alert to a doctor regarding any emergency situation. The data and information regarding the patient's health condition can now be easily shared with the doctor as well as family members [5].

The IoTs give rise to the technology to achieve an advanced level of health services [6]. Affordable, low-priced, reliable, and portable devices are now possible to be embedded; hence, flawless networking can be attained among patients, healthcare professionals, and wearable devices. The sensors of the devices are used to record signals on a regular basis, and these signals will then be correlated with certain predefined parameters and sent through the wireless network. This data will be stored in a repository, processed, and then analyzed with already stored health data [7]. Healthcare experts can utilize these records and have decision support for making an improved prognosis to treat someone in the early stages of any disease. Even in the non-availability of doctor, this analysis is capable of instructing devices to forecast future medical problems. Apart from forecasting, devices may also suggest the medicine to patients after studying the medical report databases.

The IoTs make it possible that highly advanced sensors can be implanted in the body or worn by the patient to monitor the health condition continuously. The algorithms help the health experts make the treatment personalized, and they will also reduce the cost incurred, and the result will be incredible [8].

9.2.2 MONITORING OF VITAL SIGNS THROUGH WEARABLE SMART DEVICES

The smart wearable health devices are the most innovative and growing technology now, which makes regular health-related vital sign monitoring possible. Even if you are at the office, house, walking, playing, or even sleeping, the wearable devices will be at your service all the time, continuously recording and observing your vital signs. These devices do not disturb us while we are doing any kind of daily activity, making our life easier [9]. The body of a human being has numerous physiological signs, which can be recorded from electrical signals to biochemical signs. The biosignals of humans can be acquired from various devices, as shown in Figure 9.1, and the health statistics can be observed in real time. The various vital sign monitoring wearable devices are discussed below.

   i. **Heart-Rate Monitoring (Electrocardiogram – ECG):** The heart rate is the main vital statistics that is considered as a regular monitoring necessity in the medical industry as well as in the sports industry. This

FIGURE 9.1   Vital sign monitoring through smart wearable devices in the healthcare industry.

recording gives us data regarding the physiological state by alerting us to the differences in the cycle of heart rate. This important sign is possibly acquired from R-peak (ECG) or photoplethysmography signals (PPG) [10]. ECGs are the biosignals that are used as a major diagnosis tool in medical scenarios and alerts about records of the cardiac-electrical cycle.

ii. **Electrolyte Level Monitoring:** The sweat analysis can be done by the biosensors method, which is capable of electrochemical sensing and analyzes the sweat of the body or the tears of the eyes to detect the electrolyte level of a human body. A biosensor can give real-time recordings for further analysis [11]. There are two different kinds of sensors: one is called flexible sensor and the other is called a non-flexible sensor [12, 13].

iii. **Blood Pressure (BP) Monitoring:** The BP is believed to be one of the main significant cardiopulmonary measures, which denotes the pressure applied by blood on the wall of the arteries. When the heart contracts (systole) and relaxes (diastole), BP gives blood flow-related information and information regarding oxygen being delivered to the cells. Ambulatory monitoring of BP permits BP recordings many times during the day. It can help in identifying high BP, also called hypertension. This is the biggest risk for so many people who are suffering from cardiovascular ailments [14, 15].

BP can be measured automatically with an inflatable cuff, which reads BP by comparing outside pressure and the magnitude of arterial volume pulsations [16].

iv. **Stress Monitoring:** Stress is a condition that occurs as a natural response of the human body to an external event. The main physiological reactions have differences in heartbeat rate, pulse rate, temperature of skin, dilation of pupil, and electro-dermal activity (EDA). The abnormal or stressful conditions can be identified by studying the records collected by various non-invasive sensors on wearable devices.

v. **Temperature Monitoring:** The key factor for health is the temperature of the human body. Those persons who are doing physically and mentally exhaustive tasks then the temperature needs to be monitored continuously. The temperature of the body is homoeothermic and remains at $37°$ C and can also fluctuate some time. The temperature is the result of the production of heat and the loss of heat balance in the body of a human being. It is very important to record it to bypass various components to malfunction because of high body temperatures [17]. It can be categorized into two parts: core temperature (CT) and skin temperature.

vi. **Vision Tracking:** In today's era, watching e-displays is part of our daily lives at the office, home, and also in free time or even while moving from place to place. Desktops, laptops, tablet, mobiles, etc. are now devices that have become universal [18]. Wearable devices are needed to track our vision and alert us about the status.

vii. **EEG Monitoring:** The electroencephalogram (EEG) is a method for recording brain signals and is being used to detect many mental disorders like depression, schizophrenia, and autism. Electrodes get attached to the head to record the waves that generate synchronized neuronal actions inside the brain. The EEG technology in the form of a wearable device is the most important device for the future.

viii. **Physical Activity Monitoring:** Physical activities. The tracking and monitoring and analysis of the movements of the human body provide us vital data to maintain a right and proper body posture. Regular monitoring of movements of the body enables us to detect unusual gait coordination and shaking of the hands that can help in identifying diseases like Alzheimer's, Parkinson's, and diabetes. In this way, it will help in diagnosing these diseases earlier, so treatment can be started on time.

ix. **Blood Glucose Monitoring:** One of the persistent disease conditions is diabetes, which can be detected by measuring the level of blood glucose (BG). The wearable devices will help patients with diabetes to continuously check their BG levels, and suggestive measures can also be given by the system. The Medtronic-Continuous-Glucose-Monitoring (CGM) device is able to read BG levels with a smart patch having a needle. It can also send the recorded health data in wireless mode to a wearable insulin pump to release it into the body of the wearer [19].

9.3   DIFFERENT SMART WEARABLE DEVICES

Wearable devices showcase the strength of the IoT and its benefits in the healthcare sector. These devices have sensors, and IoT enables these devices to collect information and bring it to your access through apps on your smartphone. Machine learning can help the devices to forecast the health condition of patients and take necessary actions. This emerging smart technology has entered the healthcare sector, giving rise to the "Medical Internet of Things (MIoT)." Some of the present state-of-the-art is discussed in Table 9.1.

9.4   SOLUTION AND RECOMMENDATIONS

These smart wearable devices help their users or the patients to self-monitor their vital signs regularly and decrease the number of visits to a doctor or hospital. The operational costs incurred in the treatment can be reduced this way. The health parameters measured by any of these devices can be updated to the doctors on their smartphones. Patients' conditions can be observed remotely by the doctor, and suggestive measures and medications can also be taken. These devices are capable of securing their data and keeping it confidential. By utilizing this advanced technology of the IoT, health monitoring and appropriate actions become faster and easier. But many wearable technologies are still in their prototype stages and need to be explored. There are a lot of issues in the wearable technology domain, such as user adaptation, data security and confidentiality, ethics, and the concerns regarding big data are still to be addressed so that the functions and usability of these devices can be enhanced for their real-time and practical use.

TABLE 9.1
Different Wearable Technologies and the Methodology Used

Sl. No.	Author	Technology Used	Methodology
1	[20]	ECG and ACC mobile sensors	The authors suggested a model that will be mobile monitored and will include mobile sensors that are wearable ECG and ACC. They have proposed an algorithm that can determine the interrelationship between heart rate and movements by automatically analyzing the signals of the ECG and ACC. The model was experimented on 7 healthy people while they were performing routine tasks. Then the signals from the sensors were analyzed, and they got the result that during normal physical tasks, the subjects were in a general physical state
2	[21]	ECG, galvanic skin response (GSR)	The aim of this research was to check the usefulness of wireless technology and wearable sensors to automatically record levels of stress in an ambulatory setup. A wearable sensor-enabled chest strap was used to record ECG signals by studying the autonomic function. Stress level indicator Galvanic Skin Response (GSR) was taken by placing two electrodes on the hand that is non-dominant. A function based on wireless acquisition was given as a support on the wrist. With anorexia nervosa (AN), data were collected from a group of mature adolescents in a condition of rest. ECG was used for assessments like LF/HF ratio, tachogram, power of high frequency (HF) and low frequency (LF) bands, root-mean-square-of-successive-differences (RMSSD), and mean RR intervals (meanRR). The standard deviation, area under the curve of the signal sampled, mean, variance, delta between max and min values of conductance, median, etc. are worked out using GSR. Increased mean RR and RMSSD, along with reduced HR, were observed among AN patients. Oversympathetic activity and parasympathetic prevalence were recommended, with HF increasing, LF decreasing and LF/HF decreasing. In controls, AN exhibited a reduced standard deviation, delta value, and GSR variance
3	[22]	Zigbee-compatible wireless sensor, Patch-type ECG Sensor	Wireless sensor node that was Zigbee-compatible was used by the author as a solution to wearable patch-type sensors for ECG by transferring signals through low-power wireless communication to a computer. The recorded ECG signals hold tremendous medical data for a cardiologist, such as the detection of R-peaks in ECG signals that utilize the threshold fixed value. But errors can arise if the baseline changes because of motion artifacts and change in the size of the signal. To efficiently and accurately identify the R-peak, the variable threshold technique was used. R-peak identification with the use of MIT-BIH data storage and long-term-real-time ECG were implemented for analysis and performance evaluation purposes.

(Continued)

TABLE 9.1 (*Continued*)
Different Wearable Technologies and the Methodology Used

Sl. No.	Author	Technology Used	Methodology
4	[23]	ECG detection with sensor enabled smart shirt having conductive fabric electrodes	For recording the health parameters in actual time, the author recorded acceleration signals and ECG with the help of a smart shirt with conductive fabric as an electrode to capture the body signal. For remote monitoring, information about physical tasks and physiological ECG data was transmitted to a main station and a remote server by utilizing standard IEEE 802.15.4 communication. Artifact noise was removed using an adaptive filtering method to collect clear ECG signals from the person while carrying out the physical activity.
5	[24]	Kinetic sensors of the smartphone, a self-designed ECG sensor, AFE, MCU, SD Card, Bluetooth module	Kinetic sensors within present-day smartphones, along with self-designed ECG sensors, were used as a low-power context-aware wearable by the author to monitor ECG. The wearable smart sensor for ECG included a completely integrated analog front-end (AFE), Secure Digital (SD) card, microcontroller unit (MCU), and Bluetooth module. The wearable AFE sensor design consumes only 12.5 mW of power with a convenient dimension of $58 \times 50 \times 10$ mm. Real-time ECG recording while carrying out the physical activity was possible due to the presence of kinetic sensors in the smartphone. The abnormal patterns of the ECG were detected, which helped improve arrhythmias diagnosis.
6	[25]	ECG, Raw fabric soaking in PEDOT: PSS	PEDOT: PSS as a conductive polymer was utilized in raw fabric by soaking it in it and then annealing and squeezing the material. A test of electrodes was conducted on normal subjects. Skin impedance on contact and variation in the ECG signal were observed under rest and physical activity conditions (baseline wandering, QRS detectability, power spectral density, and broadband noise). The use of these electrodes could be done both under dry and wet situations. However, dry electrodes tend to pick up noise artifacts from improper skin contact, whereas wet (saline) electrodes showed stable output and were also better than the generally used disposable gelled Ag/AgCl electrodes. With these electrodes, ECG signals were effectively measured.
7	[26]	ECG, heart rate variability (HRV), wrist worn PulseOn	Beat-to-beat identification accuracy was computed by the author from a wrist-worn and optical heart rate monitoring PulseOn (PO). 10 volunteers (2 female and 8 male; 35.9 ± 10.3 years of age) contributed to the research. HRV was recorded by using PO and Firstbeat Bodyguard 2 (BG2) devices. It was utilized as an ECG-based reference. At times of sleep, the HRV was registered. An average 99.57 percent of the heartbeats having 5.94 ms mean absolute error (MAE) in the intervals of beat-to-beat (RRI) as related to ECG founded RRI BG2 and compared to BG2 was measured with the PO. The results with PO gave an exact technique for long-duration HRV observation during sleep. The mean RMSSD difference between PO and BG2 obtained HRV recorded as 3.1 ms.

(*Continued*)

TABLE 9.1 (*Continued*)
Different Wearable Technologies and the Methodology Used

Sl. No.	Author	Technology Used	Methodology
8	[27]	ECG, PPG, smart watch-embedded sensors, RESMED S+	Present-day smart watches have many built-in sensors like gyroscope, accelerometer, and optical sensors with good processors and memory subsystems. Comparisons with usually used ECG and PPG devices were done with the optical heart rate sensor of smart watches. The result showed accuracy in the heart rate measured by the sensors of the smart watches. A commercially used medical lab-based non-contact type sleep sensor, RESMED S+, was used to compare the heart rate signal and accelerometer readings taken from the smart watch.
9	[28]	ECG, armband embedded with capacitive-coupled electrodes, Bluetooth Low Energy (BLE) protocol	Bluetooth Low Energy (BLE) was the protocol used for sending information. The protocol enabled a low-power transmission model. The model proposed by the author had built-in capacitive coupler electrodes in the armband. To make the model accurate, a filter algorithm to eliminate distractions while measuring human body movement was used.
10	[29]	ECG, belt with integrated electronics	The authors developed a belt that has in-built electronics in which a low-power module records the ECG signals and the acceleration (2-axis), and the generated data gets stored for a maximum of two days. Tests on people have also been done to analyze the performance of the belt while doing the daily of routine physical activities. The model has parameters like quality of ECG signal, uptime, and coverage of ECG signal over a day
11	[30]	ECG, blood pressure, photoplethismography (PPG) probe	The authors present a wearable clinical device for electrocardiogram (ECG) and blood pressure (BP) monitoring. Photoplethismography (PPG) probes, along with new algorithms in an online interface, were used for onspot evaluation of BP levels and physiological signal monitoring. On being compared with a commercial electronic Sphygmomanometer, the accuracy level was 94.6% for systolic BP and 92.3% for systolic BP.
12	[31]	Blood Pressure, accelerometer and optical sensor-embedded watch	The authors developed a wristwatch for monitoring blood pressure. Blood pressure was measured by recording the travel time, called the Pulse Transit Time (PTT), with the help of an accelerometer and optical sensor embedded in the watch that could detect micro-vibrations taking place on the chest wall linked to the heartbeat while the wearable watch is held against the sternum.
13	[32]	Blood pressure, smart watch with two pulse oximeters	Here, the authors propose a novel watch for current time recording and assessing blood pressure. It has two pulse oximeters: the first one is positioned on the back and the second one is on the front. When the index finger gets positioned on the front oximeter, it

(*Continued*)

TABLE 9.1 (Continued)

Different Wearable Technologies and the Methodology Used

Sl. No.	Author	Technology Used	Methodology
			starts reading two photoplethysmograms (PPG); for obtaining Pulse Transit Time, the signals are refined and cross-correlated. To estimate the BP, which is systolic and diastolic, the heart rate and the PTT recorded from the finger are treated as input to a linear model
14	[33]	Blood pressure, wristwatch and ring, PTT, PWV	Over peripheral arterial blood pressure, the calibration of non-invasive peripheral arterial sensor signals has been proposed. The attached sensor recognizes the transduction dynamics matching the peripheral arterial BP and the recorded arterial sensor signal by measuring the change in the intra-arterial hydrostatic pressure. A calibration of peripheral PTT readings to arterial BP is made by using a unique wearable sensor architecture to collect and evaluate pulse wave velocity (PWV). There are two inline photoplethysmograph sensors in this sensor architecture: one ring which reads the pulse waveform of the digital artery beside the ground of the little finger, and the other, a wrist watch, which records the pulse waveform in the ulnar artery.
15	[34]	Blood pressure and heart rate, Bluetooth, and IEEE 802.15.4 wireless technologies	Wireless wearables and ambient sensors have been described for measuring blood pressure and heart rate while carrying out routine activities. The wearable sensors are connected to different body parts and need high synchronization of time and a high sampling rate to give an analysis of the recorded signals. For current-time observation and time synchronization, Bluetooth and IEEE 802.15.4 wireless technology have been used. The results show that this wearable device gives concurrent data regarding the location and vital signs of the user with a 1-ms resolution.
16	[35]	Blood pressure, non-invasive technique, watch	The author has introduced a non-invasive tissue-informative recording technique. An experimental event of subcutaneous tissue pressure equilibrium is discovered that is concerned with the identification of the absolute value of blood pressure. A watch-like observation module was put on a dummy model to analyze the accuracy of the blood pressure reading.
17	[36]	Blood pressure, h-Shirt	This study introduced an e-textile material-based health shirt (h-Shirt) for reading arterial BP as well as physiological parameters on a regular and long-term basis by the cuffless method. Trials were made on ten and five persons accordingly for the h-Shirt. The output showed the capability of combining calibration and observation methods on the h-Shirt to design a hands-free smart wearable device in order to constantly measure BP.
18	[37]	Temperature, Belt, Negative Temperature Coefficient (NTC) resistor	The proposed wearable device with sensors has been designed to be used for premature infants. The compactness and accuracy involved in the negative temperature coefficient resistor as a temperature sensor make it fit to be used for the non-invasive neonatal temperature measurement model. A smart jacket for the

(Continued)

TABLE 9.1 (*Continued*)
Different Wearable Technologies and the Methodology Used

Sl. No.	Author	Technology Used	Methodology
			neonate is prepared with the help of conductive textile wires. A soft bamboo fabric-made dummy belt with an NTC sensor fixed to it shows the temperature reading.
19	[38]	Temperature, Infrared (IR) photodetectors	Infrared (IR) photodetectors on flexible polyimide (PI) substrates and wearable temperature sensors as flexible electronics have been described in this paper. Graphene flakes and Solar exfoliated decreased Graphene Oxide (SrGO) have been utilized as sensing materials to make sensors on a PI substrate. The present responsiveness and outer quantum efficiency of the IR photodetector for SrGO-based devices and for graphene flake are measured as 0.8 AW-1 (33.06%) and 0.4 AW-1 (16.53%), respectively. An ultrasensitive wearable has been proposed, wherein both SrGO-based devices and graphene flake showed negative temperature coefficients of -0.007429 degree C^{-1} and -0.004130 degree C^{-1}, respectively. These data are much higher as compared to any available commercial partner.
20	[39]	Temperature, wearable RFID patch	Sensor patches for wearable radiofrequency identification (RFID) built with a fabric that is conductive in nature have been proposed by the author. A similar type of design has also been put on a substrate of polyimide (PI) to demonstrate the effective performance of the proposed model. The RFID patch was prepared to be wearable and washable by utilizing a non-conductive substrate of fabric and a conductive fabric coil antenna. The flexible and comfortable nature of the conductive fabric makes it easily adaptable to clothes. The variations in the skin temperature enable the temperature measurement.
21	[40]	Temperature, advanced fabric temperature sensor, Fiber Bragg Grating (FBG)	The authors present a temperature sensor for fabric using fiber Bragg grating (FBG) sensors. The sensor was more stable and had a sensitivity of 10.61 α 0.08 pm/°C. The change in the temperature distribution due to the existence of many sources of heat as sensed by textile sensors was simulated with the help of MATLAB to analyze a real-time change in temperature. The model demonstrates increased sensitivity, good stability, and usability with the properties of comfort textiles.
22	[41]	Glucose	In this study, the authors have proposed a wearable integrated health monitoring device. It consists of a wearable smart band (for physical activity, oxygen level, and heart rate) and a sweat-based glucose sensing strip (for monitoring the glucose level). Continuous monitoring regarding physiological and electrochemical changes is done with the help of software. It also computes the glucose level for pre-exercise and post-exercise periods. The proposed integrated wearable device provides a novel health monitoring technology via integrated analysis of key metabolic and physiological health indices.

(Continued)

TABLE 9.1 (*Continued*)
Different Wearable Technologies and the Methodology Used

Sl. No.	Author	Technology Used	Methodology
23	[42]	Glucose, electrochemical glucose sensor that is enzyme-based	The study done in this paper discusses the growth of sensors that are enzyme-based electrochemical glucose sensors, including materials, structures of the device, fabrication processes, and engineering processes. Blood glucose readings for invasive and non-invasive methods using many biofluids or blood are explained. Current advancements in the procedure for developing enzyme-based glucose sensors and the related integrated systems have been discussed.
24	[43]	Glucose, In2O3 nanoribbon FET biosensors	In this paper, the authors presented In_2O_3 nanoribbon FET biosensors, which are very sensitive. This sensor has an integrated on-chip gold side gate that was coated on different surfaces, like watches, which can be used to detect glucose from body fluids (saliva and sweat). Excellent electrical performance was exhibited by shadow-mask-fabricated equipment when gold side gate electrodes provided the gate using an aqueous electrolyte. It also showed good mechanical toughness. The detection range of a glucose sensor is at least 5 orders of magnitude to 10 nM. Thus, In_2O_3 nano-ribbon devices for sensing with great efficiency to perform tasks can be utilized as essential constituents for healthcare electronics that are wearable.
25	[44]	Glucose, visible–near-infrared (Vis-NIR) spectroscopy	The authors created a new blood glucose sensor that is affordable and comfortable to wear. It has also a less data-collecting time window. It helps in the non-invasive and regular blood glucose monitoring (CGM) model. The biosensor has the capacity to recognize differences in the concentration of blood glucose in the tissue of the wrist. This proposed sensor records information regarding regular constituents of the arterial blood volume pulsation.
26	[45]	Electrolytes, Wearable potentiometric ion sensors (WPISs)	In this paper, the authors wearable potentiometric ion sensors (WPISs), which provide on-body measurements. An analysis was done on the sweat that was gathered while sports activities were performed by utilizing a proposed device consisting of ion chromatography and a pH-meter. The on-body readings were also recorded for comparison of the measures. The values were recorded (every 10–12.5 minutes) during sports activity. The proposed device consisted of pH, Cl^-, K^+, and Na^+ sensors for the detailed analysis of sweat. The array electrode was made up of multi-walled carbon nanotubes (MWCNT) and stretchable materials which has good analytical performance as well as Nernstian slopes in the anticipated physiological band of every ion analyte and drift appropriate for medium-term workout practice $(0.3 \pm 0.2$ mV h-1). The device also shows instant reaction time, a necessary refinement for measuring sweat, and good convertibility.

(Continued)

TABLE 9.1 (*Continued*)
Different Wearable Technologies and the Methodology Used

Sl. No.	Author	Technology Used	Methodology
27	[46]	Physical Activity, Triaxial Accelerometer	The aim of the authors in this study was to validate the alteration of hardware and algorithms to monitor patterns of physical activity. The equipment used was a triaxial accelerometer with the validation of timed-up and go and normal measures of balance and gait. A total of 8 subjects of old age suffering from diabetes and peripheral neuropathy (age = 77 ± 7 years) were selected. The subjects continuously wore the sensors for regular tasks performed in the gait lab. The categorization of the subjects was done on the basis of Tinetti scores (risk of falling). The proposed system was able to predict the walking duration and number of steps taken (random error <5%). The proposed device was able to monitor postural transitions as well as predict with high accuracy those at great risk of falling.
28	[47]	Stress, Poincaré-plots of PR-data	The objective of the study was to construct a new evaluation index for analysis of stress. The Poincaré plots of PR data formed the basis of the study. Inter-point distance measures of Poincaré plots of PR data formed the index. An experiment was done with a sample of seven subjects under induction of mental stress to confirm the novel stress evaluation index. Real-time change of stress level over a short-term 1-minute period was examined using PR data.
29	[48]	Stress, Posttraumatic Stress Disorder (PTSD)	The authors proposed a device that is capable of monitoring symptoms of bad dreams and tries to reduce them or gently awaken the patient if not successful. It helps in enhancing the quality of life of people who are suffering from bad dreams due to PTSD mental disorder. The device helps suppress the nightmares through sound therapy, temperature control, and aromatherapy. This proposed methodology combines the subjects into a countermeasure network and keeps monitoring the nightmare conditions. This optimization is done using machine learning techniques.
30	[49]	Stress, wearable physiological sensors	A machine learning technique has been presented in this paper for detecting stress in people adopting wearable physiological sensors. It aims to improve the quality of life of the people. The proposed method has the capability to continuously check the mental state of the subject and can categorize it into a stressful or non-stressful state. It is very efficient at detecting stress in real time.
31	[50]	Stress, AdaBoost, support vector machine, and k-nearest neighbor	The authors demonstrated an automatic stress detection device using a machine learning approach for people in different social conditions by embedding two sensors that record physiological and social responses. By using various classifiers like AdaBoost, Support Vector Machine, and k-nearest neighbor, the performance was compared. The results of the experiment show that by merging readings from both sensors, the discrimination of stressful situations from mental conditions in a controlled Trier Social Stress Test.

(Continued)

TABLE 9.1 (*Continued*)
Different Wearable Technologies and the Methodology Used

Sl. No.	Author	Technology Used	Methodology
32	[51]	Stress	In this article, the authors present a model that is based on logistics regression that combines data from psychological (using Stress Response Inventory), physiological (using Heart Rate Variability), and biochemical (using salivary cortisol) areas through a triangulation principle for attaining maximum reliability and consistency in the process of stress assessment. A mental stress index based on the correlation between salivary cortisol and Heart Rate Variability time–frequency domain characteristics was determined by this model. A group of 30 students contributed to the process of evaluating the model. The results show that mental-stress-index measurements were responsive to acute stress, and the association level could be predicted from normal subjects to a stressed person with an accuracy of 74%. This wearable sensor model can be adapted in a dynamic environment for automatic self-tracking of one's stress level.
33	[52]	Stress, fabricated stress patch	In this study, 3 sensors were integrated in a patch (25 mm × 15 mm × 72 μm) for monitoring human stress from the temperature of pulse waves and skin conductance. The skin contact region is decreased to 0.008 of the conventional single-layer multiple-sensors. The proposed device has the capability to detect multimodal biosignals, which can be further utilized for monitoring emotions.
34	[53]	Vision tracking, wearable eye tracker	To study the image in real-time scenarios, the authors have constructed a self-reliant, wearable eye tracker for examining difficult jobs. The eye tracker does not prohibit the user from natural movement or behavior and stores the peripheral vision. Wearable eye trackers may be utilized to read effectively in a variety of visual tasks, from conditional awareness to guided visual search.
35	[54]	Vision tracking, moments of eye-contact	The authors propose a framework for identifying instants of eye contact between an adult and a child. The proposed system consists of one pair of gaze-tracking glasses that are worn by an adult. The commercial gaze tracking technology technique is utilized to obtain the mature person's point of vision and join it to the child's face using computer vision video analysis to obtain their direction of gaze. Eye contact is now found in the event of concurrent, 1-to-1 gazing at faces by the dyad.

9.5   FUTURE RESEARCH DIRECTIONS

Researchers have a great interest in smart wearable device development, with a closed loop and automatic feedback to the person wearing the device to alert the wearer regarding abnormal changes in vital signs and any kind of risky behavior. These devices will work to reinforce learning and will be sufficient enough to do decision-making and analysis of the measured health records. These wearable devices will need a maximum level of sensitivity and specificity for their users and will require systems with a great degree of prediction ability. These days, the most influential electronic organizations are focusing on various areas of smart wearable devices. Few companies have initiated the early editions of wearable health devices, whereas other companies are still in the phase of prototype development.

Smart wearable devices are at a stage where adopting these devices need to be accelerated for personal as well as business use. In the upcoming years, it is probable that the most potential and normally adopted wearable device would be the combination of intelligent glasses with augmented reality. When future research will develop these products and their prices will be affordable, these devices will surely approach the maturity phase, and there will be a highly increased rate of adaptation to the innovative technology. The increased rate of popularity of smart wearable devices like fitness trackers, smart watches, wrist bands, movement sensors, smart h-shirts, smart footwear, and wearable patches may seem opulent today but will determine the healthcare industry of tomorrow.

9.6   IOT AND MACHINE LEARNING

The data generated by IoT sensors is typically unstructured and in raw form, which makes it difficult to interpret and analyze manually. This is where machine learning comes in. Machine learning algorithms can be trained on the data generated by IoT sensors to detect patterns, anomalies, and trends, which can be used to optimize processes and make predictions. Machine learning and IoT sensors have a close relationship, as IoT sensors generate a large amount of data that can be processed and analyzed using machine learning techniques to derive insights and make predictions.

For example, in a manufacturing plant, IoT sensors can be used to collect data on the temperature, pressure, and vibration of machines. Machine learning algorithms can be trained on this data to detect patterns that indicate potential machine failures. This information can be used to schedule maintenance activities proactively, thereby minimizing downtime and maximizing productivity.

Similarly, in agriculture, IoT sensors can be used to collect data on soil moisture, temperature, and humidity. Machine learning algorithms can be trained on this data to predict the best time to plant, water, and harvest crops. This information can help farmers optimize their crop yield and reduce water usage.

Similarly, in healthcare, EEG sensor along with machine learning can be used for the detection of various mental health disorders like depression, schizophrenia, and autism [55–57].

Moreover, machine learning algorithms can enable intelligent automation in IoT systems. For example, in a smart home, machine learning algorithms can analyze sensor data to learn the behavior patterns of the residents and automatically adjust the temperature, lighting, and other settings to optimize energy efficiency and comfort. This can provide a better user experience while reducing energy consumption and costs. Similarly, smart cities can use sensors along with machine learning techniques to automate decisions for smart traffic management, smart waste management, smart energy management, security and surveillance, and so on [58].

In summary, the combination of machine learning and IoT sensors can provide valuable insights and predictions, optimize processes, and enable intelligent automation in various industries. Machine learning algorithms can analyze the large amounts of data generated by IoT sensors to learn from it and make informed decisions. This relationship is essential to achieving the full potential of IoT systems.

9.7 CONCLUSION

Based on the study, it can be concluded that wearable smart technologies have emerged progressively alongside technological advances like GPS systems, electronic-based chips, Internet connectivity, Wi-Fi systems, computers, and powerful sensors. The greatest implementations of wearable devices are mainly in the healthcare industry. Today, the spread of wearable devices in the healthcare domain is in its early stages, but they are still becoming a necessity for regular and continuous health sign monitoring. The main domain for getting a breakthrough is the advancement and optimization of innovative methods to record and observe other physiological parameters with great accuracy. The wearable devices will ease the lives of people who are in need of a real-time measurement of vital signs. It will also help doctors and healthcare professionals monitor and observe the health-related signs of their patients continuously and remotely. To conclude, the future will be healthier, easier, faster, and much safer with smart wearable medical technologies.

REFERENCES

1. LeHong, H., & Velosa, A. (2014). Hype cycle for the Internet of Things, [Internet]. Stamford (CT): Gartner Inc.; 2014. Available from: https://www.gartner.com/doc/2804217/hype-cycle-internet-things
2. Haghi, M., Thurow, K., Habil, I., Stoll, R., & Habil, M. (2017). Wearable devices in medical Internet of Things. *Health Informatics Research*, *23*(1), 4–15. https://doi.org/10.4258/hir.2017.23.1.4
3. Bloom, D. E., Cafiero, E., Jané-Llopis, E., Abrahams-Gessel, S., Bloom, L. R., Fathima, S., Feigl, A. B., Gaziano, T., Hamandi, A., Mowafi, M., Pandya, A., Prettner, K., Rosenberg, L., Seligman, B., Stein, A. Z., & Weinstein, C. (2011). The Global Economic Burden of Noncommunicable Diseases. Program on the Global Demography of Aging.
4. Qaosar, M., Ahmed, S., Li, C., & Morimoto, Y. (2018). Hybrid Sensing and Wearable Smart Device for Health Monitoring and Medication: Opportunities and Challenges. In *The 2018 AAAI Spring Symposium Series*, 269–274.
5. Islam S. M. R., Kwak D., Kabir M.H., Hossain M., & Kwak, K.S. (2015). The Internet of Things for health care: A comprehensive survey. IEEE Access, *3*, 678–708.
6. Arunpradeep, N., Niranjana, G., & Suseela, G. (2020). Smart healthcare monitoring system using IoT. *International Journal of Advanced Science and Technology*, *29*(6), 2788–2796.
7. Yin, Y., Zeng, Y., Chen, X., & Fan, Y. (2016). The Internet of Things in healthcare: An overview. *Journal of Industrial Information Integration*, *1*, 3–13.

8. Sullivan, H. T., & Sahasrabudhe, S. (2017). Envisioning inclusive futures: Technology-based assistive sensory and action substitution. *Futures, 87*, 140–148.

9. Marco Di Rienzo, G. P., Brambilla, G., Ferratini, M., & Castiglioni, P. (2005). MagIC System: A New Textile-Based Wearable Device for Biological Signal Monitoring. Applicability in Daily Life and Clinical Setting. *Proceedings of the 2005 IEEE, Engineering in Medicine and Biology 27th Annual Conference 2005*; Shangai, China. 1–4 September 2005; pp. 7167–7169.

10. Chan, M., Esteve, D., Fourniols, J. Y., Escriba, C., & Campo, E. (2012). Smart wearable systems: Current status and future challenges. *Artificial Intelligence in Medicine, 56*, 137–156.

11. Banica, F. G. 2012. *Chemical Sensors and Biosensors: Fundamentals and Applications*, 1st edn. New York, NY: Wiley.

12. Segev-Bar, M., & Haick, H. (2013). Flexible sensors based on nanoparticles. *ACS Nano 7*, 8366–8378. https://doi.org/10.1021/nn402728g

13. Unno, Y., et al. (2011). Development of n-on-p silicon sensors for very high radiation environments. *Nuclear Instruments and Methods in Physics Research Section A: Accelerators Spectrometers, Detectors and Associated Equipment, 636*, 24–30. https://doi.org/10.1016/j.nima.2010.04.080

14. Elliott, M. C. A. (2012). Critical care: The eight vital signs of patient monitoring. *British Journal of Nursing, 21*, 621–625.

15. Turner, J. R., Viera, A. J., & Shimbo, D. (2015). Ambulatory blood pressure monitoring in clinical practice: A review. *American Journal of Medicine, 128*, 14–20.

16. Yilmaz, T., Foster, R., & Hao, Y. (2010). Detecting vital signs with wearable wireless sensors. *Sensors, 2010*(10), 10837–10862.

17. Xiao-Fei, T., Yuan-Ting, Z., Poon, C. C. Y., & Bonato, P. (2008). Wearable medical systems for p-health. *IEEE Reviews in Biomedical Engineering, 1*, 62–74.

18. Rosenfield, M., Howarth, P. A., & Sheedy, J. E. et al. (2012). Vision and IT displays: A whole new visual world. *Ophthalmic & Physiological Optics, 32*, 363–366.

19. Medtronic MiniMed, I. Continuous Glucose Monitoring. Available online: https://www.medtronicdiabetes.com (accessed on 7 July 2017).

20. Smoleń, M., Kańtoch, E., Augustyniak, P., & Kowalski, P. (2011). Wearable patient home monitoring based on ECG and ACC sensors. *IFMBE Proceedings, 37*, 941–944. https://doi.org/10.1007/978-3-642-23508-5_244

21. Crifaci, G., Billeci, L., Tartarisco, G., Balocchi, R., Pioggia, G., Brunori, E., Maestro, S., & Morales, M. A. (2013). ECG and GSR Measure and Analysis Using Wearable Systems: Application in Anorexia Nervosa Adolescents. In *International Symposium on Image and Signal Processing and Analysis, ISPA*, 499–504. https://doi.org/10.1109/ispa.2013.6703792

22. Kew, H. P., & Jeong, D. U. (2009). Wearable patch-type ECG using ubiquitous wireless sensor network for healthcare monitoring application. *ACM International Conference Proceeding Series, 403*, 624–630. https://doi.org/10.1145/1655925.1656038

23. Lee, Y. D., & Chung, W. Y. (2009). Wireless sensor network based wearable smart shirt for ubiquitous health and activity monitoring. *Sensors and Actuators, B: Chemical, 140*(2), 390–395. https://doi.org/10.1016/j.snb.2009.04.040

24. Miao, F., Cheng, Y., He, Y., He, Q., & Li, Y. (2015). A wearable context-aware ECG monitoring system integrated with built-in kinematic sensors of the smartphone. *Sensors (Switzerland), 15*(5), 11465–11484. https://doi.org/10.3390/s150511465

25. Pani, D., Dessi, A., Saenz-Cogollo, J. F., Barabino, G., Fraboni, B., & Bonfiglio, A. (2016). Fully textile, PEDOT: PSS based electrodes for wearable ECG monitoring systems. *IEEE Transactions on Biomedical Engineering, 63*(3), 540–549. https://doi.org/10.1109/TBME.2015.2465936

26. Parak, J., Tarniceriu, A., Renevey, P., Bertschi, M., Delgado-Gonzalo, R., & Korhonen, I. (2015). Evaluation of the beat-to-beat detection accuracy of PulseOn wearable optical heart rate monitor. *Proceedings of the Annual International Conference of the IEEE Engineering in Medicine and Biology Society, EMBS, 2015-November*, 8099–8102. https://doi.org/10.1109/EMBC.2015.7320273

27. Phan, D., Siong, L. Y., Pathirana, P. N., & Seneviratne, A. (2015). Smartwatch: Performance evaluation for long-term heart rate monitoring. *4th International Symposium on Bioelectronics and Bioinformatics, ISBB 2015*, 144–147. https://doi.org/10.1109/ISBB.2015.7344944

28. Rachim, V. P., & Chung, W. Y. (2016). Wearable noncontact armband for mobile ECG monitoring system. *IEEE Transactions on Biomedical Circuits and Systems, 10*(6), 1112–1118. https://doi.org/10.1109/TBCAS.2016.2519523

29. Mühlsteff, J., Such, O., Schmidt, R., Perkuhn, M., Reiter, H., Lauter, J., Thijs, J., Müsch, G., & Harris, M. (2004). Wearable approach for continuous ECG - And activity patient-monitoring. *Annual International Conference of the IEEE Engineering in Medicine and Biology - Proceedings, 26 III*, 2184–2187. https://doi.org/10.1109/iembs.2004.1403638

30. Marques, F. A. F., Ribeiro, D. M. D., Colunas, M. F. M., & Cunha, J. P. S. (2011). "A real time, wearable ECG and blood pressure monitoring system," 6th Iberian *Conference on Information Systems and Technologies (CISTI 2011)*, Chaves, pp. 1–4.

31. Carek, A., Conant, J., Joshi, A., Kang, H., & Inan, O. (2017). SeismoWatch: Wearable cuffless blood pressure monitoring using pulse transit time. *Proceedings of the ACM on Interactive, Mobile, Wearable and Ubiquitous Technologies, 1*(3), 1–16. https://doi.org/10.1145/3130905

32. Lazazzera, R., Belhaj, Y., & Carrault, G. (2019). A new wearable device for blood pressure estimation using photoplethysmogram. *Sensors (Switzerland), 19*(11), 1–18. https://doi.org/10.3390/s19112557

33. McCombie, D. B., Shaltis, P. A., Reisner, A. T., & Asada, H. H. (2007). Adaptive hydrostatic blood pressure calibration: Development of a wearable, autonomous pulse wave velocity blood pressure monitor. *Annual International Conference of the IEEE Engineering in Medicine and Biology - Proceedings*, 370–373. https://doi.org/10.1109/IEMBS.2007.4352301

34. Nakamura, M., Nakamura, J., Lopez, G., Shuzo, M., & Yamada, I. (2011). Collaborative processing of wearable and ambient sensor system for blood pressure monitoring. *Sensors, 11*(7), 6760–6770. https://doi.org/10.3390/s110706760

35. Woo, S. H., Choi, Y. Y., Kim, D. J., Bien, F., & Kim, J. J. (2014). Tissue-informative mechanism for wearable non-invasive continuous blood pressure monitoring. *Scientific Reports, 4*, 1–6. https://doi.org/10.1038/srep06618

36. Zhang, Y. T., Poon, C. C. Y., Chan, C. H., Tsang, M. W. W., & Wu, K. F. (2006). A health-shirt using e-textile materials for the continuous and cuffless monitoring of arterial blood pressure. *Proceedings of the 3rd IEEE-EMBS International Summer School and Symposium on Medical Devices and Biosensors, ISSS-MDBS 2006*, 86–89. https://doi.org/10.1109/ISSMDBS.2006.360104

37. Chen, W., Dols, S., Oetomo, S. B., & Feijs, L. (2011). Monitoring body temperature of newborn infants at neonatal intensive care units using wearable sensors. *Proceedings of the 5th International ICST Conference on Body Area Networks, BodyNets 2010, Mmc*, 188–194. https://doi.org/10.1145/2221924.2221960

38. Sahatiya, P., Puttapati, S. K., Srikanth, V. V. S. S., & Badhulika, S. (2016). Graphene-based wearable temperature sensor and infrared photodetector on a flexible polyimide substrate. *Flexible and Printed Electronics, 1*(2), 1–9. https://doi.org/10.1088/2058-8585/1/2/025006

39. Wen, S., Heidari, H., Vilouras, A., & Dahiya, R. (2017). A wearable fabric-based RFID skin temperature monitoring patch. *2016 IEEE SENSORS*, Orlando, FL, USA, 2016, pp. 1–3. https://doi.org/10.1109/icsens.2016.7808919

40. Xiang, Z., Wan, L., Gong, Z., Zhou, Z., Ma, Z., OuYang, X., He, Z., & Chan, C. C. (2019). Multifunctional textile platform for fiber optic wearable temperature-monitoring application. *Micromachines, 10*(12). https://doi.org/10.3390/mi10120866

41. Hong, Y. J., Lee, H., Kim, J., Lee, M., Choi, H. J., Hyeon, T., & Kim, D. H. (2018). Multifunctional wearable system that integrates sweat-based sensing and vital-sign monitoring to estimate pre-/post-exercise glucose levels. *Advanced Functional Materials, 28*(47), 1–12. https://doi.org/10.1002/adfm.201805754

42. Lee, H., Hong, Y. J., Baik, S., Hyeon, T., & Kim, D. H. (2018). Enzyme-based glucose sensor: From invasive to wearable device. *Advanced Healthcare Materials, 7*(8), 1–14. https://doi.org/10.1002/adhm.201701150

43. Liu, Q., Liu, Y., Wu, F., Cao, X., Li, Z., Alharbi, M., Abbas, A. N., Amer, M. R., & Zhou, C. (2018). Highly sensitive and wearable In2O3 nanoribbon transistor biosensors with integrated on-chip gate for glucose monitoring in body fluids. *ACS Nano, 12*(2), 1170–1178. https://doi.org/10.1021/acsnano.7b06823

44. Rachim, V. P., & Chung, W. Y. (2019). Wearable-band type visible-near infrared optical biosensor for non-invasive blood glucose monitoring. *Sensors and Actuators, B: Chemical, 286*, 173–180. https://doi.org/10.1016/j.snb.2019.01.121

45. Parrilla, M., Ortiz-Gómez, I., Cánovas, R., Salinas-Castillo, A., Cuartero, M., & Crespo, G. A. (2019). Wearable potentiometric ion patch for on-body electrolyte monitoring in sweat: Toward a validation strategy to ensure physiological relevance. *Analytical Chemistry, 91*(13), 8644–8651. https://doi.org/10.1021/acs.analchem.9b02126

46. Najafi, B., Armstrong, D. G., & Mohler, J. (2013). Novel wearable technology for assessing spontaneous daily physical activity and risk of falling in older adults with diabetes. *Journal of Diabetes Science and Technology, 7*(5), 1147–1160. https://doi.org/10.1177/193229681300700507

47. Bu, N. (2017). Stress Evaluation Index based on Poincaré Plot for Wearable Health Devices. In *2017 IEEE 19th International Conference on e-Health Networking, Applications and Services (Healthcom)*, pp. 1–6. IEEE, 2017.

48. Mcwhorter, J., Brown, L., & Khansa, L. (2017). A wearable health monitoring system for posttraumatic stress disorder. *Biologically Inspired Cognitive Architectures, 22*, 44–50. https://doi.org/10.1016/j.bica.2017.09.004

49. Sandulescu, V., Andrews, S., Ellis, D., Bellotto, N., & Mart, O. (2015). *Stress detection using wearable physiological sensors. In Artificial Computation in Biology and Medicine: International Work-Conference on the Interplay Between Natural and Artificial Computation, IWINAC 2015, Elche, Spain, June 1-5, 2015, Proceedings, Part I 6 (pp. 526-532). Springer International Publishing.*

50. Sandulescu, V., Andrews, S., Ellis, D., Bellotto, N., & Ferrandez, J. M. (2017). Stress detection using wearable physiological and sociometric sensors. *International Journal of Neural Systems, 27*(2), 1–16. https://doi.org/10.1142/S0129065716500416

51. Wu, W., Pirbhulal, S., Zhang, H., & Mukhopadhyay, S. C. (2018). Quantitative assessment for self-tracking of acute stress based on triangulation principle in a wearable sensor system. *IEEE Journal of Biomedical and Health Informatics, 23*(2), 703–713. https://doi.org/10.1109/JBHI.2018.2832069

52. Yoon, S., Sim, J. K., & Cho, Y. (2016). A flexible and wearable human stress monitoring patch. *Scientific Reports, 6*, 23468. https://doi.org/10.1038/srep23468

53. Babcock, J. (2003). *The Wearable Eyetracker: A Tool for the Study of High-Level Visual Tasks*. Rochester Institute of Technology, RIT Scholar Works.

54. Ye, Z., Li, Y., Fathi, A., Han, Y., Rozga, A., Abowd, G. D., & Rehg, J. M., 2012, September. Detecting eye contact using wearable eye-tracking glasses. In Proceedings of the 2012 ACM conference on ubiquitous computing, pp. 699–704.

55. Mahato, S., Roy, A., Verma, A., & Paul, S. (2021). Analysis of Electroencephalogram (EEG) Signals for Detection of Major Depressive Disorder (MDD) Using Feature Selection and Reduction Techniques. In *Nanoelectronics, Circuits and Communication Systems: Proceeding of NCCS 2019* (pp. 429–440). Springer, Singapore.

56. Mahato, S., Paul, S., Goyal, N., Mohanty, S. N., & Jain, S. (2023). 3EDANFIS: Three channel EEG-based depression detection technique with hybrid adaptive neuro fuzzy inference system. *Recent Patents on Engineering, 17*(6), 32–48.

57. Mahato, S., Pathak, L. K., & Kumari, K. (2021). Detection of schizophrenia using EEG signals. Data Analytics in Bioinformatics: A Machine Learning Perspective, In Editor(s): R. Satpathy, T. Choudhury, S. Satpathy, S.N. Mohanty and X. Zhang Data Analytics in Bioinformatics, Scivener Publishing, Wiley, Beverly, USA, pp. 359–390.

58. Pathak, L. K., Mahato, S., & Sweta, S. (2022). Technological Dimension of a Smart City. In: Editor(s):V. Kumar, V.Jain, B.Sharma, J. M. Chatterjee, Shrestha *Smart City Infrastructure: The Blockchain Perspective*, Scivener Publishing, Wiley, Beverly, USA pp. 247–268.

10 Different Security Breaches in Patients' Data and Prevailing Ways to Counter Them

Anup W. Burange and Vaishali M. Deshmukh

10.1 DIFFERENT SECURITY BREACHES IN HEALTHCARE DATA

Sensitive patient information has been exposed as a result of various security breaches in the healthcare sector. Patient data must be safeguarded against hostile assaults and data breaches since it is extremely sensitive and personal. Sensitive patient information, including personal identifying information like names, birth dates, and social security numbers, as well as medical data like diagnoses and treatment plans, may be exposed as a result of these breaches. A healthcare data leak may have serious repercussions. Patients whose personal information is compromised may experience identity theft, financial loss, or other adverse consequences. In addition to reputational harm and financial penalties, healthcare providers could also lose the trust of their patients. Some of the most common security breaches in patients' data include the following.

10.1.1 UNAUTHORIZED ACCESS

This type of security breach occurs when an unauthorized user accesses a patient's protected health information (PHI). This can be done through malware, hacking, social engineering, or other means. Unauthorized access to patient data can occur in a variety of ways. One way is through human error, such as when a healthcare provider fails to properly secure patient data or fails to follow data security protocols [1]. This could include, for example, leaving a laptop with patient information unsecured or failing to encrypt files containing patient data. Another way that unauthorized access can occur is through malicious software or attacks. These often involve hackers using malware or other malicious software to gain access to patient records or distributed denial of service (DDoS) attacks that aim to disrupt systems and networks, leading to unsecured patient data. Unauthorized access can also be the result of insider threats, either through accidental or intentional misuse of patient data.

10.1.2 INSUFFICIENT AUTHENTICATION

This is when an authorized user is granted access to a patient's data without sufficient authentication. This could be due to weak or default passwords or a lack of access control. Insufficient authentication of patient data typically occurs when

DOI: 10.1201/9781003388845-12

organizations fail to implement proper authentication measures. This can include not having multi-factor authentication, not enforcing the use of complex and unique passwords, or relying exclusively on static passwords that may be easily guessed. Additionally, if a system requires manual authentication processes such as physical tokens or SMS-based codes, failure to regularly change authentication settings or replace expired tokens can lead to insecure authentication. Finally, organizations may also be vulnerable if they do not regularly review and audit their authentication processes and settings to ensure they are up-to-date and secure.

10.1.3 Data Manipulation

With this type of attack, a malicious user can alter or delete patients' data without their permission. This can cause serious problems if the data are used to make medical decisions. Data manipulation with patient data can occur in many ways. It could involve the editing or altering of existing data or the entering of new data that are false or misleading. In some cases, patient data may be changed without their knowledge or consent, such as when a doctor or other healthcare provider alters information for their benefit. It can also involve the misappropriation of patient data for malicious purposes, such as using the data to commit fraud or identity theft. Data manipulation can have serious consequences, as incorrect or false data can have a lasting impact on patient care and outcomes. To prevent such manipulation, healthcare facilities should implement strict protocols and policies to ensure that patient data are securely stored and investigated if concerns arise.

10.1.4 Data Leakage

This occurs when confidential data are leaked from the healthcare system, either intentionally or unintentionally. This can include the patient's personal information, medical records, or payment information [2]. Data leakage can occur when patient data are shared inappropriately or inadvertently with unauthorized parties. It can happen when patient data are transferred from one system to another, sent via email, stored on a USB drive, or backup tapes are lost or stolen. It can also occur if the data are not properly encrypted in transit or at rest or if there are inadequacies in security protocols or access policies, allowing for unauthorized access. Additionally, improper disposal of physical paperwork or outdated equipment can lead to data leakage.

10.2 WAYS TO PROTECT CLINICAL DATA FROM SECURITY VIOLATIONS

Fortunately, there are several steps that healthcare providers can take to protect their patients' data and counter security breaches:

- **Implement strong authentication protocols:** Using strong passwords and two-factor authentication can help protect patient data from unauthorized access.

- **Use encryption:** Encrypting patient data and communications can ensure that only authorized users can access and view the data.
- **Monitor access:** Monitoring who is accessing and viewing patient data can help detect unauthorized access.
- **Educate staff:** Healthcare providers should educate their staff on the importance of protecting patient data and how to detect suspicious activity.
- **Practice good cyber hygiene:** Regularly updating software, patching systems, and using firewalls and antivirus software can help protect against cyberattacks.

By implementing the above measures, healthcare providers can help ensure that their patients' data are secure and protected from malicious attacks [3].

10.2.1   USE OF MACHINE LEARNING IN COUNTERING SECURITY INFRINGEMENT

Security breaches in patients' data can have serious consequences for both healthcare providers and individuals. Fortunately, machine learning (ML) can help organizations reduce the risk of such attacks and protect their data [4].

10.2.2   IDENTIFYING VULNERABILITIES

ML may be used to identify internal and external sources of patient data vulnerabilities and possible threats. ML algorithms can find trends or behaviors that point to a vulnerability by examining huge databases of patient data. For instance, a ML model might be used to find irregularities in user account changes or access patterns.

10.2.3   IMPROVED AUTHENTICATION

ML can also help organizations improve their authentication processes. Algorithms can be used to analyze large collections of user data to detect patterns that could indicate a fraudulent attempt to access a system. This can be used to create more secure authentication systems that are less vulnerable to attack.

10.2.4   DATA ENCRYPTION

ML can be used to securely encrypt data, making it much harder for hackers to access it. Encryption algorithms can use techniques such as natural language processing to analyze user data and generate complex, difficult-to-guess encryption keys. This makes it virtually impossible for anyone other than the intended recipient to decrypt the data.

10.2.5   ALARMING UNAUTHORIZED ACCESS

Once a potential security breach has been identified, it is important to respond quickly to minimize the damage. ML can be used to create alarm systems that detect when unauthorized access has occurred and alert the relevant personnel.

10.3 ROLE OF ARTIFICIAL INTELLIGENCE AND MACHINE LEARNING IN IMPROVING DATA SECURITY

ML can be used to detect security breaches in patients' data and help protect it from malicious actors. ML algorithms can analyze data patterns to detect signs of intrusion and alert security personnel. ML models can also be used to automatically update security parameters based on data analysis and track changes in user behavior. Additionally, ML models can be used to detect fraudulent activities and identify potential threats before they cause harm. By leveraging the power of ML, healthcare organizations can ensure that their patients data are kept safe and secure [5]. By assisting in the detection and prevention of security breaches, ML plays a significant role in healthcare security. Large volumes of data may be processed by ML algorithms to find patterns and anomalies that can be used to spot possible security risks. ML models can assess whether a person has permission to view a particular piece of information or whether their activity is suspect and requires additional investigation by examining trends in user behavior.

Overall, the use of ML in healthcare security can help ensure that sensitive patient information is kept confidential and secure. As healthcare organizations increasingly rely on digital systems to store and manage patient data, robust security measures must be put in place to protect this information from unauthorized access or theft. By leveraging the power of ML, healthcare providers can improve the security of their systems and safeguard the privacy and confidentiality of their patients' data.

10.3.1 FASTER DATA COLLECTION

ML is used for faster data collection and processing in healthcare by leveraging wearable technology to compile real-time data, which can then be quickly processed by ML algorithms. Healthcare workers gather real-time data using wearable technology, which ML can swiftly evaluate and learn from. Wearable devices such as fitness trackers and smartwatches can collect a wealth of data on a patient's vital signs, activity levels, and other health metrics. ML algorithms can then be trained to analyze these data and identify patterns that may indicate potential health issues. By processing this data in real time, healthcare providers can quickly identify potential problems and take action to address them before they become more serious. This can be especially valuable in situations where rapid intervention is critical, such as in emergency medicine or intensive care settings.

ML may be used to evaluate enormous datasets in addition to real-time data collection to spot trends and patterns that human analysts might miss. This can aid medical professionals in creating better treatment strategies and enhancing patient outcomes. Overall, using ML to speed up data collection and processing in the healthcare industry has potential to completely change how the treatment is provided. Healthcare practitioners may enhance the speed and accuracy of diagnoses, lower the risk of mistakes, and ultimately deliver better care to their patients by utilizing the power of wearable technologies and advanced data analytics.

10.3.2 ACCELERATED DRUG DISCOVERY AND DEVELOPMENT

Artificial intelligence (AI) and ML are increasingly being used in accelerated drug discovery and development. AI and ML enable more effective approaches to complex problems associated with drug discovery through rapid and massive number-crunching capabilities. AI and ML systems can find promising compounds and forecast their therapeutic potential by evaluating enormous volumes of data on pharmacological targets. These algorithms can also be applied to improve medicine dosage and lower the possibility of negative side effects.

One major advantage of using AI and ML in drug discovery is the ability to accelerate the process. ML models can be trained on existing data to predict the efficacy and safety of new compounds, reducing the need for time-consuming and expensive animal testing. This can help speed up the drug development process, potentially bringing life-saving treatments to market more quickly. Another important use of AI and ML in drug discovery is the ability to identify new drug targets and repurpose existing drugs for new indications. By analyzing large amounts of data on disease mechanisms and drug interactions, AI and ML algorithms can identify new targets for drug development and discover new uses for existing drugs. Overall, the use of AI and ML in accelerated drug discovery and development has the potential to revolutionize the way that new drugs are discovered, developed, and brought to market. By leveraging the power of these advanced technologies, researchers can identify promising compounds more quickly and efficiently, potentially bringing new treatments to patients faster than ever before.

10.3.3 COST-EFFICIENT PROCESSES

AI and ML have the potential to significantly improve cost efficiency in healthcare processes by automating routine tasks, reducing errors, and providing personalized care. One area where AI and ML can help is in streamlining administrative processes, such as billing and scheduling. By automating these tasks, healthcare providers can save time and reduce errors, which can ultimately lower costs. ML algorithms can swiftly search through electronic health records (EHRs) for particular patient data, make patient appointments, and automate a variety of tasks. The ability to concentrate on more critical issues allows healthcare professionals to do so.

Making healthcare decisions is a different area where AI and ML might be useful. Having access to a wealth of patient data, AI algorithms can assist medical professionals in selecting the best course of therapy, potentially minimizing the need for expensive and pointless operations. In addition, AI and ML can also help with patient monitoring and management, allowing healthcare providers to better predict and prevent potential health issues. This can lead to earlier interventions and lower healthcare costs over time. Overall, AI and ML have the potential to greatly improve cost efficiency in healthcare processes by reducing errors, streamlining tasks, and providing more personalized care. It is important to keep in mind that these technologies don't have the same level of dependability as clinical knowledge and judgment; therefore, they shouldn't be used as a substitute for such things.

10.3.4 PRECISE PERSONALIZED TREATMENT

By analyzing vast amounts of data, ML technology can help healthcare professionals create precise medication solutions that are tailored to each individual's features. Moreover, ML algorithms can forecast how patients would respond to certain medications, enabling healthcare professionals to anticipate patients' requirements [6]. AI and ML are being increasingly used in healthcare to generate precisely personalized treatment plans for patients.

Here are some ways in which AI and ML can be used to generate personalized treatment plans:

- **Predictive Analytics:** To forecast future health risks and consequences, AI and ML systems may assess patient data, including medical history, genetics, lifestyle choices, and environmental variables. Based on these predictions, personalized treatment plans can be developed to prevent or manage these risks.
- **Precision Medicine:** By analyzing large amounts of genetic and clinical data, AI and ML algorithms can identify specific biomarkers that can guide treatment decisions. Precision medicine is an individualized treatment for patients based on their particular genetic makeup and other biological traits, and it may be developed with the use of AI and ML.
- **Medical Imaging:** Medical pictures like MRI scans and X-rays may be analyzed by AI and ML algorithms to identify and diagnose illnesses at an early stage. This helps in developing personalized treatment plans that can improve patient outcomes.
- **Drug Discovery:** The use of AI and ML in the medication development process allows for the identification of novel therapeutic targets and the formulation of personalized treatment plans based on a patient's genetic profile. AI and ML algorithms can find potential pharmacological targets that can be exploited to create novel medicines by evaluating vast volumes of genetic data.
- **Electronic Health Records:** To find patterns and trends in patient data, AI and ML may be used to analyze EHRs. By spotting these patterns, individualized treatment programs that take into consideration a patient's medical past, present health state, and other elements may be created.

AI and ML are powerful tools that can be used to generate precisely personalized treatment plans for patients. These technologies can assist medical practitioners in creating individualized treatment plans that enhance patient outcomes by analyzing vast volumes of data and spotting patterns and trends.

10.3.5 PREDICTING THE SIDE EFFECTS OF A DRUG

AI and ML can be used to predict the side effects of drugs by analyzing a patient's past medical history and body characteristics.

Here are a few ways in which AI and ML can be used for this purpose:

- **Data Analysis:** AI and ML algorithms can analyze large amounts of data, including electronic medical records, to identify patterns that can be used to predict the likelihood of side effects based on patient characteristics.

- **Predictive Modeling:** Using ML models, it is possible to build predictive models that can identify which patients are most at risk for specific side effects based on their individual characteristics and medical history.
- **Drug Interactions:** ML algorithms can also be used to identify potential drug interactions that could increase the risk of side effects. This information can be used by healthcare providers to make more informed decisions about prescribing medications.
- **Personalized Medicine:** AI and ML can be used to develop personalized medicine by identifying which patients are most likely to respond well to certain medications based on their characteristics.

The use of AI and ML can help healthcare providers better understand which patients are most at risk for side effects and make more informed decisions about prescribing medications. This can ultimately lead to better patient outcomes and improved healthcare overall.

10.3.6 PROTECTING THE IDENTITY OF PATIENT WORLDWIDE

In the techniques listed below, AI and ML may be utilized to safeguard patients' identities everywhere:

- **Anonymization of Data:** One of the primary ways AI and ML can be used to protect patient identity is through the anonymization of data. This involves removing all identifiable information, such as name, address, and other personal details, from healthcare records before they are used for analysis or research.
- **Differential Privacy:** Another approach is using differential privacy techniques. This involves adding noise to data, which preserves the overall patterns of the data but makes it more difficult to identify specific individuals. This can help protect patient privacy while still allowing researchers to analyze the data.
- **Secure Data Sharing:** AI and ML can also be used to enable secure data sharing between healthcare providers while maintaining patient privacy. For example, homomorphic encryption techniques can be used to encrypt data in such a way that it can still be analyzed by ML algorithms without exposing the underlying data.
- **Federated Learning:** Another technique is federated learning, which allows ML models to be trained using data from multiple sources without having to transfer the data. Instead, the models are trained on the data in a distributed manner, with the results being aggregated and used to improve the overall model.

AI and ML can be used to protect patient identity by anonymizing data, using differential privacy techniques, enabling secure data sharing, and using federated learning. These techniques can help ensure that patient privacy is protected while still allowing researchers and healthcare providers to benefit from the insights provided by healthcare data.

10.3.7 DATA LEAKAGE AND DATA MANIPULATION PREVENTION USING ML

ML is an important tool for preventing data leakage and manipulation of patient data. It can be used in conjunction with traditional techniques to detect suspicious activity and alert authorities to potential breaches or other issues [7]. The algorithms can monitor user activity, detect anomalies, and identify patterns that could indicate malicious activity. ML can also be used to identify and classify sensitive data, helping organizations secure and protect patient data.

ML is also a powerful tool for manipulating patient data. It can be used to automate data entry and retrieval as well as generate analytics that can help medical professionals make more informed decisions. By leveraging predictive analytics, healthcare organizations can better understand the health of their patients and provide personalized, targeted treatment that leads to better outcomes. Additionally, ML can be used to identify trends and patterns in patient data, enabling healthcare organizations to more accurately diagnose and treat illnesses.

10.3.8 IMPROVED AUTHENTICATION AND IDENTIFYING VULNERABILITIES AND PREVENTING UNAUTHORIZED ACCESS USING ML

The use of ML can enhance authentication and identify vulnerabilities in systems. It can be used to detect any suspicious activity or identify any weak authentication points, such as weak passwords or outdated software. By leveraging algorithms, ML can detect any unauthorized access attempts and alert authorities to possible breaches. Additionally, ML can be used to identify and authenticate users by recognizing patterns in their behavior and activities. This can be used for both in-person and online authentication, ensuring that only authorized users can access sensitive data.

Moreover, ML is used to identify potential vulnerabilities in systems. By scanning and analyzing data, ML can detect any potential weaknesses in a system and alert administrators to take the necessary steps to protect their networks [8]. This can include patching any outdated software, implementing stronger passwords, and taking other measures to ensure system security. ML can be an important tool for ensuring the security of sensitive data and systems.

ML can be used to prevent unauthorized access and insufficient authentication. It can be used to detect any suspicious activity or identify any weak authentication points, such as weak passwords or outdated software. By leveraging algorithms, ML can detect any unauthorized access attempts and alert authorities to possible breaches [9].

Another important use of ML in healthcare security is to streamline the workflow for security professionals. By automating routine tasks and flagging potential security threats, ML can increase efficiency and reduce the risk of human error. This frees up security professionals to focus on more complex tasks and ensures that security measures are being implemented effectively.

10.4 CREATING SECURED ROUTING FOR CONFIDENTIAL DATA IN IOT

In the following approaches, AI and ML may be utilized to secure routing data:

- **Intrusion Detection:** ML algorithms can be used to detect and prevent unauthorized access to network routing data. These algorithms can analyze network traffic and identify patterns that indicate an intrusion attempt, such as unusual data volume, frequency, and source of data packets.
- **Predictive Maintenance:** AI and ML can be used to monitor and predict network failures before they occur. By analyzing routing data, ML models can detect patterns that indicate a potential network issue and alert network administrators to take preventive measures.
- **Encryption and Decryption:** ML algorithms can also be used to encrypt and decrypt routing data to protect it from unauthorized access. By using advanced encryption techniques, ML models can ensure that routing data are protected while in transit.
- **Threat Intelligence:** AI and ML can be used to collect and analyze threat intelligence data, which can be used to detect and prevent attacks on routing data. By analyzing historical data, ML algorithms can identify trends and patterns that indicate potential threats, allowing network administrators to take proactive measures to prevent security breaches.

AI and ML can be used to provide security to routing data by detecting and preventing intrusions, predicting network failures, encrypting and decrypting data, and collecting and analyzing threat intelligence data. These techniques can help ensure that routing data are secure and protected from unauthorized access [10].

10.4.1 RPL PROTOCOL'S SECURITY

RPL (Routing Protocol for Low-Power and Lossy Networks) is a widely used routing protocol for IoT (Internet of Things) networks. It is designed specifically to support networks with low-power devices that may have limited processing and memory capabilities and may experience frequent packet loss [11]. RPL is a distance-vector routing protocol that uses a directed acyclic graph (DAG) to represent the network topology. The DAG consists of nodes and edges that represent the network links. Each node in the DAG is assigned a rank, which is used to determine the preferred path for routing packets. RPL uses a proactive approach to routing, which means that nodes constantly exchange routing information with their neighbors to maintain an up-to-date view of the network topology. This allows RPL to quickly adapt to changes in the network, such as node failures or changes in traffic patterns. One of the key features of RPL is its support for different routing metrics, which allow the protocol to optimize routing based on different criteria, such as energy consumption, latency, and packet loss. This makes RPL highly customizable and suitable for a wide range of IoT applications. RPL is a robust and efficient routing protocol that is well suited for IoT networks with low-power devices and limited resources.

10.4.2   Use of AI and ML for the RPL Protocol's Security

ML can also be used to detect any potential vulnerabilities in an RPL's routing system [12]. By scanning and analyzing data, ML can detect any potential weaknesses in a system and alert administrators to take the necessary steps to protect their networks. This can include patching any outdated software, implementing stronger passwords, and taking other measures to ensure system security. Additionally, ML can help optimize routing paths in an RPL network by examining network performance and finding the most efficient routing paths. This can help ensure that data are transferred quickly and securely while also reducing energy consumption.

ML can be used to protect patient data from security breaches by detecting vulnerabilities, improving authentication processes, encrypting data, and alarming about unauthorized access [13]. With proper implementation, healthcare providers can protect their data and reduce the risk of serious security breaches. AI and ML techniques can be used to enhance the security of RPL.

Mentioned below are some ways in which AI and ML can be applied to RPL security:

- **Intrusion detection:** ML algorithms can be trained to identify anomalous behavior or patterns that may indicate an intrusion or attack in RPL networks. This can help detect and prevent security threats before they can cause damage to the network.
- **Threat analysis:** AI can be used to analyze network traffic and identify potential threats or vulnerabilities in RPL networks. This can help network administrators take proactive measures to mitigate security risks and prevent attacks [14].
- **Secure routing:** ML can be used to develop secure routing algorithms that can protect against routing attacks, such as black hole attacks, gray hole attacks, and wormhole attacks. These algorithms can identify secure paths for routing data and avoid compromised nodes.
- **Trust management:** AI can be used to develop trust management systems that can evaluate the trustworthiness of nodes in RPL networks. This can help prevent attacks by identifying malicious nodes and preventing them from participating in network activities.
- **Attack prediction:** ML can be used to predict potential attacks in RPL networks based on historical data and network behavior. This can help network administrators take proactive measures to prevent attacks and improve network security.

AI and ML techniques can be used to improve the security of RPL networks by detecting and preventing security threats, developing secure routing algorithms, managing trust, and predicting potential attacks.

10.5   CONCLUSION

AI and ML have numerous benefits for the healthcare sector, including early detection and diagnosis, personalized treatment, medical imaging analysis, drug discovery, and predictive analytics. They can also be useful in preventing security breaches of patients' data by monitoring network traffic, detecting anomalies, conducting predictive analytics, and automating responses to security breaches. Overall, AI and ML technologies have the potential to improve patient outcomes, enhance the quality of care, and ensure the security of patient data in the healthcare sector.

REFERENCES

1. Seh, A. H. *et al.*, "Healthcare data breaches: Insights and implications," *Healthcare.*, vol. 8, no. 2, 2020, https://doi.org/10.3390/healthcare8020133
2. Almulihi, A. H., Alassery, F., Khan, A. I., Shukla, S., Gupta, B. K., and Kumar, R., "Analyzing the implications of healthcare data breaches through computational technique," *Intell. Autom. Soft Comput.*, vol. 32, no. 3, pp. 1763–1779, 2022, https://doi.org/10.32604/IASC.2022.023460
3. Keshta, I., and Odeh, A., "Security and privacy of electronic health records: Concerns and challenges," *Egypt. Inform. J.*, vol. 22, no. 2, pp. 177–183, 2021, https://doi.org/10.1016/j.eij.2020.07.003
4. Gururaj, H. L., Pooja, R., & Pavan, K. (2022). "Machine learning (ML) methods to identify data breaches," in *Machine Learning (ML) Methods to Identify Data Breaches*, 10.4018/978-1-6684-3991-3.ch004, 2022.
5. Toh, C., and Brody, J. P., "Applications of machine learning in healthcare," Smart Manufacturing - When Artificial Intelligence Meets Internet of Things, 2021, https://doi.org/10.5772/intechopen.92297
6. Jain, S., Sharma, R. K., Aggarwal, V., and Kumar, C., "Human disease diagnosis using machine learning," Lecture Notes on Data Engineering and Communications Technologies, vol. 57, pp. 689–696, 2021, https://doi.org/10.1007/978-981-15-9509-7_56
7. Swain, D., Ballal, P., Dolase, V., Dash, B., and Santhappan, J., An Efficient Heart Disease Prediction System Using Machine Learning, vol. 1101, 2020. https://doi.org/10.1007/978-981-15-1884-3_4
8. Munonye, K., and Péter, M., "Machine learning approach to vulnerability detection in OAuth 2.0 authentication and authorization flow," *International Journal of Information Security*, vol. 21, no. 2, pp. 223–237, 2022, https://doi.org/10.1007/s10207-021-00551-w
9. Păvăloaia, V. D., and Husac, G., "Tracking unauthorized access using machine learning and PCA for face recognition developments," *Inf*ormation, vol. 14, no. 1, 2023, https://doi.org/10.3390/info14010025
10. Tahsien, S. M., Karimipour, H., and Spachos, P., "Machine learning based solutions for security of Internet of Things (IoT): A survey," *Journal of Network and Computer App*lications, vol. 161, no. April, 2020, https://doi.org/10.1016/j.jnca.2020.102630
11. Almusaylim, Z. A., Alhumam, A., and Jhanjhi, N. Z., "Proposing a secure RPL based Internet of Things routing protocol: A review," *Ad Hoc Netw.*, vol. 101, 2020, https://doi.org/10.1016/j.adhoc.2020.102096
12. Raghavendra, T., Anand, M., Selvi, M., Thangaramya, K., Santhosh Kumar, S., and Kannan, A., "An intelligent RPL attack detection using machine learning-based intrusion detection system for Internet of Things," *Procedia Comput. Sci.*, vol. 215, no. 2022, pp. 61–70, 2022, https://doi.org/10.1016/j.procs.2022.12.007
13. Tiwari, S. M., Jain, S., Abraham, A., and Shandilya, S., "Secure semantic smart healthcare (S3HC)," *J. Web Eng.*, Vol. 17, no. 8, pp. 617–646, 2019, https://doi.org/10.13052/jwe1540-9589.1782
14. Sezer, E., Bursa, O., Can, O., and Unalir, M. O., "Semantic Web Technologies for IoT-Based Health Care Information Systems," *The Tenth International Conference on Advances in Semantic Processing*, pp. 45–48, 2016.

Part III

Security Aspects of ML

11 The Intersection of Biometrics Technology and Machine Learning

A Scientometrics Analysis

Mousumi Karmakar and Keshav Sinha

11.1 INTRODUCTION

The use of biometrics for identification can be traced back to ancient Babylon, where fingerprints were used on clay tablets for business transactions. However, the modern history of biometrics began in the late 19th and early 20th centuries with the development of fingerprint recognition as a reliable identification method. In the late 1800s, an Englishman named Edward Henry developed a systematic approach for classifying fingerprints, which laid the foundation for the widespread use of fingerprints for identification purposes. In the early 1900s, fingerprint recognition was first used for criminal investigations and later for military purposes, such as identifying soldiers and verifying the identities of military personnel (Garfinkel, 2015). In the late 20th century, computer technology and the miniaturization of components made it possible to automate the capturing, storing, and comparing of biometric data. It paved the way for the widespread adoption of biometrics in various applications, such as access control, time and attendance systems, and border control. In recent years, the rise of mobile technology and the Internet of Things (IoTs) has driven the growth of biometrics in various applications, including mobile devices, online banking, and physical security systems. The increasing demand for secure and convenient authentication methods has also led to the development of new biometric technologies, such as facial and iris recognition, which are becoming increasingly popular in various applications. The history of biometrics spans several centuries and has seen the evolution of fingerprint recognition from a manual process to a highly automated and sophisticated technology used in various applications. The need for secure and convenient identification methods, technological advances, and the increasing demand for biometric solutions in multiple applications drive the continued growth of biometrics.

11.2 BACKGROUND OF THE WORK

Biometrics is a field of technology that focuses on measuring and analyzing individuals' unique physical or behavioral characteristics to identify them. It is typically done through sophisticated software and hardware systems that collect and analyze data on

DOI: 10.1201/9781003388845-14

these characteristics and compare them against a database of known individuals to verify a person's identity. It is unique to each individual and is not easily duplicated, lost, or forgotten like traditional forms of identification such as passwords or PINs. It makes biometrics a highly secure and reliable identification method, particularly in applications where security is paramount. The most commonly used biometric identifiers include fingerprints, facial recognition, iris scans, and voice recognition. Fingerprint recognition, for example, involves capturing an image of a person's fingerprints and then using pattern recognition algorithms to compare the captured image against a database of known individuals. Facial recognition uses artificial intelligence and machine learning (ML) algorithms to compare the unique features of a person's face against a database of known individuals (Bortolato et al., 2020).

Iris recognition is another popular biometric identifier and involves capturing an image of a person's iris and using algorithms to compare the captured image against a database of known individuals (Yuan & Ebrahimi, 2017). The method is considered highly secure as the iris is unique to each individual and does not change over time. On the other hand, voice recognition involves capturing a sample of a person's voice and using algorithms to compare it against a database of known individuals. This method is becoming increasingly popular as it is non-intrusive and can be operated remotely, making it ideal for applications such as phone-based banking and customer service. In recent years, biometrics have become increasingly widespread and are being used in various applications, including but not limited to security systems, electronic devices, and financial transactions. For example, biometric authentication is becoming increasingly common on smartphones and laptops, allowing users to unlock their devices simply by using their fingerprints or facial recognition.

Biometrics is also being used in the financial sector, where it is being used to provide secure and convenient access to financial services such as mobile banking. It involves using biometric identification to verify a person's identity before allowing them to access their financial information or make transactions. While biometrics offers many advantages over traditional forms of identification, it raises some concerns regarding privacy and security (Ribaric et al., 2016). For example, once a person's biometric data has been captured, it can be difficult to change if it falls into the wrong hands. Additionally, there is a risk that biometric data could be used for malicious purposes, such as identity theft or unauthorized access to sensitive information.

To address these concerns, organizations must implement strong security measures to protect biometric data and ensure it is used responsibly and ethically. It can include implementing strict access controls, regularly monitoring for unauthorized access and providing education and training on the proper use of biometrics to all employees and stakeholders (Cunningham & Truta, 2008).

11.2.1 BIOMETRIC AUTHENTICATION AND VERIFICATION

Biometric authentication and verification are two different processes that are used in the field of biometrics. Biometric authentication confirms a person's claimed identity by comparing their biometric data against a stored reference. It is typically done by capturing a sample of the person's biometric data (such as a fingerprint or facial recognition) and comparing it against a reference stored in a database (Sinha et al., 2022).

If the biometric data matches the reference, the person is authenticated and granted access to the relevant system or service. Biometric verification, conversely, is the process of confirming that a person is who they claim to be by comparing their biometric data against a reference. Unlike authentication, verification only confirms the person's identity rather than granting access to a system or service (Sinha et al., 2020). In practical terms, biometric authentication is often used to access secure methods, such as financial transactions, online accounts, and other applications where security is paramount. Biometric verification is typically used for less critical applications, such as verifying a person's identity for demographic or marketing purposes. It is important to note that biometric authentication and verification are not foolproof, and there is always a risk of false matches or rejections. Using high-quality biometric technologies and implementing strong security measures to protect biometric data is essential.

11.2.2 MACHINE LEARNING FOR BIOMETRICS

ML is a field of artificial intelligence increasingly used to enhance biometric security. ML algorithms can be used to analyze large amounts of biometric data to improve the accuracy and reliability of biometric systems. One common application of ML in biometrics is developing biometric recognition systems. These systems use ML algorithms to learn patterns in biometric data and use this knowledge to make more accurate and reliable decisions about a person's identity. For example, a facial recognition system can be trained on an extensive database of face images, allowing it to learn the unique features of each face and make more accurate identifications (Andrade et al., 2013). Another application of ML in biometrics is developing biometric spoof detection systems. These systems use ML algorithms to detect attempts to fool a biometric system, such as using a fake fingerprint or face to gain access to a secure method (Acquisti et al., 2014). By learning the characteristics of genuine biometric data and identifying anomalies, these systems can help prevent unauthorized access to secure systems. Finally, ML can improve biometric systems' usability and user experience. For example, ML algorithms can analyze user data to identify common difficulties or issues with the system, such as problems with capturing high-quality biometric data (Sinha et al., 2021). This information can then improve the system's design and make it more user-friendly. In summary, ML is an important area of artificial intelligence increasingly used to enhance biometric security. By analyzing large amounts of biometric data, ML algorithms can improve the accuracy and reliability of biometric systems, detect attempts to fool the system, and improve the system's user experience.

11.3 THEORETICAL FRAMEWORK FOR MACHINE LEARNING IN BIOMETRIC

Recent trends in the use of ML for biometric applications include:

- **Increased Accuracy:** With advances in ML algorithms and computing power, the accuracy of biometric recognition systems has significantly improved. It has led to the more widespread adoption of biometric technologies in security, finance, and healthcare.

- **Integration with Other Technologies:** ML is integrated with other technologies such as IoT, cloud computing, and blockchain to create more secure and efficient biometric systems. For instance, biometric data can be securely stored and processed in the cloud, while blockchain can be used to ensure the privacy and integrity of the data.
- **Personalization and Context Awareness:** ML creates more personalized and context-aware biometric systems. For example, facial recognition systems can be trained to recognize different expressions and emotions, making them more robust and accurate.
- **Adoption in Emerging Markets:** Biometric technologies, including ML-based systems, are growing rapidly in emerging markets. It is due to increasing smartphone adoption, the need for secure financial transactions, and the growing demand for identity verification.
- **Focus on Privacy and Security:** As biometric technologies become more widespread, there is a growing concern about privacy and security. ML is being used to address these concerns by developing more secure and privacy-preserving biometric systems that protect personal information and prevent unauthorized access.

11.3.1 PRE-PROCESSING STEPS IN SCIENTOMETRICS

In scientometrics, pre-processing refers to the steps taken to prepare the data for analysis (Kajikawa et al., 2006). The following are some common pre-processing steps in scientometrics:

- **Data Collection:** The first step is collecting relevant data, such as scientific papers, patents, and other scientific and technological outputs. This data may be sourced from online databases, such as Web of Science or Google Scholar, or from manual searches.
- **Data Cleaning:** The collected data must be cleaned to remove inconsistencies, errors, or irrelevant information. It may involve correcting errors in the data, removing duplicate records, and standardizing the data format.
- **Data Transformation:** The data must be transformed into a format that can be analyzed. It may involve converting the data into a numerical or categorical format, such as counting the number of papers or patents each year or grouping the data by author, institution, or geographic region.
- **Data Reduction:** The data must be manageable, as large datasets can be challenging to analyze. It may involve aggregating the data into summary statistics, such as the mean or median, or selecting a subset representative of the larger dataset.
- **Data Visualization:** The transformed and reduced data can be visualized to gain insights and identify patterns and trends. It may involve creating graphs, charts, and maps to represent the data and help understand the relationships between variables.

The specific pre-processing steps used in scientometrics may vary depending on the type of data and the research question being studied. However, these steps are generally required to prepare the data for analysis and ensure the results are accurate and meaningful.

11.3.2 BIBLIOMETRIC ANALYSIS IN SCIENTOMETRICS

Bibliometric analysis is a subfield of scientometrics that focuses on analyzing scientific and technological literature, such as scientific papers, patents, and conference proceedings (Nakamura et al., 2015). The following are some standard bibliometric methods and techniques:

- **Citation Analysis:** Citation analysis involves the analysis of the citation patterns of scientific papers, such as the number of citations received by an article or the number of citations received by an author. This method is used to assess the impact of scientific works, identify the most influential authors and institutions, and track research fields' development (Asatani et al., 2018).
- **Co-citation Analysis:** Co-citation analysis involves the analysis of the co-citation relationships between scientific papers, such as the number of times two articles are cited together. This method is used to identify the most related works and the key topics in a field.
- **Co-authorship Analysis:** Co-authorship analysis involves the analysis of the co-authorship relationships between authors, such as the number of papers written by two authors together. This method assesses the level of collaboration between authors and identifies the most collaborative research networks.
- **Social Network Analysis:** Social network analysis involves the analysis of the social relationships between authors, institutions, and countries, such as the number of connections between authors or institutions. This method is used to identify the most influential authors, institutions, and governments in a field and to understand the distribution of expertise.
- **Keyword Analysis:** Keyword analysis involves the analysis of the keywords used in scientific papers, such as the frequency of use of specific keywords or the relationships between keywords. This method is used to identify the key topics and subtopics in a field and to track the development of research fields.

The bibliometric analysis provides valuable insights into the impact, collaboration, and evolution of scientific and technological fields and can be used to support research and innovation policy and decision-making.

11.4 DATA COLLECTION AND PRE-PROCESSING

For this study, we collected data from the Scopus database from 2002 to 2022, with 3,130 records. The data has been collected using the advanced search feature of Scopus. The search string employed was ({biometric} AND {machine learning}) OR ({biometrics} AND {ml}). The string was searched in the title, abstract, and keyword of the papers using the TITLE-ABS-KEY fieldcode. The Boolean operators "AND"

Authors	Title	Year	Source title	Cited by	DOI	Affiliations
Gu H., Gao Z., Wu F.	Selection of optimal features for iris recogni...	2005	Lecture Notes in Computer Science	11.0	10.1007/11427445_14	Institute of Artificial Intelligence, Zhejiang...
Lu X., Jain A.K.	Ethnicity identification from face images	2004	Proceedings of SPIE - The International Societ...	115.0	10.1117/12.542847	Dept. of Comp. Sci. and Engineering, Michigan ...
Toh K.-A., Tran Q.-L., Srinivasan D.	Benchmarking a reduced multivariate polynomial...	2004	IEEE Transactions on Pattern Analysis and Mach...	118.0	10.1109/TPAMI.2004.3	Institute for Infocomm Research, 21 Heng Mui K...

FIGURE 11.1   Raw data.

and "OR" have the usual meaning. For example, using the search string XX AND YY, those records containing the terms "XX" and "YY" were fetched. The phrase enclosed within {ZZ} was used to find the exact match of the string "ZZ." The snapshot of raw data is presented in Figure 11.1.

The data were then pre-processed to remove duplicate and null-values records, resulting in 1,972 publications. Figure 11.2 presents the detailed methodology of data processing and analysis. Firstly, we identified the publication growth over the years (Singh et al., 2021). For this, we grouped the data by year and counted the number of papers each year. Secondly, the average citation count (CPP) is computed each year. Each year, papers with at least one citation have been grouped and averaged out for citations. Thirdly, a co-authorship analysis was performed. The "Author" field was exploited for this purpose. It has all the author names of the paper separated by a comma. The data has been split on the "comma," and we counted the number of authors. Fourthly, the collaboration pattern has been analyzed. We computationally extracted the country from the "Affiliations" field. Fifthly, the top contributing institutions have been identified. Regular expressions have been employed to capture the institution names within the "Affiliations" field. Lastly, the highly active journals were explored using the "Source title" field. All the computations were done using scripts written in the Python programming language (Karmakar et al., 2023).

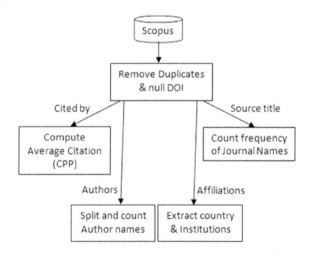

FIGURE 11.2   Data pre-processing and analysis.

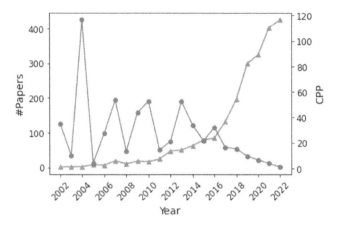

FIGURE 11.3   Year-wise publication growth and citation trend.

11.5   RESULTS AND DISCUSSION

Figure 11.3 presents the publication growth and citation trend over 21 years (2002–2022). During 2002–2004, only 1–2 papers were published in the field. Interestingly, from 2005 to 2010, an alternative pattern of increase and decrease has been observed. It can be observed that the highest number of 392 papers will be published in the year 2022. Interestingly, 2012 and 2013 have approximately the same number of papers, 41 and 43, respectively. A continuous decrease has been observed in the research output from 2011 to 2022. The CPP value ranges from 1.11 to 116.5. The citation value in 2018 witnessed the highest citation value of 3,006. The CPP plot has evidenced a continuous fall between 2017 and 2022. Interestingly, the highest CPP, 116.5, was obtained in 2004 for only two publications with 233 total citations. One of the possible reasons for such a high citation impact could be that these are the base/initial studies in the domain. The lowest CPP value, 1.11, is obtained in 2022, followed by 4.24 in 2021. The recent and relatively new studies require more time to acquire citation impact. Overall, the results suggest a positive trend in publication count, whereas no consistent pattern has been observed in the citation pattern.

Table 11.1 exhibits the co-authorship analysis of research outputs during the period. The results show that three authors have written the most (494 papers), constituting 25.05% of the total research output. The collaboration of two to four authors has been equally popular over the years, with 421 and 414 papers, respectively. Interestingly, 4.92% (97) of papers are written by single authors without collaboration. At most, 239 authors have contributed to writing the paper with the DOI "10.1016/S2589-7500(20)30131-X." The second-largest collaboration has been observed with 159 authors, followed by 28 authors resulting in a single paper.

The research collaboration has also been studied from domestic and international perspectives. The collaboration analysis could reveal the most productive countries in the domain. The analysis would help better understand the knowledge exchange between India and other international countries. We have investigated India's role

TABLE 11.1
Co-authorship Trend

#Authors	TP	%Papers	#Authors	TP	%Papers
1	255	11.55	12	6	0.27
2	451	20.43	13	3	0.14
3	514	23.28	14	5	0.23
4	427	19.34	15	3	0.14
5	257	11.64	17	2	0.09
6	156	7.07	18	2	0.09
7	53	2.4	21	2	0.09
8	28	1.27	27	1	0.05
9	18	0.82	28	1	0.05
10	10	0.45	159	1	0.05
11	12	0.54	239	1	0.05

in the global biometrics–ML field. Figure 11.4 shows that India has published 356 papers, i.e., 18% of the total papers without international collaboration. India is the first-ranked country, publishing the most papers without any foreign affiliation. The United States ranked second with 241 papers. It is considered that in the India–international collaboration, there are only 50 papers, which constitute only 2.55% of the total papers. India has its largest international collaboration share of 16% with the United States, whereas it is 6% with the United Kingdom. India's other collaborators are Saudi Arabia, Malaysia, Japan, Pakistan, etc. Foreign countries are highly active in the area. The international countries are working collaboratively to a large extent and contribute 79.33% to the world's output. In an international collaboration, the United States also appears at the top. Other countries are Canada, China, Australia, Brazil, Macau, etc.

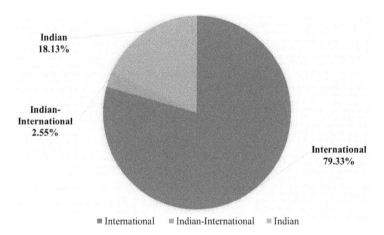

FIGURE 11.4   Collaboration trend.

TABLE 11.2
Top 10 Journals

Journal Title	No. of Publications
Lecture Notes in Computer Science	85
IEEE Access	50
ACM International Conference Proceeding Series	40
Advances in Intelligent Systems and Computing	31
Multimedia Tools and Applications	26
Proceedings of SPIE – The International Society for Optical Engineering	25
Sensors	24
IEEE Transactions on Image Processing	23
Communications in Computer and Information Science	23
IEEE Transactions on Pattern Analysis and Machine Intelligence	21

Table 11.2 shows the popular journals in the biometrics-ML area. *Lecture Notes in Computer Science* is the top journal, in which 85 papers have been published. *IEEE Access* and *ACM International Conference Proceeding Series* are the 2nd and 3rd most active journals, with 50 and 40 publications, respectively. *Communications in Computer and Information Science* ranks 9th with 23 papers, whereas *IEEE Transactions on Pattern Analysis and Machine Intelligence* appears at the 10th position with 21 publications. This analysis will help researchers identify potential venues for their research work.

Table 11.3 lists the top 10 most productive institutions in the domain. Nanyang Technological University, Singapore, has produced the maximum number of papers (16). Hangzhou Dianzi University in China is the second-most productive institution. It can be observed that Michigan University (Michigan) and Purdue University (Indiana) have the same number of papers, i.e., 11. Interestingly, the Vellore Institute of Technology (India), the University of California, Khalifa University (UAE),

TABLE 11.3
Top 10 Institutions

Institutions	No. of Publications
Nanyang Technological University	16
Hangzhou Dianzi University	12
Michigan State University	11
Purdue University	11
Vellore Institute of Technology	10
University of California	10
Khalifa University	10
Zhejiang University	10
Harbin Institute of Technology	9
University of Macau	9

and Zhejiang University (China) have all published 10 papers. Harbin Institute of Technology and the University of Macau appear at the bottom with 9 papers.

11.6 CONCLUSION

In conclusion, biometric technology has seen rapid growth and advancements over the past few years. Integrating ML, biometric authentication, and verification has become more reliable and efficient. Using biometric data for ML has opened up a new frontier for biometric research. The recent trend analysis for ML in biometrics has shown promising results, with more studies and applications being developed. Scientometrics plays a crucial role in the trend analysis of ML in biometrics. This chapter presents a scientometrics analysis of Scopus data spanning 20 years, aimed at identifying recent trends in the growth of publications, citation patterns, institutional affiliations, co-authorship, collaboration patterns, and journal profiles in the field of biometrics. The number of published papers in the field was relatively low, with only 1–2 papers published from 2002 to 2004. However, the number of published papers increased steadily over time, reaching its peak with 392 papers published in 2022. The results also suggest a positive trend in publication counts, but no consistent pattern was observed in citation patterns. The most prominent form of collaboration in the field was three-author collaboration. The study revealed that India contributed 18% of the papers without international collaborators. The analysis helps quantify and analyze research growth, development, and impact in a particular field. The pre-processing steps in scientometrics, such as data cleaning and normalization, are essential to ensuring accurate and reliable results. Overall, biometrics and ML have created a new era in biometrics research and applications, potentially revolutionizing how we authenticate and verify identity. With the continuous advancements in technology and the increasing demand for secure and efficient authentication methods, the future of biometrics and ML in biometrics looks bright and promising.

CONFLICT OF INTEREST

The authors declare that they have no conflict of interest.

REFERENCES

Acquisti, A., Gross, R., & Stutzman, F. (2014). Face recognition and privacy in the age of augmented reality. Journal of Privacy and Confidentiality, 6(2). https://doi.org/10.29012/jpc.v6i2.638

Andrade, N. N. G., de, Martin, A., & Monteleone, S. (2013). "All the better to see you with, my dear": Facial recognition and privacy in online social networks. IEEE Security & Privacy, 11(3), 21–28. https://doi.org/10.1109/msp.2013.22

Asatani, K., Mori, J., Ochi, M., & Sakata, I. (2018). Detecting trends in academic research from a citation network using network representation learning. PLoS One, 13(5), e0197260. https://doi.org/10.1371/journal.pone.0197260

Belter, C. W. (2015). Citation analysis as a literature search method for systematic reviews. Journal of the Association for Information Science and Technology, 67(11), 2766–2777. Portico. https://doi.org/10.1002/asi.23605

Bortolato, B., Ivanovska, M., Rot, P., Krizaj, J., Terhorst, P., Damer, N., Peer, P., & Struc, V. (2020). Learning privacy-enhancing face representations through feature disentanglement. 2020 15th IEEE International Conference on Automatic Face and Gesture Recognition (FG 2020). https://doi.org/10.1109/fg47880.2020.00007

Cunningham, S., & Truta, T. M. (2008). Protecting privacy in recorded conversations. Proceedings of the 2008 International Workshop on Privacy and Anonymity in Information Society. https://doi.org/10.1145/1379287.1379295

Garfinkel, S. L. (2015). De-identification of personal information. https://doi.org/10.6028/nist.ir.8053

Kajikawa, Y., Abe, K., & Noda, S. (2006). Filling the gap between researchers studying different materials and different methods: A proposal for structured keywords. Journal of Information Science, 32(6), 511–524. https://doi.org/10.1177/0165551506067125

Karmakar, M., Singh, V. K., & Banshal, S. K. (2023). Measuring altmetric events: The need for longer observation period and article level computations. Global Knowledge, Memory and Communication. https://doi.org/10.1108/gkmc-08-2022-0203

Morales, A., Fierrez, J., Vera-Rodriguez, R., & Tolosana, R. (2021). SensitiveNets: Learning agnostic representations with application to face images. IEEE Transactions on Pattern Analysis and Machine Intelligence, 43(6), 2158–2164. https://doi.org/10.1109/tpami.2020.3015420

Nakamura, H., Suzuki, S., Sakata, I., & Kajikawa, Y. (2015). Knowledge combination modeling: The measurement of knowledge similarity between different technological domains. Technological Forecasting and Social Change, 94, 187–201. https://doi.org/10.1016/j.techfore.2014.09.009

Ribaric, S., Ariyaeeinia, A., & Pavesic, N. (2016). De-identification for privacy protection in multimedia content: A survey. Signal Processing: Image Communication, 47, 131–151. https://doi.org/10.1016/j.image.2016.05.020

Singh, V. K., Singh, P., Karmakar, M., Leta, J., & Mayr, P. (2021). The journal coverage of Web of Science, Scopus and Dimensions: A comparative analysis. Scientometrics, 126(6), 5113–5142. https://doi.org/10.1007/s11192-021-03948-5

Sinha, K., Paul, P., & Amritanjali, A. (2021). Randomized block size (RBS) model for secure data storage in distributed server. KSII Transactions on Internet and Information Systems (TIIS), 15(12), 4508–4530. https://doi.org/10.3837/tiis.2021.12.014

Sinha, K., Paul, P., & Amritanjali, A. (2022). An improved pseudorandom sequence generator and its application to image encryption. KSII Transactions on Internet and Information Systems (TIIS), 16(4), 1307–1329. https://doi.org/10.3837/tiis.2022.04.012

Sinha, K., Priya, A., & Paul, P. (2020). K-RSA: Secure data storage technique for multimedia in cloud data server. Journal of Intelligent & Fuzzy Systems, 39(3), 3297–3314. https://doi.org/10.3233/JIFS-191687

Yuan, L., & Ebrahimi, T. (2017). Image privacy protection with secure JPEG transmorphing. IET Signal Processing, 11(9), 1031–1038. https://doi.org/10.1049/iet-spr.2016.0756

12 Can ML Be Used in Cybersecurity?

Naghma Khatoon, Sharmistha Roy,
and Ritushree Narayan

12.1 INTRODUCTION

The word cyber means virtual reality. It comes from two terms "cyber" and "security". Cyber is a term that is being collectively used for groups of computers in networks or information technology, and security means we have to secure the network from attacks. It is that world where every work is based on technology. Cybersecurity is a line of defence versus intrusions on all internet-connected devices, including hardware, software, programs, and data. Beginning with mobile banking and ending with online purchasing, the digitization era has created numerous opportunities for everyone, notably businesses and companies. The likelihood of cybercrime increases as we become increasingly connected to digital assets. Crimes committed using or dependent on technology are referred to as cybercrimes. It is a general term for any illegal operations carried out through the use of components of communication technology, including the internet, cyberspace, as well as the world wide web (www). Some current trends and challenges in cybersecurity include the following, which is also depicted in Figure 12.1.

12.1.1 RANSOMWARE ATTACKS

These are becoming more frequent and sophisticated, with hackers encrypting victims' data and demanding payment for the decryption key. Malicious software (malware) assaults known as ransomware encrypt a victim's files and demand payment (often in cryptocurrency) in return for the decryption key. Attacks using ransomware may be extremely damaging to both people and businesses since they can result in large financial losses, harm to one's reputation, and an interruption of daily activities. To protect yourself from ransomware attacks, here are some best practices:

- **Backup your data regularly:** Regular backups can help you restore your files in case of a ransomware attack. Make sure to keep your backup files in a secure location.
- **Maintain software updates:** Ransomware assaults frequently take advantage of software flaws. Maintain the most recent security updates on the operating system, your internet browser, and other applications.
- **Use antivirus software:** Antivirus software can detect and prevent ransomware attacks. Make sure to use reputable antivirus software and keep it up-to-date.

DOI: 10.1201/9781003388845-15

FIGURE 12.1 Different types of cyberattacks.

- **Be cautious of suspicious emails and links:** Ransomware attacks often come from phishing emails or malicious links. Be wary of emails or links from unknown sources, and do not download attachments or click on links unless you are certain they are safe.
- **Educate yourself and your employees:** Educate yourself and your employees on how to identify and avoid ransomware attacks. Teach them to be cautious of suspicious emails and links and to report any suspicious activity to IT.
- If you do become a victim of a ransomware attack, do not pay the ransom. Paying the ransom only encourages the attackers to continue their criminal activities. Instead, report the attack to law enforcement and seek the help of a reputable cybersecurity professional to help you recover your files.

12.1.2 Cloud Security

As more organizations adopt cloud technology, securing sensitive data stored in the cloud has become a major concern. Cloud security refers to the set of technologies, policies, procedures, and controls used to protect cloud computing resources, data, and infrastructure. Cloud security is important because it addresses the unique security challenges that arise when data and applications are hosted in a cloud environment.

Here are some best practices for cloud security:

- **Choose a reputable cloud provider:** Before selecting a cloud provider, research their security policies and certifications. Look for providers that have strong security measures and regularly test and update their systems.
- **Use strong authentication:** Use strong authentication measures, such as multi-factor authentication, to prevent unauthorized access to your cloud accounts.

- **Encrypt your data:** Encrypt your data both in transit and at rest to prevent unauthorized access. Use strong encryption protocols and key management practices.
- **Monitor your cloud environment:** Use monitoring tools to track activity in your cloud environment and detect suspicious activity. Set up alerts to notify you of any potential security threats.
- **Implement access controls:** Use access controls to limit access to your cloud resources. Use role-based access control (RBAC) to grant permissions based on user roles and responsibilities.
- **Regularly test your security:** Regularly test your cloud security controls to identify vulnerabilities and address any weaknesses. Conduct regular security audits and penetration testing to identify potential security risks.
- **Train your employees:** Educate your employees on cloud security best practices and provide regular training to ensure they are aware of the latest security threats and how to avoid them.

By following these best practices, you can help ensure the security of your cloud environment and protect your data and resources from potential security threats.

12.1.3 ARTIFICIAL INTELLIGENCE AND MACHINE LEARNING

These tools can help cybersecurity, but they may also be employed by hackers to automate assaults and avoid detection. Creating systems that can carry out operations that ordinarily require human intellect, including observation, reasoning, learning, and decision-making, is the goal of the areas of artificial intelligence (AI) and machine learning (ML), two closely related branches of computer science.

AI is a broader field that encompasses a range of approaches, from rule-based systems to deep learning, that enable machines to exhibit intelligent behaviour. The goal of ML (ML), a branch of AI, is to train computers to acquire knowledge about data as well as make predictions or judgements based on that data.

Various sectors apply AI and ML in the following ways, as examples:

- **Healthcare:** To diagnose illnesses and provide individualized treatment regimens, ML and AI are utilized to analyse patient data as well as medical pictures.
- **Finance:** Financial data is analysed using AI and ML to look for fraud and other abnormalities.
- **Retailing:** Retailing as a ML and AI are used to analyse customer data in order to forecast purchasing trends and enhance marketing plans.
- **Manufacturing:** Production process optimization and downtime reduction are achieved using AI and ML.
- **Transportation:** A Study AI and ML are applied to boost the management of supply chains and logistics, optimize traffic flow, and forecast maintenance needs.

However, with the increasing use of AI and ML, there are also concerns around the ethics and biases that may be built into these systems. It is important to ensure that AI and ML systems are transparent, fair, and accountable, and that they do not reinforce or perpetuate existing biases and inequalities.

12.1.4 Internet of Things (IoT) Security

There are new security risks brought on by the growing number of gadgets that are connected in households and companies that need to be fixed. The network of networked devices, sensors, and other types of items known as the IoT are equipped with software, sensors, and network connections, enabling them to gather and share data. The IoT has revolutionized how we live and work, but it also presents special security issues because of the vast number of linked devices and the possibility for network assaults to spread swiftly. Here are some best practices for IoT security:

- **Secure devices and networks:** Ensure that all IoT devices are secured with strong passwords and up-to-date firmware and software. Set up secure networks with firewalls and other security measures to protect against unauthorized access.
- **Use encryption:** Encrypt all data that is transmitted between IoT devices and networks to prevent interception and tampering.
- **Monitor for vulnerabilities:** Regularly scan for vulnerabilities and patch security weaknesses as soon as possible to prevent attacks.
- **Implement access controls:** Use access controls to limit access to IoT devices and networks. To assign rights according to user roles and responsibilities, utilize role-based access control (RBAC).
- **Use a secure data management strategy:** Develop a secure data management strategy to protect sensitive data and ensure that it is not shared with unauthorized parties.
- **Train your employees:** Educate your employees on IoT security best practices and provide regular training to ensure they are aware of the latest security threats and how to avoid them.
- **Have a response plan in place:** Create an incident response strategy that explains what you do in the event of an IoT device or network safety breach or other issue.

By following these best practices, you can help ensure the security of your IoT devices and networks and protect your data and resources from potential security threats.

The remainder of the essay is organized as follows. The literature review of the linked study is included in Section 12.2. We provide a quick explanation of what cyber law is and its significance in Section 12.3. Section 12.4 provides a brief introduction to ML, deep learning, and AI. The application uses ML for cybersecurity, as shown in Section 12.5. Section 12.6 presents several ML algorithm types for cybersecurity. This chapter concludes with Section 12.7.

12.2 LITERATURE SURVEY

In Ref. [1], the authors explain an ML method for identifying Rank assaults inside a smart hospital setting utilizing centralized anomaly-based Intrusion detection system

(IDS) that was proposed by the author. The suggested work's main requirements are adaptability, portability, and historical learning. Because ML classifiers have a low power consumption, the authors, for example, simply used Only Support Vector Machines for the classification stage. With this sporadic placement of hostile nodes, the authors created four different scenarios within the simulation environment. They then evaluated their methodology using various attacker node counts. While the first scenario just consists of typical network traffic trends as training material for IDS, the next three instances each incorporate various combinations of hostile nodes. The experimental finding demonstrates that the suggested IDS' DR rises as maliciousness rises.

According to relevant literature, the author of [2] focused on the consequences of different alterations made to conventional ML/DL algorithms on the vulnerabilities faced with digital communications systems and wireless networks. By briefly outlining the most well-liked datasets that are used to train and test the models, a quality study of these cyberattack data has already been carried out. To encourage upcoming researchers and supporters, descriptions of open challenges that are yet unsolved and new study areas have been offered.

The research in Ref. [3] by the authors employed binary classification algorithms, which can distinguish between two states. Whenever binary classifiers disagree, their accuracy is compared to reaching a decision. The development of multi-class classification techniques to serve as the basic expertise is a workable alternative course of action. These classifiers would require the use of a novel method to be merged into an ensemble. Future research might focus on an approach like this. We may say that weights produced by metaheuristic algorithms can increase intrusion detection systems' accuracy. We have seen some variations in classification accuracy for various datasets, as is typically the case with randomized algorithms. This shows that by using various optimization techniques that are also based on meta-heuristics, additional progress may be made.

In Ref. [4], the authors proposed a system to safeguard patient records from future cyberattacks. The suggested system also needs to be updated periodically with fresh cyberattack data. The model's performance might be enhanced and kept current by periodic fine-tuning of the most recent cyberattack data, but it is a laborious and time-consuming operation. Future research will also concentrate on the creation of self-supervised learning neural network architects that will allow systems such as intrusion detection to automatically adapt to novel threats without even needing manual re-training or fine-tuning, as well as making use of the most recent data sets to boost equilibrium as opposed to reweighing strategies to improve the model's fairness.

In Ref. [5] The recommended model was tested using the dataset covered in this study, which provides a wide variety of assaults and a large number of cases. The collection includes network information gathered across eight distinct sessions. Seven sessions were taken into account, but one session—which just provides typical traffic data—was missed. By choosing characteristics based on Pearson's correlation coefficient, we improved the original dataset. We also eliminated occurrences from the dataset that were redundant or duplicate. Utilizing the measurement parameters of the confusion matrix, the model was evaluated. The proposed model has a 98.73% classification accuracy rate and a low FP rate. Compared to all other classifiers, the approach employed just under 58% of the total attributes for each sub-dataset, or close to half of the entire attributes.

12.3 WHAT IS CYBER LAW?

The phrase "cyber law" refers to a body of legislation that regulates matters pertaining to the Internet, electronic components, and communication technologies, including computers, software, hardware, and information systems. It alludes to the laws, rules, and policies that control the Internet, online activity, and technological matters. Rights in intellectual property, confidentiality, privacy, data protection, e-commerce, and cybercrime are just a few of the legal concerns it covers. The main objective of cyber law is to ensure the safe and secure use of technology and protect individuals, businesses, and governments from cyber threats.

12.3.1 IMPORTANCE OF CYBER LAW

Today, everyone is concerned about cyber legislation. This is mostly due to the fact that we all use the internet every day in some capacity. While doing e-commerce transactions, net banking, sending emails, etc., we utilize the internet to create any online accounts. Cyber laws play a crucial role in regulating and protecting the Internet and technology-related activities. Here are some of the reasons why cyber laws are important:

- **Protecting individuals' rights:** Cyber laws aid in defending people's rights, including the freedom of speech, the right to confidentiality, and the defence against cybercrime.
- **Maintaining online security:** Cyber laws help to ensure the security of online activities by regulating the use of encryption and other security measures.
- **Preventing cybercrime:** Cyber laws play a vital role in preventing and prosecuting cybercrime, such as hacking, identity theft, and online fraud.
- **Regulating e-commerce:** Cyber laws help to regulate online transactions and ensure the protection of consumers in online commerce.
- **Protecting intellectual property:** Cyber laws help to protect the rights of individuals and businesses with regards to their intellectual property, such as patents, trademarks, and copyrights.
- **Promoting innovation and growth:** By providing a legal framework for the use of technology and the Internet, cyber laws help to promote innovation and growth in the technology sector.

12.4 MACHINE LEARNING, DEEP LEARNING, AND ARTIFICIAL INTELLIGENCE

The goal of the "machine learning" area of AI is to develop algorithms and mathematical models that can detect patterns in data and draw conclusions or forecasts without being explicitly told to do so. With so many uses in fields like marketing, banking, and healthcare, it has attracted a lot of interest in recent years. In precisely this new technological era, businesses and developers from all over the world have started concentrating on ML and AI for cybersecurity. Deep learning and machine learning are terms that are frequently used figuratively in technology. As illustrated

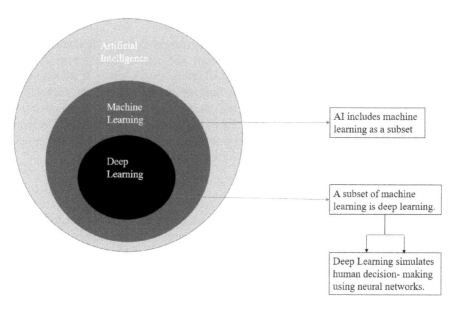

The figure contains the following labels:
- Artificial Intelligence
- Machine Learning
- Deep Learning
- AI includes machine learning as a subset
- A subset of machine learning is deep learning.
- Deep Learning simulates human decision- making using neural networks.

FIGURE 12.2   Artificial intelligence umbrella.

in Figure 12.2, both of them fall within the category of AI. AI is a broad term that refers to everything that makes a machine smarter (AI). Although ML is used in conjunction with AI, it is just a subset of AI. The intelligent system that can really self-learn and is dependent on the algorithm is referred to as ML. As a result, ML systems develop their intelligence over time without human involvement. It creates intelligent systems using statistical learning methods. On the other hand, deep learning is ML that has been applied to huge data sets. This branch of AI is a method that takes its cues from how the human brain processes data. Thus, ML is used in the majority of AI projects since intelligent behaviour necessitates extensive learning.

Among the various types of computer vision are learning algorithms such as supervised learning, unsupervised learning, semi-supervised learning, reinforcement learning, and deep learning. The choice of method relies just on the nature of the issue as well as the type of information available. Different types of ML take different approaches to problems. The most popular type of ML, supervised learning, aims to train a model using labelled information to make forecasts on brand-new, untainted data. On the other hand, unsupervised learning includes discovering patterns or correlations in data without using labelled data.

Artificial neural networks are used in deep learning, a branch of ML, to model intricate data patterns. It has revolutionized the fields of both vision in computers and natural language processing and has proved especially effective in tasks like picture and speech recognition. ML has also been used for developing personalized experiences, such as recommendation systems, fraud detection, and predictive maintenance. Despite its many benefits, ML also poses some ethical and societal concerns, including issues of bias, privacy, and accountability. Overall, ML has significantly impacted various industries and has the potential to revolutionize many more in the future.

12.5 USES OF ML FOR CYBERSECURITY

Individuals and organizations may use a variety of security measures to stay safe, including multi-factor authentication, strong passwords, routine software and system updates, and data backups. It is also important to stay informed about the latest security threats and best practices. Data security has never been higher, thanks to ML's ability to automate threat identification and fight even without human intervention. With the development of AI and ML, many businesses have begun to employ them as a potent defence against sophisticated cyberattacks and intrusions.

ML has become an increasingly important tool in the field of cybersecurity due to its ability to analyse large amounts of data and identify patterns that are indicative of security threats. ML algorithms have the potential to play a significant role in detecting and preventing cybercrimes. ML algorithms can be trained to detect and respond to a variety of cyber threats, including malware, network intrusions, and phishing attacks. Here are some ways in which ML algorithms can be used to detect and respond to cyber threats:

IDSs are one of the most common applications of ML in cybersecurity. An IDS uses algorithms to analyse network traffic and identify any anomalies that might indicate a security breach. For example, an IDS might detect an unusual spike in network traffic from a specific IP address, which could indicate a Denial of Service attack.

Antivirus software also relies on ML algorithms to identify and respond to malware. Antivirus software uses ML to analyse file behaviour and detect any signs of malicious activity. For example, an antivirus program might detect that a file is attempting to modify system files, which is a common characteristic of malware.

Another common application of ML in cybersecurity is email filtering systems. Email filtering systems use ML algorithms to analyse email messages and identify any messages that are likely to be spam or phishing attacks. For example, an email filtering system might analyse the content of an email message to determine if it contains links to known phishing websites or if it has a high probability of being a phishing attack based on previous training data.

- **Threat detection:** ML algorithms can be trained on large amounts of data to identify unusual behaviour that may indicate a cyberattack. For example, ML algorithms can analyse network traffic to detect unusual patterns of behaviour, such as increased traffic from a single IP address or an unusual increase in traffic during certain times of day.
- **Anomaly detection:** ML algorithms can be used to detect anomalies in network traffic and system logs. This can help to identify potential security breaches, such as unauthorized access to sensitive data.
- **Phishing protection:** ML algorithms can be trained to detect and block phishing attacks, which are a common type of cyberattack. Phishing attacks typically involve an attacker sending an email or message that appears to be from a trusted source, but which actually contains a link or attachment that leads to a malicious website or downloads malware onto the victim's computer. ML algorithms can be trained to identify and block these types

of attacks by analysing the content of emails or messages and the behaviour of links and attachments.

- **Fraud detection:** ML algorithms can be used to identify and prevent fraud by analysing patterns in large amounts of data. This can help financial institutions to detect and prevent fraud in real time by identifying unusual patterns of behaviour, such as a sudden increase in the amount of money being spent from a single account.
- **Automated response:** With the help of ML, organizations can automate their response to cyber threats, reducing the time and resources required to resolve incidents. For example, ML algorithms can be used to automatically quarantine infected systems, update security systems, and block suspicious traffic.

In addition to these applications, ML algorithms can also be used to improve the overall security of computer systems. For example, ML algorithms can be used to analyse security logs to identify weaknesses in security systems and recommend improvements.

While ML algorithms have the potential to be a valuable tool in the fight against cybercrime, it is important to remember that they are not a silver bullet. ML algorithms can only be as effective as the data they are trained on, and they are not immune to hacking and can be fooled by attackers who understand how they work. Therefore, it is important to use ML as part of a comprehensive cybersecurity strategy that includes multiple layers of protection.

12.6 THE ML ALGORITHMS FOR CYBERSECURITY

There are several different types of ML algorithms that can be used for cybersecurity purposes. Some of the most commonly used algorithms include the following:

- **Anomaly detection algorithms:** These algorithms detect unusual or unexpected behaviour in a system, which can indicate the presence of a cyber threat. Anomaly detection algorithms can be used to analyse network traffic, system logs, or other sources of data to identify anomalies.
- **Supervised learning algorithms:** These algorithms are trained on labelled data, where the outcome or label is known in advance. They can be used for tasks such as classifying emails as spam or phishing attacks or detecting malicious software.
- **Unsupervised learning algorithms:** These algorithms are trained on unlabelled data and are used to identify patterns or relationships in the data. They can be used for tasks such as detecting clusters of related data, which can be used to identify potential cyber threats.
- **Reinforcement learning algorithms:** These algorithms use rewards and punishments to learn how to perform tasks. They can be used to optimize network security policies by learning how to respond to different types of cyber threats.

- **Deep learning algorithms:** These methods may be used to find patterns in massive volumes of data since they are a form of artificial neural network. They may be used for activities like voice and picture recognition, which are relevant to issues with cybersecurity like finding viruses in image files. It is important to note that different ML algorithms may be better suited for different types of cybersecurity tasks and that the best approach will depend on the specific problem being solved and the type of data being analysed.

12.7 CONCLUSION

Cyber world refers to the virtual realm created by the Internet and interconnected computer systems, which contains various forms of digital information and online communities. Cybersecurity refers to the practices and technologies aimed at protecting these systems, networks, and digital assets from unauthorized access, theft, and damage, ensuring the confidentiality, integrity, and availability of data and resources in the cyber world. The use of ML in cybersecurity has been growing rapidly in recent years, as the amount of data generated by cyberattacks continues to increase. By automating the process of analysing and responding to cyber threats, ML algorithms can help organizations stay ahead of cyberattacks and prevent data breaches. ML has the potential to be a valuable tool in the fight against cyber threats, but it should not be relied upon as the sole solution. Organizations should use it as part of a comprehensive security strategy that includes multiple layers of protection.

REFERENCES

1. Said, A.M., Yahyaoui, A., Yaakoubi, F., Abdellatif, T. (2020). Machine learning based rank attack detection for smart hospital infrastructure. In: Jmaiel, M., Mokhtari, M., Abdulrazak, B., Aloulou, H., Kallel, S. (eds.). *The Impact of Digital Technologies on Public Health in Developed and Developing Countries. ICOST 2020.* Lecture Notes in Computer Science, vol 12157, 28–40.
2. Gupta C., Johri J.; Srinivasan K., et al. (2022). A systematic review on machine learning and deep learning models for electronic information security in mobile networks. *Sensor*, 22(5). https://doi.org/10.3390/s22052017
3. Aburomman A.A., Reaz M.B.I. (2016). A novel SVM-kNN-PSO ensemble method for intrusion detection system. *Applied Soft Computing*, 38, 360–372. https://doi.org/10.1016/j.asoc.2015.10.011
4. Kumar M.A., Samiayya D., Vincent P.M.D.R., et.al. (2021). A hybrid framework for intrusion detection in healthcare systems using deep learning. *Frontiers in Public Health*, 9, 824898. https://doi.org/10.3389/fpubh.2021.824898
5. Henry A., Gautam S., Khanna S., et al. (2023). Composition of hybrid deep learning model and feature optimization for intrusion detection system. *Sensor*, 23(2), 890. https://doi.org/10.3390/s23020890

13 GAN Cryptography

Purushottam Singh, Prashant Pranav, and Sandip Dutta

13.1 INTRODUCTION

The Creator of the universe created the most intelligent living organism on the planet, known as "Humans." Does the question arise of why humans are the most intelligent creatures? The answer can be simpler or complex! But in simpler terms, we can say that humans can solve every problem efficiently and effectively. Of course, we can't solve every problem by ourselves, so the machine era arrived, and in that same machine era, the computer was introduced. Undoubtedly, the invention of the digital computer revolutionized the human capacity to solve problems, but it was still just a machine. We needed a mechanism by which the machines could be intelligent – Artificial Intelligence. For devices to be smart, it was not easy to develop a method, i.e., a mathematical model to describe intelligence. In the current era, machine intelligence dominates every part of human life, from medicine to entertainment.

The problem of dealing with network security is very concerning for data privacy. Of course, the network can be secured with various methods. Cryptography is one of the methods used to secure data communication through the use of codes. Cryptography allows us to secure the data and make sure that the data are transmitted to only those people who are meant to process and understand them. Cryptography prevents unauthorized access to data around the world. The word cryptography is made up of two words "Crypt," which means hidden, and "graphy," means writing. This method was secure in the past, but in the present, high-performance computing methods can break the code and access the messages.

Let's see the different methods used in the past and present to secure the data.

Many companies share the database with different data scientists outside of their organization. Here the following question arises: will data be secured outside of the organization? One method that can be used to secure the data is data anonymization. However, this will not secure the whole dataset as the other part of the database is not anonymized, leading to the prediction of the whole dataset. Thus, data anonymization cannot be a method at the current time to secure the data outside the organization, as it is an era of machine learning and artificial intelligence.

Another method that is used to secure the data is "Homomorphic Encryption," which allows users to transit the calculation and computation of the encrypted data without performing decryption on it. But the main problem with homomorphic encryption is that it is not differentiable and computationally inefficient.

DOI: 10.1201/9781003388845-16

The use of artificial intelligence-leading neural networks improves the cryptosystem. The team at Google Brain came up with the "Generative Adversarial Network" solution.

Using a generative adversarial network (GAN) [1] in cryptography enhances the security capability of the communication network. The main idea was to develop a model of a cryptographic system using a neural network that allows the data to be more secure than other models.

Before understanding the current scenario, let us see how machine intelligence evolved.

13.2   NEURAL NETWORK AND CRYPTOGRAPHY HISTORY

It all started in 1943 when famous neurophysiologist Warren McCulloch collaborated with genius mathematician Walter Pitts. They performed research together and contributed a research paper [2] explaining the working of neurons. They built an electrical circuit modeling a simple neural network.

Later in 1962, Bernard Widrow and Ted Hoff [3] introduced a learning model which was based on the value of the weight (i.e., 0 or 1) and adjusting in accordance with the rule. This idea was basically based on the big error method. If any active perceptron faces a big error, then it should adjust its weight to make it distributed across the whole network. This distribution ensures that the error is eliminated.

After some time, a paper was published describing the leading extension of single-layered neural networks to multiple-layer neural networks.

The practical application of neural networks [4] was very rare. Some of the philosophical ideas led to dread based on "Thinking Machines."

Later, the advancement of technology based on neural networks produced high-capability thinking machines that comforted humans. David Rumelhart [5] patches the new idea of a backpropagation network, allowing the distribution of errors faced by pattern recognition throughout the network. The backpropagation network uses many layers of neural networks. But as many layers need to be iterated, the backpropagation layer network was called "Slow Learner."

The fundamental concept of the neural network implementation was that if the neural network works in nature, it must work in computer technology.

The advancement of neural networks needs hardware development because of their neural functions. For example, machines for chess playing named Deep Blue depend upon the hardware built especially for them. Some of the machine's efficiency was increased by implementing the neural network.

For example, in the airline industry, if a person has to travel, he must visit the airport 2 to 3 hours early to make board possible. This amount of time is wasted on all the passengers, as security checking takes time. In Finland, the airport authority tells passengers to visit only before 16 minutes of flight time. This only happened due to artificial intelligence implemented on the CT scanner allowing fast security checks with enhanced capability. Advanced technologies in the application of neural networks help solve complex problems for humans.

Now let's see the brief history of cryptography.

In 1917, Gilbert Vernam created the one-time pad, which is believed to be an unbreakable cipher. In 1949, Claude Shannon's *Communication Theory of Secrecy*

Systems established the mathematical principles of cryptography. Whitfield Diffie and Martin Hellman introduced the concept of public-key cryptography in their 1976 publication *New Directions in Cryptography*. A year later, Ron Rivest, Adi Shamir, and Leonard Adleman developed RSA, the first practical implementation of public-key cryptography. David Chaum invented the blind signature, the first digital signature scheme, in 1982. The Data Encryption Standard (DES), which was used for 20 years, was retired in 1985 due to concerns about its security. Phil Zimmermann's creation of PGP, an email encryption program, in 1991 was widely adopted. Bruce Schneier's *Applied Cryptography*, in 1997, is a significant book that discusses the practical implementation of cryptographic algorithms. The Advanced Encryption Standard (AES), which replaced DES, was adopted as a government standard for encryption in 2001. Finally, Satoshi Nakamoto's 2008 publication of the Bitcoin whitepaper introduced the concept of blockchain technology and a decentralized digital currency. These advancements have significantly influenced the field of cryptography, paving the way for new developments in secure communication and data protection.

13.3   NEURAL NETWORK

Artificial neural networks [6], also referred to as neural networks, are intelligent computing systems designed based on biological neural networks that work in the human brain.

The neural network consists of a layered structure that defines how the human brain is connected hierarchically at each level. The standard function of the human brain is to process information, leading the information to enter the brain, and layer by layer, each level of neuron performs its particular job by processing the information. For example, when we pass through a restaurant, our brain responds to the smell of the cooked cake in the following stages:

- **Data input:** The aroma of the freshly baked cake.
- **Thought:** It reminds me of my last birthday.
- **Decision-making:** I think I will purchase a cake.
- **Memory:** Oh no! I have already taken my lunch.
- **Reasoning:** But I can have more snacks.
- **Action:** Give me one pound of freshly baked strawberry cake.

The above example shows how the brain works in different cycle stages.

There are three layers of neurons. The information is passed from one layer of the neuron to another, as our brain does.

1. **The input layer:** The entry point for the information/data.
2. **The hidden layer:** The layer of the neuron in which the information is processed so that the needs can be associated.
3. **The output layer:** This is the last layer of the neural network where the system decides how it will proceed based on the data/information.

The neural network plays a vital role in the computer network and security.

13.4   GENERATIVE ADVERSARIAL NETWORK

A GAN [7] is a modified version of deep learning architecture with a pair of competing models, leading to a zero-sum game framework. It generates new and synthetic data similar to the known dataset. The motto of GANs is to learn, analyze, and capture the data. GANs are basically used for unsupervised learning techniques. The GAN framework was designed and developed by Ian J. Goodfellow in 2014. GANs were basically developed for the improvement of image quality.

There are two components of GANs, which are as follows:

1. **Generator:** The work of the generator is to create the synthetic dataset.
2. **Discriminator:** It is just the opposite of the generator; it processes the evaluation of the dataset generated by the generator and determines whether it is fake or real.

Here, both components of GAN, i.e., generator and discriminator, are neural networks. The generator-processed output directly passes through the discriminator as the input. The discriminator used the backpropagation method to classify the data and send it to the generator to perform weight updating. The generator is always penalized by the discriminator for unlikely outputs. During the data training process, the generator produces the fake result data and passes them to the discriminator to evaluate. During the evaluation, the discriminator learns quickly and informs the victim that the data are fake.

13.4.1.   APPLICATION OF A GENERATIVE ADVERSARIAL NETWORK

GANs were basically developed for the improvement of image quality. However, in the present time, the implementation has been done in a very wide area of computer science.

The application of GANs has rapidly increased. Some of the applications of GANs are as follows:

- **Image Synthesis:** GANs are used for image synthesis, which allows the process of generating a large set of training data that provides the best variety and distribution during dataset generation.
- **Anomaly Detection:** It is also known as outlier detection; in this process, unexpected events or items are identified which are significantly different from the defined norm or function. There are many data points that don't fit with normal patterns. GANs are used to solve these problems, leading to medical diagnosis, fraud detection, etc.
- **Text-to-Image Synthesis:** One of the most effective implementations of the GANs is the text-to-image synthesis, which allows the system to generate a realistic synthesis image in accordance with the description given in the natural text language.
- **Image-to-Image Translation:** It is basically used to map the image in association with an input image and an output image, allowing object transfiguration and photo enhancement.

13.5 CRYPTOGRAPHY

The Term "Cryptography" is made up of two keywords: "Crypt," which means hidden, and "graphy," which means writing. Cryptography [8] is a technique in which data are secured. The data are transferred to those who are meant to understand and process them. The cryptography technique uses code to convert plain text into secure code. In the case of transmitting electronic data, there is a particular set of rules known as an algorithm, consisting of mathematical functions. The data are then encrypted with that set of algorithms. This allows intruders or hackers to find it hard to decrypt or decode. This algorithm, constituting a mathematical function, allows the system to generate the cryptographic key and digital signatures. These allow us to secure data privacy and digital transactions associated with the network.

The technique used in current-age cryptography is to convert ordinary text into cipher text with the help of an algorithm. That intended information is passed to only those intended recipients. The intended receiver will only be able to process the text data and decode or decrypt them, a process known as decryption.

13.5.1 FEATURES OF CRYPTOGRAPHY

1. **Authentication:** The identities of the sender and receiver will be confirmed during data transmission. The data origination and destination will also be confirmed.
2. **Integrity:** Data modification cannot be done during the transition between sender and receiver. No addition of extra information is allowed throughout the transition.
3. **Confidentiality:** Information will be fetched by only those people those for whom it is intended; no other person can access the information.
4. **Non-repudiation:** This feature allows the sender from where the data originated to not deny sending data/information at a later stage.

13.5.2 TYPES OF CRYPTOGRAPHY

1. **Symmetric Key Cryptography:** It is an encryption technique in which a single common key is used by the sender and receiver to encrypt and decrypt the data. This cryptography technique is the fastest and simplest encryption technique. The most common problem faced by symmetric key cryptography is the exchange of keys in a secure manner. The data encryption system (DES) is a popular example of symmetric key cryptography.
2. **Asymmetric Key Cryptography:** In this cryptography technique, a pair of keys is used to perform encryption and decryption of data. One pair of key is known as the "Public Key," and the other is the "Private Key." The public key is intended to be used in the process of encryption. The private key is intended to be used in the process of decryption. The public key can be known to the whole population but cannot be used for data decryption; only the intended receiver can perform decryption as he/she only knows the private key.

3. **Hash Function:** In the hash function method, no key is used in this algorithm. A cryptographic hash function has the ability to take input data (often called a "message") and return a fixed-size string of bytes, which is typically a digest that is unique (to the best extent possible) to each unique input. This process makes it impossible to read plain text. The hash function is used by many operating systems to encrypt the password.

13.5.3 APPLICATION OF CRYPTOGRAPHY

Some of the applications of cryptography are stated in the following:

- Electronic signature
- Digital currencies
- Security of data during transmission
- Cryptocurrencies
- Digital computer passwords
- Authentication
- Security of data in storage

13.6 GENERATIVE ADVERSARIAL NEURAL CRYPTOGRAPHY

As we have already seen, in the concept of GANs and cryptography, data privacy is very concerning for everyone. The data shared by different organizations to process are vulnerable to everyone, leading to data theft. The introduction of GANs in computer science allows researchers to expand their field into different areas. Cryptography cannot secure the dataset as it uses an algorithm that can be broken by quantum computing (QC) technology. The researcher must work hard to sustain the balance between data security and data theft.

Data anonymization seemed to be the solution for a specific period of time, but the problem with data anonymization was that the level of security we were expecting was not fulfilled. Data anonymization has the issue of inference. For example, any MNC could share the sales dataset with a third-party organization to perform data operations. Let us assume there is no obscure of department or organization in the dataset. Still, some clever data scientist or engineer could figure it out by performing basic inferences on the dataset. There is a statement about anonymization:

If the data in the dataset that is not obscured can be used to predict the obscured data, then the anonymization may not be a suitable solution.

Recently, the development of techniques like homomorphic encryption and secure multi-party computation with zero-knowledge proofs has played a crucial role in advancing machine learning methods. GANs cryptography, although not as well-known, is part of that unique group and possesses a robust theoretical foundation, making it a promising solution for ensuring data privacy in the machine learning process.

GAN cryptography [1] is a technique that overcomes the problems of both methods, anonymization and homographic encryption. The Google Brain team introduced this concept, allowing the combined use of GANs and cryptography. They explained that using the neural network in network security ensures complex solutions for data theft. GAN cryptography is a method that exists between data anonymization and homomorphic encryption.

Neural networks, while incredibly powerful for many tasks, have their limitations, especially when it comes to cryptographic operations. Specifically, they often struggle with XOR operations, making these calculations time-consuming. However, a redeeming quality is that neural networks consistently demonstrate the ability to safeguard data confidentiality when interfaced with other neural networks. To delve deeper into the realm of GAN cryptography, it's essential first to grasp some fundamental components integral to the neural network process:

- **Encryptor:** The plain text and shared key will be the input; both the plain text and shared key will be in a binary sequence to generate encrypted text.
- **Decryptor:** Encrypted text and a shared key will be the input to generate the decrypted text in the output form.
- **Eavesdropper:** only encrypted text will be taken as input; it will try to decrypt the encrypted text intercepted by it.

There are generally three layers used in generative adversarial network cryptography, as follows:

1. Convolution layer
2. Fully connected dense layer
3. Flatten layer

Let us see an example of how GAN cryptography works.

In this GAN cryptography scenario, there are three parties involved: Alice, Bob, and Eve. Alice and Bob are two parties who want to communicate with each other, and Eve is the party who wishes to eavesdrop on their communications. The security feature aims to maintain confidentiality (not integrity), and the adversary involved is a passive attacker who has the ability to intercept communications but has limited capabilities.

In a situation described, Alice wants to send a confidential message, "P," to Bob. Alice inputs the message "P," and the output produced is "C" (where "P" represents plaintext and "C" represents ciphertext). Both Bob and Eve receive the "C" and try to retrieve the original message "P." These actions can be represented by "PBob" and "PEve," respectively. Alice and Bob have an advantage over Eve as they share a secret key "K." This secret key "K," is used as extra input by Alice and Bob. Casually, the objectives of the participants can be described as follows: Eve's objective is straightforward, to recreate "P" accurately, meaning to reduce the difference between "P" and "P_{Eve}." On the other hand, Alice and Bob want to communicate effectively, reducing the difference between "P" and "PBob," while also concealing their communication from Eve.

"The outcome of the GAN cryptography tests were noteworthy, around 8500 training cycles, both Bob and Eve began to recover the original message. At about 10,500 training cycles, the Alice and Bob networks appeared to understand this, causing Eve's error rate to increase again. To put it simply, Bob was able to adapt to Eve's actions and secure the communication, enhancing its efficiency at the same time."

Alice and Bob utilized generative adversarial network methods to communicate while learning to overcome Eve effectively. The unique aspect is that Alice and Bob do not have prior knowledge of the cryptography algorithms they will use to achieve their objective or the techniques that Eve will employ. Based on GAN principles, Alice and Bob are trained to defeat the strongest version of Eve instead of a fixed one.

The team at Google Brain modified the GAN cryptography design during research to create a model where Alice and Bob still share a key. In this model, Alice receives inputs "A," "B," and "C," and produces "D-public" along with a ciphertext. Both Bob and Eve have access to Alice's output. Bob uses them to create a refined estimate of "D," while Eve tries to uncover "C." The objective is to prove that through adversarial training, it is possible to approximate "D" without disclosing "C," and that by combining this approximation with encrypted information and the key, a more accurate approximation of "D" can be obtained.

At last, to determine if the system is effectively hiding information, the researchers employed a separate evaluator named "Blind Eve." Blind Eve attempts to guess "C" based only on her knowledge of the distribution of "C." However, the actual Eve has access to the intermediate output ("D-public") and the ciphertext in addition to the information known to Blind Eve. If the reconstruction error of Eve becomes the same as that of Blind Eve, it shows that Eve is unable to extract information from the public estimate and the ciphertext. This is exactly what happened. After a few training steps, Eve's advantage over Blind Eve becomes negligible, indicating that Eve cannot reconstruct any more information about "C" than what is possible by knowing just the distribution of "C" values.

The above example shows how effective GAN cryptography is. Data security is achieved very efficiently and effectively. GAN cryptography will show beautiful results in the future as new research and implementation go on.

13.6.1 Advantages of GAN Cryptography

- **Security:** GANs can produce cryptographic keys that are more secure and harder to predict than traditional techniques, thereby improving the security of encrypted data.
- **Robustness:** GANs have demonstrated resistance to attacks like tampering, manipulation, and deletion of watermarked data, thus guaranteeing the authenticity and reliability of the information.
- **Versatility:** GANs can perform various cryptographic tasks such as watermarking, generating random numbers, encrypting data, and producing keys.

- **Efficiency:** GANs are capable of efficiently learning from large amounts of data and processing high-dimensional data such as images, audio, and video, making them appropriate for a range of multimedia applications.
- **Deep Learning Capabilities:** GANs utilize deep learning to comprehend intricate connections between input and output data and adjust to changing circumstances.

13.6.2 LIMITATION OF GAN CRYPTOGRAPHY

GAN cryptography is a relatively new approach to encryption that uses GANs to create cryptographic keys, but it also has some limitations:

- **Computational Complexity:** The process of generating keys using GANs is computationally intensive and requires significant resources, which limits its practical applications.
- **Limited Scalability:** GAN-based cryptography is currently limited in scalability as it requires a large amount of data to train the GAN model, which can be difficult to obtain in some applications.
- **Limited robustness:** GAN-based cryptography is still in the experimental stage and has not been thoroughly tested in real-world scenarios. Its robustness and reliability are still unknown.
- **Vulnerability to attacks:** GAN-based cryptography is susceptible to attacks, such as adversarial attacks and gradient-based attacks, which could compromise the security of the encryption.

13.6.3 STATE-OF-THE-ART

GANs are a type of deep learning algorithm that has shown promise for use in cryptography. GAN cryptography involves using GANs to generate cryptographic keys, which can be used for various cryptographic operations.

Currently, the state-of-the-art in GAN is still in the research and development phase. However, there have been several promising developments in recent years, including:

- **Data Encryption:** GANs have been used for data encryption by transforming the data into an image and then using an image-to-image translation GAN to encrypt the image.
- **Multi-party GAN:** Multi-party GANs involve using multiple GANs in a distributed system to generate cryptographic keys that are secure even if one or more of the GANs are compromised. This approach has shown promise in improving the security of GAN cryptography.
- **Key Generation:** GANs have been used to generate more secure and unpredictable cryptographic keys than traditional methods.
- **Random Number Generation:** GANs have been used to generate high-quality random numbers, which are crucial in cryptography for encryption and key generation tasks.

Overall, GAN cryptography is still a developing field. However, more research and development are needed to address its limitations and ensure its security in practical settings.

13.6.4 Applications of GAN Cryptography

GANs have shown promise for several applications in cryptography, which include the following:

- **Deep Learning Based Key Generation:** One approach to GAN cryptography involves training a GAN to generate cryptographic keys directly from random noise inputs. This approach has been shown to be effective in producing high-quality cryptographic keys that are resistant to attacks.
- **Privacy-Preserving Computations:** GAN's cryptography can be used to generate synthetic data that is protected by a GAN cryptographic layer of encryption which is almost impossible to decrypt, preserving sensitive data while allowing computations on it.
- **Authentication:** GAN cryptography can be used to create secure authentication, leading to a complex layer of encryption in the network.
- **Anomaly Detection:** GANs can be utilized to identify deviations in encrypted data, thereby aiding in thwarting cyber assaults.
- **Digital Watermarking:** GANs can embed digital watermarks securely and effectively in images, audio, and video data, thus aiding in the protection of copyright and ownership of multimedia content.

Overall, GAN cryptography has a wide range of potential applications, and ongoing research is exploring new ways to leverage this technology to improve the security and privacy of data and communications.

13.7 CONCLUSION

In conclusion, GANs have shown promising results in the field of cryptography, particularly in generating secure keys and obfuscating sensitive data. GAN-based cryptography techniques offer several advantages, such as their ability to generate large numbers of secure keys quickly and their resistance to attack from both classical and quantum computers. However, there are potential risks and limitations that need to be addressed, such as the possibility of adversarial attacks and the need for a large amount of training data. Overall, GAN cryptography holds great potential for enhancing the security of various applications and systems, and further research and development are necessary to fully realize its potential capabilities.

REFERENCES

1. Abadi, M., & Andersen, D. G. (2016). Learning to protect communications with adversarial neural cryptography. *arXiv preprint arXiv:1610.06918*.
2. McCulloch, Warren S., and Walter Pitts. (1943). "A logical calculus of the ideas immanent in nervous activity." *The Bulletin of Mathematical Biophysics*, 5, 115–133.

3. Widrow, B., & Hoff, M. E. (1960). Adaptive switching circuits. Stanford Univ Ca Stanford Electronics Labs.

4. Bishop, Chris M. (1994). Neural networks and their applications. *Review of Scientific Instruments*, 65(6), 1803–1832.

5. Rumelhart, D. E., Hinton, G. E., & Williams, R. J. (1986). Learning representations by back-propagating errors. *Nature*, 323(6088), 533–536.

6. Krogh, Anders. (2008). What are artificial neural networks? *Nature Biotechnology*, 26(2), 195–197.

7. Goodfellow, I., Pouget-Abadie, J., Mirza, M., Xu, B., Warde-Farley, D., Ozair, S., … & Bengio, Y. (2020). Generative adversarial networks. *Communications of the ACM*, 63(11), 139–144.

8. Kessler, G. C. (2003). An overview of cryptography. http://www.garykessler.net/library/crypto.html

14 Security Aspects of Patient's Data in a Medical Diagnostic System

Ankita Kumari

14.1 INTRODUCTION

In today's digital world, healthcare systems have become highly dependent on information technology (IT) to provide better, more efficient patient care. As a result, medical diagnostic procedures have emerged, which are highly sophisticated and automated, utilising big data analytics, artificial intelligence (AI), machine learning (ML), and the Internet of Things (IoT). However, the use of such technologies in healthcare also poses significant security risks, especially when it comes to protecting patient data. This article will explore the security aspects of patient data in a medical diagnostic system.

Medical data security refers to the measures and practices to protect and secure medical information from unauthorised access, theft, or damage. Medical data are often some of the most sensitive and personal information an individual can possess. As such, proper security measures must be in place to protect it. Medical data security covers various aspects of information protection, including confidentiality, privacy, and integrity. Confidentiality restricts access to information only to those who need to know. Privacy refers to the security of personal information from unauthorised disclosure or use. Integrity refers to the accuracy and consistency of data and information protection from unauthorised modification or destruction. Various technologies, processes, and policies ensure medical data security. For example, encryption technologies can scramble sensitive information and prevent unauthorised access. Access control systems can restrict access to medical data based on a person's role and responsibilities. Physical security measures, such as locked cabinets and limited access to data centres, can be used to protect against theft or damage to data.

Moreover, organisations must comply with regulations such as the Health Insurance Portability and Accountability Act (HIPAA) in the United States and the General Data Protection Regulation (GDPR) in Europe, which set standards for protecting personal health information. These regulations require organisations to implement administrative, physical, and technical safeguards to protect the privacy and security of medical data. In addition to these technical measures, organisations must implement policies and procedures that define how medical data should be

DOI: 10.1201/9781003388845-17

handled and protected. This includes guidelines for access control, data backup and recovery, incident response, and employee training. Medical data security is critical in healthcare, protecting individuals' sensitive information from theft, unauthorised access, or damage. By implementing strong security measures and adhering to industry regulations, organisations can ensure the privacy and security of medical data and build trust with their patients, employees, and partners.

Medical records are comprehensive documentation of a patient's health information, including their medical history, diagnoses, treatments, test results, medications, and other relevant details. These records can be maintained in paper or electronic form to support the diagnosis, treatment, and management of a patient's health.

Medical records serve as a central repository of information about a patient's health and are critical for ensuring continuity of care. They provide a comprehensive picture of a patient's health history and are used by healthcare providers to make informed decisions about diagnosis, treatment, and care.

Medical records also play an essential role in research and public health. They can be used to track disease trends, monitor the effectiveness of treatments, and inform public health policy. Additionally, they are essential for insurance purposes and can be used to support insurance claims. Medical records are a critical component of the healthcare system, serving as a comprehensive and centralised source of information about a patient's health history and treatment.

Patient data can be categorised into several types: medical records, personal identification information (PII), financial information, and health-related data. Medical records contain information about a patient's medical history, diagnoses, and treatments, which is critical for providing appropriate care. PII includes the patient's name, date of birth, address, and social security number. Financial information provides insurance details, payment history, and billing information. Health-related data may include genetic information, test results, and images, among other things.

A medical diagnostic system is a set of procedures, technologies, and processes that healthcare providers use to identify the presence and nature of a disease or medical condition in a patient. The goal of a diagnostic system is to provide accurate and reliable information that can be used to develop a treatment plan and improve patient outcomes. Diagnostic systems typically involve a combination of medical history and physical examination, laboratory tests, imaging studies, and other diagnostic procedures. During a diagnostic evaluation, a healthcare provider may ask questions about the patient's symptoms, medical history, and lifestyle and perform a physical examination to gather information about the patient's current health status.

Laboratory tests are a critical component of the diagnostic process. These tests use samples of blood, urine, or other bodily fluids to identify the presence of diseases, genetic disorders, or other medical conditions. Standard laboratory tests include blood tests for glucose, cholesterol, and liver function and urine tests for protein, glucose, and other disease markers.

Imaging studies, such as X-rays, CT scans, MRI scans, and PET scans, are also commonly used in the diagnostic process. These studies provide detailed images of the inside of the body, allowing healthcare providers to see the structure and function of organs, bones, and other tissues. Imaging studies can be used to identify abnormalities, such as tumours, herniated discs, or clogged arteries, which may be causing symptoms.

In some cases, more invasive diagnostic procedures, such as biopsies, endoscopies, or angiograms, may be required. These procedures involve collecting a tissue sample or performing an imaging study using a contrast agent introduced into the body. The samples or images obtained during these procedures can provide critical information about the nature of a disease or condition.

The diagnostic process results are then used to develop a treatment plan. Treatment may involve medication, surgery, lifestyle changes, or other therapeutic interventions, depending on the nature and severity of the medical condition. The goal of treatment is to manage symptoms, slow or stop the progression of the disease, and improve the patient's quality of life.

The medical diagnostic system is a complex and sophisticated process critical to adequate healthcare. By combining medical history, physical examination, laboratory tests, imaging studies, and other diagnostic procedures, healthcare providers can identify the presence and nature of a medical condition, develop a treatment plan, and improve patient outcomes.

14.2   RELATED WORK

According to Dhanalakshmi & George [1], cloud computing raises serious security issues, especially privacy and data integrity. It is critical to appropriately store, process, and exchange these data on cloud storage platforms because the healthcare sector generates and manages an enormous amount of data. However, the specific location of the stored data is frequently unknown, and unauthorised parties may access it during delivery and storage. Additionally, data analysis applications dealing with large healthcare information systems need a robust security approach that provides scalability and privacy protection to fulfil the demands of computing, communication, and storage operations. This study suggests adopting RSA algorithms for e-healthcare systems to overcome these problems, which can increase the effectiveness of cloud-based systems and guarantee the security and integrity of data transfer from medical facilities to the cloud. By utilising this cutting-edge strategy, healthcare companies may better retain cloud computing's advantages while protecting sensitive data.

A solution to the demanding data security requirements of Internet of Medical Things (IoMT) applications is put forth in [2]. According to the paper, several IoMT applications cannot be widely adopted because of data circulation and utilisation limitations. SEMMI is intended to be a secure, effective, and intelligent decision-making tool for intelligent medical devices. The KNN classification algorithm is used in an example application in the article. The data is transferred, calculated, and stored in ciphertext, preventing theft or leakage by nefarious parties. The approach accomplishes the four design goals listed in the study, as shown by theoretical and experimental findings. The programme's members don't have to remain online, lowering the participant cost. To demonstrate the scheme's flexibility, the paper also addresses the possibilities of employing it in neural network applications and creates a federated learning algorithm. The paper outlines a novel approach to tackling security issues with IoMT applications and shows how the suggested strategy may be applied in practical situations.

The IoMT-Fog-Cloud architecture is described in this work [3] for health systems. This architecture was created to secure e-health applications by guaranteeing the secret exchange of data and safeguarding patient privacy. Context-aware Ciphertext-Policy ABE (Cx-CP-ABE), a new addition to the CP-ABE method, was introduced to accomplish this goal. This novel solution integrates blockchain and context awareness to improve security at the data access control management level, ensure data integrity, and keep track of data sharing. They conducted various tests to show how well the Cx-CP-ABE approach protects patient data confidentiality. They also mentioned that health data might be collected in actual usage scenarios with the proper integration abilities and blockchain knowledge. They intended to improve our model by using machine learning in their subsequent work to safeguard the cloud computing environment, including numerous connected objects. Overall, they feel that their suggested architecture represents a substantial advancement in developing e-health applications and has the potential to raise the standard of healthcare services.

According to Azzaoui et al. [4], cloud-based systems' quantum computation can dramatically increase intelligent healthcare environments' computational power and security. Their suggested architecture combines two cutting-edge technologies to provide smart healthcare applications with higher service quality and safety. Utilising blockchain technology, they can lessen the need for a quantum machine on the client side and enable secure access to trustworthy devices and clients for quantum cloud services. A quantum terminal (a quantum image) at the edge layer converts conventional bits into qubits and vice versa. In addition, fully blind computation guarantees that the Quantum Cloud can fulfil complicated requirements from healthcare clients while upholding the highest data and computation security levels. They examined the Grover searching data to confirm our suggested architecture's security. They examined the Grover searching algorithm over completely encrypted data on the Quantum Cloud to verify the security of our proposed architecture. According to their research, the Q-OTP (Quantum One-Time Pad) provides 100 percent security. The viability of a blockchain-based delegated quantum cloud architecture for medical big data security is shown through simulation results. They will use this architecture in the future to better quantify quantum error rates by doing various computations on accurate medical data.

Implementing digitalisation in the healthcare sector necessitates changes in employment expectations, processes, regulations, and activities, as mentioned in [5]. To effectively incorporate digitalisation into the professional environment and ensure patient security, it is essential to assess the digitalisation capabilities of healthcare professionals. Adopting digital health systems and other health information technology can potentially replace outdated paper-based health record systems in developing economies effectively. As a result, healthcare organisations are increasingly embracing various digital technologies to improve their measures. The rapid adoption of these technologies can be attributed to factors such as the availability of dependable, affordable, and low-power equipment or software systems, increased internet usage, and the success of high-profile initiatives in numerous countries. Adopting digital advancements in the healthcare industry is expected to result in significant cost savings and increased efficiency, especially given the short timeframes for delivering healthcare services. In developing nations, digital health systems can potentially enhance healthcare performance and assist in achieving strategic objectives. However, implementing digitalisation in healthcare is frequently hindered by context-specific challenges that impede success. Healthcare organisations must focus on the social environment of the workplace and foster a positive attitude if they want to improve their response to digitalisation. Practical, organisational, and collaborative support is necessary to implement new technology successfully. Despite the potential advantages of healthcare digitalisation, some researchers have noted that not all computerised healthcare systems live up to expectations. It is essential to recognise that projected improvements resulting from digitalisation may not always materialise as predicted.

In [6], the study evaluated an end-to-end secure remote-control system that utilised contemporary mobile communication on ECHONET Lite devices. The system's performance was also tested in the current mobile internet environment. Results demonstrated that the suggested approach might control ECHONET Lite devices without requiring a particular server while retaining network performance similar to traditional remote-control solutions. All internet messages were encrypted as part of the proposed technology's control over ECHONET, and the server did not keep track of previous operations. As a result, a safe and dependable remote-control system that safeguards users' privacy was established.

The suggested approach in [7] has important ramifications for healthcare service providers since it enables them to choose the safest healthcare system. Healthcare providers can guarantee the privacy and confidentiality of patient's medical records by using a solution like this. Healthcare service providers are entrusted with the guardianship of patient medical records and are accountable for their security. The scientific method was created and confirmed on a strong scientific basis, which would make the decision-making process of healthcare service providers in selecting a healthcare system more precise and evidence-based. The suggested approach can also be a thorough benchmarking and assessment framework for future researchers and software developers interested in creating blockchain-based healthcare sector 4.0 technologies. A comparable methodology can be used to address similar issues.

The authors of [8] concentrate on the security issues of implantable medical devices (IMDs) that can operate independently and in a network. The writers thoroughly review the incentives that might lead potential attackers to exploit these devices and the different attacks that might be conducted against them. Even though there haven't been any confirmed security lapses with IMDs in real-world scenarios, research teams have demonstrated that they are susceptible to security breaches that could endanger patients' lives. The authors suggest several security measures that can be implemented to lessen the attack surface for IMDs and mitigate these risks. IMDs can offer customers significant medical benefits and convenience despite security risks. It is crucial to understand that they are not impervious to security dangers. Patients will have more faith in these medical solutions if the security issues involved in their design, development, installation, and use are rigorously investigated and improved. To safeguard the safety and well-being of patients, the medical industry must take these security issues seriously and invest in developing secure IMDs.

Their work [9] examines recent research in this field and focuses on the security of AI-based COVID-19 detection systems. These investigations show that deep learning models are susceptible to adversarial attacks, which is concerning considering the crucial role that a correct COVID-19 diagnosis plays in containing the outbreak. When creating AI-based COVID-19 systems, it is crucial to consider attack and defence strategies to solve this problem. They intend to investigate the function of various attack and defence methods in their upcoming study using diverse methodologies and datasets from other sources. They seek a more thorough examination of the flaws and potential fixes for boosting the security of AI-based COVID-19 detection systems.

IoT-based solutions, including e-healthcare, connected medical solutions, and IoMT with IoT sensor support, have extensively impacted the healthcare sector. The expansion of these apps has made it possible for healthcare professionals to offer patients more precise, predictive, and successful medication services and tactics, including doctors, nurses, hospitals, and clinics. To fulfil the increasing expectations of the digital society, it is essential to integrate IoT-based sensors into the current e-healthcare services. To enhance sensor-centric knowledge and comprehension of their usability, they offered a taxonomic market capitalisation structure for IoT-based sensors in the study [10]. These sensors have been divided into many classes, and their significance has been highlighted. Additionally, they have conducted a comparative analysis of existing survey literature, highlighting the novelty and uniqueness of our study. Furthermore, they have discussed the lessons from this extensive and in-depth study, providing recommendations and future directions for practitioners. They have also suggested when to use which type of sensor and how. Lastly, they have addressed various security and privacy issues associated with sensor data and proposed ways to mitigate them. Overall, this paper presents a novel contribution to the dissemination of IoT-based sensor-centric e-healthcare services, paving the way for readers and practitioners to think about and utilise IoT-based sensors for the benefit of humanity.

14.3   IMPORTANCE OF SECURING A PATIENT'S HEALTH RECORD

Security is of utmost importance regarding patient data for several reasons. Patient data, such as medical records, diagnostic reports, and test results, contain sensitive and confidential information that needs to be protected to ensure the privacy and safety of the patients. Here are some reasons why security is essential in terms of patient's data:

- **Protecting patients' privacy:** Patient data contain sensitive information that must be kept confidential. These include personal information like name, address, and date of birth, as well as medical information such as diagnoses, test results, and treatments. Patient privacy must be protected to prevent unauthorised access, use, or disclosure of this information.
- **Preventing identity theft:** Patient data can be used to steal identities, leading to significant financial loss, damage to reputation, and other negative consequences. Security measures, such as encryption and access controls,

can help prevent identity theft by limiting access to patient data to authorised individuals.

- **Protecting against medical fraud:** Patient data can be used to commit medical fraud, such as submitting false insurance claims or prescribing unnecessary treatments. Security measures can help prevent these types of fraud by limiting access to patient data to authorised individuals and ensuring that only appropriate treatments are prescribed.
- **Ensuring continuity of care:** patient data are critical for providing appropriate and timely medical care. If patient data are compromised, it can lead to delays in treatment or incorrect diagnoses, which can have severe consequences for patients' health. Security measures can help ensure that patient data are available when needed, and accurate and up-to-date.
- **Compliance with regulations:** Healthcare organisations must comply with various regulations related to patient data, including HIPAA, HITECH, and the GDPR. Failure to comply with these regulations can result in significant fines and legal penalties. Security measures can help ensure that healthcare organisations remain compliant with these regulations.

Security is essential in terms of patient data to ensure the privacy and safety of patients, prevent identity theft and medical fraud, ensure continuity of care, and comply with regulations. Healthcare organisations must take appropriate security measures to protect patient data and maintain the trust of their patients.

14.4   SIGNIFICANT ASPECTS OF SECURITY

Security is a broad and complex field encompassing various aspects of protecting people, property, and information. Security is generally concerned with preventing, detecting, and responding to threats that can harm individuals, organisations, or communities. To fully understand the significant aspects of security, it is helpful to break them down into several key categories:

- **Physical Security:** This is the aspect of security that deals with protecting physical assets, such as buildings, equipment, and people, from theft, damage, or unauthorised access. Physical security measures include access controls (e.g., keys, access cards, biometric scanners), CCTV cameras, security guards, fences, and alarms. These measures deter would-be intruders and prevent unauthorised access to sensitive areas.
- **Information Security:** This is the aspect of security that deals with protecting digital assets, such as data, systems, and networks, from cyber threats. Information security measures include firewalls, antivirus software, intrusion detection systems, encryption, and user authentication. These measures are designed to prevent unauthorised access, data breaches, and other cyberattacks that can compromise sensitive information.
- **Operational Security:** This security aspect ensures business operations' continuity and prevents disruptions caused by natural disasters, technological failures, or other unforeseen events. Active security measures can include

business continuity planning, disaster recovery planning, redundant systems, and backup generators. These measures are designed to minimise the impact of unexpected events and help organisations quickly recover from disruptions.

- **Personnel Security:** This aspect of security ensures the trustworthiness of employees and other personnel with access to sensitive information or assets. Personnel security measures can include background checks, security clearance screenings, and security policies and procedures training. These measures are designed to prevent insider threats, such as theft or sabotage, and ensure that only trustworthy individuals can access sensitive information.
- **Crisis Management:** This is the aspect of security that deals with responding to emergencies, such as natural disasters, terrorist attacks, or other catastrophic events. Crisis management measures can include emergency response plans, communication protocols, and drills or simulations. These measures ensure that organisations are prepared to respond quickly and effectively to crises, minimising the impact on people, property, and operations.

Security encompasses protecting people, property, and information from multiple threats. These aspects include physical security, information security, operational security, personnel security, and crisis management, all of which are essential for ensuring the safety and security of individuals and organisations.

14.5 TYPES OF MEDICAL DATA AND WAYS TO SECURE MEDICAL HEALTH RECORDS

Medical data refer to information about an individual's health or medical history. This can include demographic information, medical diagnoses, lab test results, imaging studies, medication history, and more. As medical data are sensitive, it is essential to secure them to ensure patient privacy and confidentiality. This article will discuss different types of medical data and how we can secure them.

Types of medical data:

- **Electronic Health Records (EHRs):** EHRs contain a patient's medical history, including diagnoses, treatments, medications, and test results. EHRs are stored in a digital format and can be accessed by healthcare providers and patients.
- **Medical Images:** Medical images include X-rays, CT scans, MRI scans, and ultrasounds. These images are used to diagnose medical conditions and are stored in digital format.
- **Lab Results:** Lab results include blood, urine, and other medical tests that provide information about a patient's health status.
- **Prescription Information:** Prescription information includes a patient's medication history, current and past prescriptions, dosage, and frequency.

Medical patient data security is a critical aspect of healthcare security for maintaining patient information's privacy, confidentiality, and integrity. Medical patient data include a wide range of sensitive information, such as personal identification, medical history, diagnostic test results, medication orders, and treatment plans. As such, it is crucial to implement robust security measures to protect this information from unauthorised access, disclosure, and alteration.

The following are some of the critical security aspects that are important for protecting medical patient data:

a. **Access Controls:** Access controls are essential to medical patient data security. They ensure that only authorised personnel have access to patient information. Access controls can include authentication and authorisation mechanisms, such as passwords, biometrics, and access cards, that verify the user's identity and determine their level of access to patient data. Implementing access controls to prevent unauthorised access to patient information and ensuring that only authorised individuals can modify or delete data is important.

b. **Encryption:** Encryption is the process of encoding data to be unreadable by unauthorised users. Encryption is essential for protecting medical patient data stored and transmitted electronically. This includes data stored in EHRs and transmitted over the Internet through email or web-based applications. Encryption can help prevent unauthorised access to patient data by ensuring that the data are only readable by authorised users with the appropriate decryption keys.

c. **Data Backup and Recovery:** Data backup and recovery are essential to medical patient data security. Regular backups of patient data ensure that the data can be recovered in the event of data loss or corruption. Additionally, backup data can be used to test recovery processes and identify vulnerabilities in the backup and recovery systems. Backup and recovery processes should be tested regularly to ensure that they are practical and can be relied upon during a security incident.

d. **Audit Logs:** Audit logs are records of events on a computer system, such as access attempts, data modifications, and system errors. Audit logs are an essential aspect of security for medical patient data because they can be used to track and identify suspicious activities, such as unauthorised access attempts or data modifications. Audit logs should be reviewed regularly to detect and investigate unusual or suspicious activity.

e. **Physical Security:** Physical security is important for medical patient data security. Physical security measures can include access controls, such as security cameras, access cards, and biometric scanners, that prevent unauthorised access to physical areas where patient data are stored. Additionally, physical security measures should be implemented to protect physical devices, such as computers and servers, that store patient data.

f. **Medical Patient Data Security:** It is an essential aspect of healthcare security that requires a multi-faceted approach to protect patient information. This includes implementing access controls, encryption, data backup and recovery processes, audit logs, and physical security measures. By implementing robust security measures, healthcare organisations can ensure that patient data remain confidential and secure.

14.6 HEALTHCARE INFORMATION SYSTEMS (HIS) AND WHY IS IT IMPORTANT?

Healthcare Information Systems (HISs) are computerised systems that manage and store healthcare information. Healthcare providers use these systems to access and manage patient records, medical histories, treatment plans, laboratory results, and billing information. HIS is designed to improve healthcare delivery by providing healthcare professionals with easy access to patient information. This ensures that doctors and nurses have all the information required to make informed decisions about patient care. In addition, HIS systems help reduce medical errors by ensuring that accurate and up-to-date information is always available. HIS systems are also designed to streamline administrative processes such as patient registration, appointment scheduling, and billing. This reduces the workload for healthcare providers and allows them to focus on patient care. HIS systems also improve billing accuracy by automating the process and reducing the risk of errors. Data analysis is another important feature of HIS systems. These systems collect and store large amounts of data that can be analysed to identify trends and patterns. This information can be used to develop new treatment protocols and improve healthcare delivery. HIS systems also provide healthcare providers with access to real-time data, allowing them to make informed decisions quickly. HIS is an essential component of modern healthcare delivery. It gives healthcare professionals quick access to patient information, streamlines administrative processes, reduces medical errors, and improves data analysis. As technology advances, HIS systems will become even more critical to delivering high-quality healthcare.

There are several reasons why HIS is important:

- **Improved Patient Care:** HIS systems provide healthcare professionals with quick access to a patient's medical history and treatment plan. This ensures that doctors and nurses have all the necessary information to provide the best care possible. It also reduces the risk of medical errors and allows for more efficient communication between healthcare providers.
- **Efficient Operations:** HIS systems streamline administrative processes by automating patient registration, appointment scheduling, and billing tasks. This saves time and reduces errors, allowing healthcare providers to focus on patient care.
- **Data Analysis:** HIS systems collect and store large amounts of data, which can be analysed to identify trends and patterns. This information can be used to improve healthcare delivery and develop new treatment protocols.
- **Cost Savings:** HIS systems can help reduce healthcare costs by improving efficiency and reducing errors. This can lead to lower costs for patients and providers alike.

HIS is important because it helps healthcare providers deliver better care, improve patient outcomes, and reduce costs. With the continued growth of technology, HIS systems will play an increasingly vital role in modern healthcare.

14.7 THE IMPORTANCE OF SECURING PATIENTS DATA

Medical data security is of utmost importance because medical data contain sensitive and confidential information about an individual's health, which can have severe consequences if accessed by unauthorised personnel. This article will discuss an example to illustrate the importance of medical data security.

One of the most significant medical data breaches occurred in 2015, when Anthem Inc., one of the largest health insurers in the United States, reported that it had suffered a data breach. Hackers gained unauthorised access to the company's database, which contained the personal and medical information of 80 million individuals, including names, birth dates, social security numbers, medical identification numbers, and other sensitive information. This breach was one of the largest in history, and the information stolen is estimated to be worth over $2 billion on the black market.

The Anthem data breach demonstrates the significant impact of medical data security breaches on individuals and organisations. The stolen information can be used to commit identity theft, financial fraud, and other crimes. The breach exposed sensitive medical information, including medical conditions, medications, and treatments, which can be used to discriminate against individuals in employment, insurance, and other areas. For example, an individual with a history of mental illness or substance abuse may be denied work or insurance coverage due to the stigma associated with these conditions.

Furthermore, medical data security breaches can have significant financial and reputational consequences for organisations. The cost of investigating and remediating a breach can be high, as can the cost of legal settlements and regulatory fines. Additionally, breaches can damage an organisation's reputation, leading to a loss of customers and revenue.

Medical data security is critically important for several reasons, including protecting patient privacy, maintaining the integrity of medical records, and ensuring that sensitive medical information is not misused or stolen. Here's an example that illustrates why medical data security is so essential:

Imagine that a hospital's electronic medical records system is hacked and the hackers gain access to all patient records. Among the records are those of a high-profile politician currently running for office. The records reveal that the politician has a history of substance abuse and has been treated for depression. This information is leaked to the media, becoming a significant scandal derailing the politician's campaign.

In this scenario, there are several ways in which medical data security has been compromised. First, the hospital's electronic medical records system was not adequately secured, allowing hackers to gain unauthorised access. Second, the hackers could view and copy patient records, violating the privacy of the patients whose records were stolen. Finally, the stolen medical information was used for nefarious purposes, causing harm to a high-profile individual and potentially damaging the hospital's reputation.

This example illustrates why medical data security is crucial. Medical records contain sensitive and personal information about patients. If this information falls into the wrong hands, it can be used to harm individuals, damage reputations, and even commit identity theft or fraud. Therefore, healthcare organisations must take steps to protect patient data, such as implementing robust security protocols, training employees on data security best practices, and regularly auditing their systems for vulnerabilities.

If a patient's data get hacked by a hacker, it can have several adverse effects on the patient, including:

- **Identity theft:** Hackers can use personal information such as name, address, social security number, and date of birth to steal a patient's identity, open fraudulent accounts, or take out loans in their name.
- **Medical identity theft:** Hackers can fraudulently use a patient's medical information to obtain medical services or prescription drugs. This can lead to the patient's medical records being corrupted with inaccurate details, negatively impacting their future medical care.
- **Financial loss:** Patients may incur financial losses due to fraudulent transactions using their stolen information and may have to pay for expenses related to resolving identity theft.
- **Emotional distress:** Patients may experience emotional pain, anxiety, or fear about potentially misusing their personal information.
- **Loss of privacy:** Patients may feel that their privacy has been violated, leading to a loss of trust in the healthcare system and a reluctance to share their personal information. A data breach can have significant negative impacts on patients, and healthcare organisations must take steps to protect patient data from hackers.

14.8 USING ARTIFICIAL INTELLIGENCE TO SECURE PATIENT HEALTH RECORD

Artificial Intelligence (AI) refers to developing computer systems that can perform tasks that usually require human intelligence, such as learning, problem-solving, decision-making, and language understanding. AI is a broad field encompassing a range of subfields, including machine learning, natural language processing, computer vision, robotics, and expert systems.

Machine learning is a branch of artificial intelligence that involves developing algorithms and statistical models that enable computers to learn from data and make predictions or decisions based on that learning. Machine learning algorithms are trained on large datasets and use statistical techniques to identify patterns and relationships in the data, which can then be used to make predictions or decisions about new, unseen data. Machine learning can be used to detect and prevent security breaches such as unauthorised access or data theft. Machine learning algorithms can be trained to identify behaviour patterns indicative of a security threat, such as unusual login activity or attempts to access sensitive data. Once these patterns are identified, the system can automatically take action to prevent the threat, such as locking the account or alerting security personnel.

Machine learning can also identify and mitigate vulnerabilities in medical systems and devices. By analysing data from sensors and other sources, machine learning algorithms can identify potential security vulnerabilities and recommend actions to reduce them.

Machine learning is a subset of AI that focuses on developing algorithms that can learn from data and improve performance over time. This involves training the algorithm on a large dataset and then using that data to make predictions or classifications on new data. Several machine learning types exist, including supervised, unsupervised, and reinforcement learning.

Natural language processing (NLP) is another subset of AI that focuses on teaching computers to understand and generate human language. This involves developing algorithms to recognise speech, translate languages, and analyse text.

Computer vision is a field of AI that enables computers to interpret and understand visual information from the world around them. This involves developing algorithms to recognise objects, faces, and gestures in images and videos.

Robotics is a field of AI that focuses on developing machines that can perform tasks autonomously. This involves integrating AI technologies, such as computer vision and machine learning, into robots to enable them to perceive and interact with their environment.

Expert systems are another type of AI technology that uses a knowledge base and rules to solve complex problems in specific domains. Expert systems are typically used in medicine, finance, and law to support decisions and improve productivity.

Overall, AI technologies are becoming increasingly sophisticated and are transforming many industries, from healthcare to finance to manufacturing.

Artificial Intelligence (AI) has the potential to enhance the security of medical data and protect it from hackers. Here are some ways AI can help in securing medical data:

- **Threat Detection and Prevention:** AI can analyse vast amounts of data and detect patterns that indicate potential threats or security breaches. AI algorithms can be trained to identify and prevent unauthorised access attempts, malware attacks, and other security threats. For example, AI-based intrusion detection systems can continuously monitor network traffic and alert security teams of suspicious activities, such as attempted data exhilaration.
- **Predictive Analysis:** AI algorithms can be trained to predict potential security threats before they happen. For instance, machine learning models can analyse historical data to identify patterns of suspicious activity and predict future attacks.
- **Anomaly Detection:** AI can help detect unusual patterns in medical data that may indicate a security breach. For example, machine learning models can detect unusual medical record access patterns or unauthorised patient data changes.
- **Encryption and Decryption:** AI can assist in encrypting and decrypting medical data, making it more secure against cyberattacks. AI-based encryption algorithms can encrypt data in transit or at rest, making it difficult for hackers to access and read sensitive information.

- **Identity Verification:** AI-based authentication systems can help verify the identity of users accessing medical data. Facial recognition, voice recognition, and other biometric technologies can be used to ensure that only authorised users are granted access to medical data.

One example of AI being used to secure medical data is machine learning algorithms to detect and prevent cyberattacks in healthcare systems. For instance, AI-powered security solutions such as Dark Trace can see and respond to threats in real-time using unsupervised machine learning to identify anomalous behaviour on networks, devices, and applications. Another example is using AI to encrypt medical data using advanced encryption algorithms, such as homomorphism encryption. This allows for the secure processing and analysis of medical data without decrypting it, thereby reducing the risk of data breaches.

AI can potentially play a significant role in securing medical data from hackers. AI-based threat detection, predictive analysis, anomaly detection, encryption, and identity verification systems can help protect sensitive medical data and prevent unauthorised access while ensuring that healthcare providers can provide efficient and effective patient care.

14.9 CONCLUSIONS

Medical data security is essential for protecting patient privacy, preventing medical identity theft, avoiding medical errors, protecting against cyberattacks, and facilitating medical research. Healthcare organisations must prioritise medical data security by implementing proper security measures and ensuring that only authorised personnel can access patient information. Failure to do so can result in serious consequences for patients and healthcare providers.

With the increasing use of electronic medical records and diagnostic systems, the security of patient data has become a critical concern for healthcare providers. This chapter discusses the security aspects of patient data in a medical diagnostic system. It also discusses the importance of patient data confidentiality, achieved through access controls, authentication, and encryption. It highlights the significance of ensuring that patient data are only accessible to authorised personnel and are not susceptible to unauthorised access or theft. The integrity of patient data is also a crucial aspect of its security. This involves ensuring that the data are accurate, complete, and have not been modified or tampered with. Data validation, access logs, and system auditing are essential measures for maintaining the integrity of patient data. This chapter also emphasises the importance of ensuring the availability of patient data. This includes system redundancy, disaster recovery plans, and data backup to ensure healthcare providers can access relevant patient data when needed. The security of patient data in a medical diagnostic system is critical for adequate healthcare. Patient data's confidentiality, integrity, and availability must be prioritised through appropriate security measures to ensure that patient data remain secure and protected from unauthorised access or theft.

REFERENCES

1. Dhanalakshmi, G., & George, V. S. (2022). Security threats and approaches in e-health cloud architecture system with big data strategy using cryptographic algorithms. *Materials Today: Proceedings, 62*, 4752–4757.
2. Li, C., Yang, L., Yu, S., Qin, W., & Ma, J. (2022). SEMMI: Multi-party security decision-making scheme for linear functions in the internet of medical things. *Information Sciences, 612*, 151–167.
3. Annane, B., Alti, A., & Lakehal, A. (2022). Blockchain based context-aware CP-ABE schema for Internet of Medical Things security. *Array, 14*, 100150.
4. Azzaoui, A. E., Sharma, P. K., & Park, J. H. (2022). Blockchain-based delegated Quantum Cloud architecture for medical big data security. *Journal of Network and Computer Applications, 198*, 103304.
5. Paul, M., Maglaras, L., Ferrag, M. A., & AlMomani, I. (2023). Digitization of healthcare sector: A study on privacy and security concerns. *ICT Express, 9*, 571–588.
6. Venu, D., Babu, J., Saravanakumar, R., Borda, R. F. C., Abd Algani, Y. M., & Bala, B. K. (2022). End-to-end security in embedded system for modern mobile communication technologies. *Measurement: Sensors, 23*, 100393.
7. Qahtan, S., Yatim, K., Zulzalil, H., Osman, M. H., Zaidan, A. A., & Alsattar, H. A. (2023). Review of healthcare industry 4.0 application-based blockchain in terms of security and privacy development attributes: Comprehensive taxonomy, open issues and challenges and recommended solution. *Journal of Network and Computer Applications, 209*, 103529.
8. Hassija, V., Chamola, V., Bajpai, B. C., & Zeadally, S. (2021). Security issues in implantable medical devices: Fact or fiction? *Sustainable Cities and Society, 66*, 102552.
9. Shamshiri, S., & Sohn, I. (2022). Security methods for AI based COVID-19 analysis system: A survey. *ICT Express, 8*, 555–562.
10. Ray, P. P., Dash, D., & Kumar, N. (2020). Sensors for internet of medical things: State-of-the-art, security and privacy issues, challenges and future directions. *Computer Communications, 160*, 111–131.

Index

For Product Safety Concerns and Information please contact our EU
representative GPSR@taylorandfrancis.com
Taylor & Francis Verlag GmbH, Kaufingerstraße 24, 80331 München, Germany

www.ingramcontent.com/pod-product-compliance
Ingram Content Group UK Ltd.
Pitfield, Milton Keynes, MK11 3LW, UK
UKHW021829240425
457818UK00006B/128